D1485511

THE PILGRIM PRINCESS

THE
PILGRIM PRINCESS

A Life of Princess Zinaida Volkonsky

MARIA FAIRWEATHER

Constable · London

First published in Great Britain 1999
by Constable and Company Limited,
3 The Lanchesters,
162 Fulham Palace Road,
London W6 9ER
Copyright © Maria Fairweather 1999
ISBN 0 09 480040 5
The right of Maria Fairweather to be identified as the author
of this work has been asserted by her in accordance with
the Copyright, Designs and Patents Act 1988

Set in Monotype Garamond 12pt by
Rowland Phototypesetting Limited
Printed in Great Britain by
St Edmundsbury Press Ltd,
both of Bury St Edmunds, Suffolk

A CIP catalogue record for this book
is available from the British Library

For Patrick

Contents

Illustrations

Alexander Sergeivich Pushkin by I. I. Vivien 1826 (*State Pushkin Museum, Moscow*)

Dimitry Venevitnov by P. F. Sokolov 1827 (*State Pushkin Museum, Moscow*)

Zinaida at the ball, in her Moscow salon

A ball at Zinaida's Moscow house in the late 1820s

Party at the Villa Volkonsky, Rome, by G. Gagrin

Sketch of Gogol at the Villa Volkonsky, attributed to F. Bruni

Zinaida Volkonsky in 1822 and 1855

Zinaida's original villa in Rome, as it is today (*photograph by the author*)

Memorial to Zinaida, in the garden of the Villa Volkonsky, Rome (*photograph by the author*)

Cardinal Consalvi

Memorial tablet to Zinaida, Nikita Volkonsky and Maria Vlasova

Acknowledgements

I am most grateful to the following without whose help and encouragement over the past five years, this book would have been much the poorer. They have greatly contributed to whatever merit it may have. The faults are, of course, all mine.

I should like to thank the staff of the British Library, the London Library, The Biblioteca Apostolica Vaticana, the Bibliothèque de L'École Française de Rome, The National Library in Moscow, The Houghton Library, Harvard and the Staff of the British Council in Rome for kind permission to use their microfilm scanner and printer.

In Russia, Olga Adamishina and Polly Gray gave me guidance on illustrations, Professor Bocharov gave me the benefit of his knowledge when he visited the Villa Volkonsky, as did Professor Fridkin. I am very grateful to Mrs Elena Rapoport of the State Pushkin Museum for her enthusiastic guided tour of Pushkin's former house in Moscow, and for supplying photographs. I should like to thank the Director of the State Pushkin Museum and the Director of the Pushkin Museum in Kishinev, Republic of Moldova, for their kind permission to use illustrations.

In Rome, I am most grateful to Bianca Riccio for help with research, to Princess Elena Volkonsky Ciccognani, Elena Cardenas Malagodi and Dottessa Wanda Gasparowicz. Special thanks to Mrs Jo Trippa, social secretary at the Villa Volkonsky, for always knowing where to find anything and for her invaluable help in running our lives while we were there. My warmest thanks to all the staff at Villa Volkonsky. I am immensely indebted to Don Michele Colagiovanni of the Collegio Missionari del Preziossimo Sangue del Nostro Signore Gesu Christo in Rome, for giving me his own books, and for his unstinting help and advice, as well as access to material in the Order's archives, all of which threw invaluable light on Zinaida Volkonsky's last years.

In England I am most grateful to Martin Drury and Alistair Lang for their help with the painting of the Allied Sovereigns at Petworth and to Doctor Pauline Munro and Doctor Michael Johnson for material on the Beloselsky Palace in St Petersburg. Above all I should like to thank all my friends, especially, Marina Berry, Jill Braithwaite, Ellen Dahrendorf, Linda and Laurence Kelly, Nina Lobanov, Susan Richards, Gaia Servadio and Ben Whitaker who have read all or part of the book in its various stages, supplied me with articles, books and photocopies of relevant material and offered varied, sometimes contradictory but invaluable advice and encouragement. I am very grateful to Rodric Braithwaite and Derek Thomas for finding paintings of Zinaida in all sorts of unlikely places in Russia and the former Soviet Union, and for sharing their expert knowledge of things Russian and Italian. My thanks to Adrian Berry for initiating me into the mysteries of computer technology, and I should like to thank Victoria Glendinning and Christine Sutherland for their kind interest and advice. I am very grateful to my publisher, Ben Glazebrook and Krystyna Niedenthal at Constable and to my agent, Christopher Sinclair Stevenson. My thanks too to Richard Cohen and Pat Chetwin. I am especially grateful to Mary Sandys, for asking all the right questions, and for steering me on to the paths of biographical righteousness. I have learnt much from her.

Last but foremost, I should like to thank all my family for their kind interest, particularly my very busy daughters Catherine and Natasha, not only for their practical and literary help and advice, but also for their unfailing encouragement and the bossy, active and warmhearted interest they always take in my life. My son-in-law Richard Beeston's kindness, help and frequent shelter in Moscow, made research there an unalloyed pleasure. My husband, Patrick to whom I dedicate this book with love and gratitude, as well as providing all the above, set my punctuation on more orthodox lines. He has shared our bedroom and frequently our bed, with my book for several years without a murmur. Had he not taken me to live at the Villa Volkonsky, this book would not have been written, but as I often pointed out to him when we were there, but for him, it would have been finished sooner.

London May 1999.

Introduction

In the summer of 1992 a posting to Italy completed my husband's diplomatic career, in a city where it had begun so happily more than thirty years before, and we returned to Rome. We were both delighted at this poetic closing of the circle, and looked forward to the prospect of living at the Villa Volkonsky, the residence of the British ambassador to Italy since 1946.

I knew, of course, that the original villa had been built by a Russian princess. Half Russian myself, I was intrigued by her and determined to find out more. Who was she and why had she come to Rome? As I began my research I realised at once that here was no ordinary woman, no mere princess in search of art or romance or a better climate, although at various times in her life Zinaida Volkonsky had been in search of all three. It was then that I decided to try and write her life story.

One day, a couple of months after our arrival, a call was put through to me from 'a foreign professor'. 'You don't know me,' said the voice at the other end in heavily Russian-accented English, 'but I am a great lover of Pushkin, and I would like to come and talk to you about Princess Volkonsky who was a friend of the poet's, and about whom we are making a television film.' Caught off my guard, I exclaimed in Russian that I too loved Pushkin and was particularly interested in Zinaida Volkonsky. There followed a long conversation about Pushkin only possible among Russians. The professor came to make his film and in the course of his visit I was confirmed in my intention to write about someone in whom I was growing daily more interested. While interviewing me for his film, the professor asked me to describe what I felt about the Princess. I did so, telling him and the Russian television audience what I knew of her, and of her connection with the villa. 'Cut,' said he suddenly. Then, turning to me: 'Now tell me what she means to you. Speak from your soul.'

Amused at the time at this very Russian view of things, I did my best. Later, after three years of serious research, necessarily, constantly interrupted by the duties and pleasures which are the lot of ambassadors' wives, I realised that 'soul' was the most important aspect of Zinaida Volkonsky's complex and fascinating character.

Even now, she is not easy to classify. Society beauty, richly gifted artist, aspiring intellectual; worldly, powerful, brave, original, practical, reckless, emotionally fragile; 'sinner' as she saw herself, and Christian mystic; profoundly Western but deeply Russian – she was all of those things. Perhaps one is struck most by her sincerity, her humanity and her constant struggle towards the light. Zinaida's life, as it took her from the gilded ballrooms of imperial St Petersburg to – after she left the Villa Volkonsky – a small house in Rome, seemed to me a true pilgrimage.

The winter of 1862 was particularly cold in Rome. Down one of the narrow streets between St John the Lateran and the Piazza di Spagna, one might have seen an old woman, dressed in black, slowly making her way along the mean and narrow streets of that poor district. As she walked home to the small house in the Via dei Avignonesi which she shared with a few nuns, she came across a beggar woman, shivering in her thin rags. The old woman saw at a glance that what was most needed were some warm clothes. On impulse, she pulled the beggar into the shelter of a church porch nearby, where, taking off her warm flannel petticoat, she gave it to her. Thoroughly chilled by the time she got home, she went to bed. The next morning she was feverish, too ill even for Mass, as had been her daily habit for so many years. As she lay in her simple bed, lovingly tended by the nuns, Princess Zinaida Alexandrovna Volkonsky knew that her long pilgrimage was almost over. Soon she would be with her Maker, as she earnestly believed and longed for with all her heart. So ended the life of a woman remarkable by the standards of any age.

Zinaida Alexandrovna Volkonsky (née Beloselsky-Belosersky) was born into the highest ranks of the Russian aristocracy in 1789, the year of the fall of the Bastille in France. She died in Rome in 1862. In her lifetime, the revolution in France and the industrial revolution in Britain unleashed unprecedented political and social change as wave upon wave of wars, and nationalist uprisings, changed the map of Europe.

All biography is also a part of history. If in the first part of this book I have concentrated more on events than on Zinaida's personal life, it is because much of the evidence of her early life was destroyed, probably by a loving son, perhaps to protect her honour. Above all, though, it is because her early years were completely overshadowed by momentous historical events and by the colossal figures on the world's stage. Napoleon and his rival, Tsar Alexander, who was Zinaida's love and her lifelong friend, but also Wellington, Talleyrand and Metternich were the main protagonists, all but Napoleon himself known to her. As lady-in-waiting to Alexander's mother, the Empress Dowager, Maria Feodorovna, Zinaida married Prince Nikita Grigorievich Volkonsky, one of the Tsar's aides-de-camp. Zinaida was always a part of the Tsar's inner circle. After Napoleon's ill-fated invasion of Russia and the burning of Moscow, she travelled across Europe as a member of Alexander's suite throughout the German and French campaigns.

Zinaida was dogged by depressive illness all her life. Greatly gifted, she had inherited a genuine love of music from her father, composed music and opera and played both the piano and the harp. Above all she was famous for her beautiful voice, which was admired throughout Europe, and possessed a considerable talent for acting although her social position made anything but private performances impossible. A friend of both Rossini and Donizetti, she had helped to make Rossini's music known in France. Stendhal, who knew about music, wrote that she 'sang like an angel' and he praised her compositions.

The end of the Napoleonic wars found the Princess in Paris and then London for the peace celebrations where, young, beautiful and well-educated as she was, she enjoyed life in the salons and ballrooms of the two capitals. She remained a part of the Imperial suite in Vienna throughout the Congress. It was during the Congress of Vienna that she became a friend of Cardinal Consalvi, the powerful and charming Secretary of State at the Vatican. His friendship and guidance then and later, at a difficult time in her life, meant much to them both and was probably a decisive influence on her decision later to become a Roman Catholic.

It was as hostess of the foremost literary and musical salon of her time that Zinaida Volkonsky became a legend in her own lifetime in Russia. In her magnificent Moscow palace in the years 1824–29 she played an important role in the history of Russian culture at a time when Russia was entering on what came to be known as her Golden Age of literature. Although she could not be counted a great writer herself, she was nevertheless good enough to be elected the first woman honorary member of the Society of History and Russian Antiquities. More importantly the foremost Russian literary critic of his time, V. Belinsky, later wrote that 'in the Pushkin period of Russian literature one can speak of only four women's names'. One of the four was that of Princess Z. A. Volkonsky.

In her house, immortalised by the Polish poet Mickiewicz, who recalled the Princess in a white dress, floating across ebony tiles, she entertained Pushkin, the poets Zhukovsky, Koslov, Venevitinov and Baratinsky, as well as most of the leading intellectuals of the time. Here she also comforted her tragic young sister-in-law Maria, on the eve of her departure for Siberia to join her husband, Zinaida's brother-in-law Sergei Volkonsky, who had been exiled for his part in the Decembrist revolt of 1825.

Zinaida's influence in Russia continued after her death. Some Russian scholars believe that both Pushkin and Tolstoy based fictional characters on her life. Two of Pushkin's stories are about a society woman called Zinaida Volskaya and bear striking similarities to Zinaida's early life, while it is thought that Tolstoy may have based the character of Helene in *War and Peace* on Zinaida. Nobody could have been less like the cold and selfish Helene than Zinaida, but the beautiful, talented and glamorous Princess, looking to the West and to the Catholic Church, as well as speaking 'that refined French which our grandparents not only spoke, but thought in', as Tolstoy put it in the opening chapter of his great novel, represented everything that he had come to hate.

In 1829, the Princess left Russia never to live there again. She settled in Rome, where she converted to the Roman Catholic faith a few years later.

In 1830 Zinaida bought a large estate near St John the Lateran. Here she built a summer villa and began to plan her garden, which to this day is one of the loveliest in Rome. In the next decade, she welcomed all the Russians of note who came to Rome and entertained many famous artists in her Roman salon, among them Canova, Thorvaldsen, Cammucini, Vernet and Ivanov, Walter Scott, Mickiewicz, Stendhal, Victor Hugo, Fennimore Cooper, Donizetti and Glinka. Above all Nikolai Gogol's life in Rome is closely associated with Zinaida Volkonsky's. Gogol loved the gardens of the villa and spent hours lying on the terrace, gazing at the sky and marvelling at its blueness. In the cool grotto which Zinaida created in one of the arches of the aqueduct which runs through the garden, Gogol worked on *Dead Souls*.

Although today the wonderful views over the Roman Campagna and towards the distant Sabine and Alban hills, so often mentioned by Zinaida's contemporaries, have been blocked out by the buildings which rose as Rome expanded after the 1870s (when a part of the estate was sold to build the much larger villa, now the ambassador's residence), the garden within its high walls remains a magically romantic place. To me it always seemed a truly European garden. Here in the flying arches of the aqueduct and the Roman tombs and statuary was history and architecture, here the lovely natural sweep of an English garden, the untamed romantic wildness of a Russian one, the climate and colour of the Mediterranean.

Stretching out along the ancient aqueduct Zinaida's former villa is covered in the spring with thick purple coils of wisteria, studded with white and yellow Banksia roses. Along the aqueduct's shaded walks, waves of iris stretch their elegant heads through the sculptural leaves of acanthus. Under the umbrella pines the lawns are carpeted with violets, their light scent the timid woodwind notes to the more insistent ones of wisteria, lilac and mimosa, and above them all the heady trumpet call of lemon and orange blossom. After such an overture, summer comes in with a symphony of scent and colour – sweet peas and jasmine, lime blossom and gardenia, peonies and lilies, but above all the scent of roses. Just as they were described in Zinaida's day, roses tumble from the aqueduct, some clinging to its narrow bricks, some leaning against its warm walls. There are roses along the yew hedge, roses crowning ancient Roman heads, climbing up broken fragments of Roman columns, decking the austere dark green of the cypresses. From the villa's terraces and the upper arches of the aqueduct one sees a different garden. The heavy heads of the umbrella pines are still above us, their elegant branches providing perfect perches at night for the owls, between their silent swoops into the darkened garden. The shaggy crowns of palms rise above cedar and cypress, oak and lime, above carob and the purple-flowering pawlonia, above the scented white acacias and the huge magnolia grandifloras, their glossy dark green leaves a perfect foil for the ivory chalices of the flowers. Late summer brings fruit trees laden with apricots, peaches, cherries and plums, and then in autumn the pale wild cyclamen and pink autumn lilies return. Bronzed leathery pomegranates spill their ruby seed followed by persimmons, glowing like orange globes from the bare trees, each standing in a pool of saffron leaves. The winter garden belongs to the citrus trees. Oranges and lemons, tangerines and kumquat glimmer festively among the aromatic, shiny foliage, until February when the first delicate white clouds of almond blossom once again announce the spring.

The garden of the Villa Volkonsky together with Zinaida's Allée des Mémoires, which she had created to commemorate her friends, many of whom are among the great names of European culture, could not be a more fitting memorial to a woman who had been called the Northern Corinne, after the eponymous heroine in Madame de Staël's novel, and whom Pushkin himself had once hailed as 'Queen of the Muses and of Beauty'.

PART I

Childhood and Youth
Through War and Peace

1

Childhood: Her Father's Daughter

'Happy the family that called him father.'

PRINCESS ZINAIDA VOLKONSKY

In a quiet corner of the garden of the Villa Volkonsky in Rome, half hidden by fern and acanthus, stands the most important memorial in Princess Zinaida Volkonsky's Allée des Mémoires. Among the memorial tablets and urns one stands out. The simple inscription in Russian, 'To my father, friend and teacher', gives the measure of her loss. Then in French is written:

> Under his roof, I have seen the unfortunate consoled, poets and scholars celebrated and cherished, strangers welcomed like brothers, servants cared for and happy. His speech was eloquent, his acts generous and pure. Happy the family that called him father.

The choice of Russian for the simple statement of what her father had meant to her, and of French for the more formal and conventional funerary inscription, is telling, for Zinaida Volkonsky, in spite of a French upbringing and a life spent largely in western Europe, remained very much a Russian: spontaneous, generous, soulful, but inclined to excess and mysticism.

Zinaida, the second of three daughters (a first-born son, Hippolite, had died in infancy), was born to Prince Alexander Mikhailovich Beloselsky and his wife Varvara Yakovlevna, née Tatishchev, in

Dresden on 3 December 1789.[1] Zinaida did not remember her mother, who died on 25 November 1792, little more than eighteen months after the birth of her third daughter Natalia (born in March 1791), when Zinaida was only three. Writing about her in an autobiographical sketch, Zinaida recalled that her mother had died in Turin.

> I knew nothing of the details of her death, nor about her religious views. It was impossible to talk of her with my father. He loved and mourned her so deeply that he hadn't even the strength to unwrap the paper in which there was a lock of her hair. His hands would tremble, as once again he put away the precious relic.[2]

At the time of Zinaida's birth, her father had for nine years been the Empress Catherine's ambassador to the Saxon court, a post to which he succeeded on the death of his much older half-brother Andrei Mikhailovich. A decade earlier, the twenty-six-year-old Alexander had described his travels in a letter to a friend, which by chance fell into the Empress Catherine's hands. She was impressed:

> *Voila une lettre parfaitement bien écrite et encore mieux pensée, où trouveroit-on des gens si celui la n'étoit pas employé? J'ai ordoné de m'aporter la liste des vacances, et je le placerai en Cour étrangère.'* [sic] Ekaterina.[3]

Soon after the Empress's ukase, in May 1780, Alexander Beloselsky found himself posted to Dresden.

Zinaida's father was a member of a distinguished noble family with roots stretching back to the troubled times of the Tartar invasions in the mid-thirteenth century. The youngest of four children and the only son of his father's second marriage to Countess Natalia Grigorievna Tchernishev, he was born in 1752. His father, Vice-Admiral Mikhail Andreevich (1702–55), who had had a distinguished naval career under Peter the Great, died when Alexander was three. Alexander had a liberal education mostly in Germany where his tutor, Dieudonné Thiébault, a former Jesuit, a member of the Berlin Academy of Sciences and secretary to King Frederick of Prussia, was an important influence and remained a lifelong friend. His first taste of diplomatic life had been as a boy of sixteen, when he served as Cavalier de l'Ambassade to the Russian Embassy in London where his uncle, Admiral of the Fleet Count Ivan Grigorevich Tchernishev, was briefly ambassador. Alexander, encouraged by his tutor, early showed great love for all the arts, in particular for music. His health was delicate from childhood. This, together with an impetuous nature and a tendency always to speak his mind, caused his tutor some worry. When Alexander was still only twenty and a lieutenant in the Guards in St Petersburg, Thiébault wrote to him affectionately, warning him to guard against his high spirits and directness, and to look after his health:

> You have a weak chest, be careful my dear Prince if you wish to live! – You are by nature extremely attached to your freedom ... and you are a little proud, you will have to take care, since you cannot bear to be a slave! ... You will always be very dear to me, and whatever concerns you will always be of the most lively interest to me.[4]

In common with many young noblemen of his time, the Prince travelled extensively in Europe. Unlike most, he impressed both Voltaire and Rousseau. A letter survives from Voltaire to the twenty-three-year-old Alexander, dated 27 February 1775: 'Sir, An old man of eighty-one was afforded some measure of relief from his cruel ills by the charming letter in prose and poetry, with which you did him honour, in a language which is not your own, and in which you write better than all our young courtiers.' To this, Voltaire added some verses of his own in which he praised the Prince, flatteringly tracing his descent from Ovid and Orpheus, ending his letter 'with respect from the old man of Ferney'.[5]

A letter from Jean-Jacques Rousseau, dated 27 May 1775, in reply to one from the Prince, reflects the bitterness and isolation of Rousseau's last years. Persecuted after the publication of *Emile* in 1862, Rousseau left his native Geneva for France. Mourning the loss of his native land, 'now he lives only to suffer', he tells the Prince, asking him not to write again, for he wouldn't have the strength to answer him, but to come and see him when the Prince is in Paris. Rousseau begs that his letter be burnt in case it is misinterpreted.[6]

Alexander's serious interest in the arts was matched by a great capacity for pleasure and fun. A visit to Italy, when he was still only twenty-four, produced a learned book on Italian music, *De la Musique en Italie* published in 1788, as a result of which he was made a foreign member of the Institute of Bologna. The book created quite a stir in France and Italy. In Italy too, he began to keep a journal – his *Vademecum*, in which he gives a lively account of his travels and of contemporary society.

Diplomacy provided an ideal opportunity for Alexander Beloselsky to combine service with a growing passion for collecting and gave him leisure for writing. He was no mere dilettante, however. From the outset he showed great ability as a diplomat. A broad and liberal education, an understanding of human nature, considerable analytical abilities and boundless energy and curiosity, together with a wide range of contacts, made his diplomatic reports as interesting as they were personal. He was never able to fully reconcile one of the classic diplomatic dilemmas: the wish to report the truth as he saw it and the need to please his political masters. His relations with his superiors were always troubled. Almost as soon as he arrived in Dresden in 1780, he was having to eat humble pie for ignoring the advice of the Foreign Minister, Count Osterman, to tone down his lively despatches: 'Sire, I accept with profound submission Your Excellency's reproaches regarding my conduct. I am conscious of having done wrong, and will do all in my power to be wiser and more prudent in future.' Prudence, alas, was not in his nature. He would always go his own way, a trait he passed on to his daughter Zinaida.[7]

In Dresden, happily married and enjoying his first diplomatic post in a country he knew well, the Prince quickly made his embassy a centre for people of wit and culture. Letters and diaries by contemporaries bear witness to his charm, his abilities as a raconteur, his sudden and catching laugh, and his exceptional talent for acting. The much-travelled Count Komarovsky noted that, as a comic actor particularly, Beloselsky had no equal in Russia or Europe.

Although he enjoyed his first embassy, the Prince was aware that Dresden was a relative backwater. He sent back enthusiastic reports

about the Dresden Academy of Art and wrote to the Empress personally, on matters of art, collecting works on her behalf, but as early as
September 1780 he also wrote to her for guidance: the letter shows
that, for all his independent spirit, when it came to the Empress the
Prince understood the imperatives of dealing with an absolute Monarch, addressing her in terms which today seem grovelling:

> I take the liberty of throwing myself at the sacred feet of your
> Imperial Majesty to ask for a favour, which in her goodness she
> might perhaps grant. I have had the honour of serving your Majesty
> in a place where I am unfortunately unable not only to justify your
> attention, but even to interest it, as I believe.[8]

Meanwhile he enjoyed his own literary and intellectual pursuits. In
1784, with the help of Marmontel, the Prince published a collection
of his poems, the three 'Epistles' to the English, to the French and
to the citizens of the Republic of San Marino in which he reflects
on their national characteristics.[9] He also wrote the preface to *Circe*,
a cantata by Seidlemann.[10] A letter from Mozart to his wife, dated
16 April 1789, speaks of his having been to dinner at the Russian
ambassador's where he (Mozart) had played a great deal.[11] Among
his other friends and correspondents were Condorcet and Joseph De
Maistre. In 1790 he published a philosophical tract on man's cognitive
faculties, his *Dianologie, ou Tableau Philosophique de L'Entendement*, which
he sent to Kant. Kant's reply it seems, showed that the Prince had
impressed him.[12]

In October 1789, shortly before Zinaida's birth, Alexander begged
the Empress for a new posting. France was in revolution and émigrés
were flooding to his house. He longed to be closer to the action. Perhaps
to his surprise, the request was granted. In January he was appointed
ambassador to the court of Victor Amadeus III of Savoy, in Turin.

The Prince did not immediately take up his new post, however. Ill
health, as well as the birth of his third daughter Natalia in March
1791, must have been partly responsible for the delay. A letter to
Count Osterman from Vienna, where the Prince spent some time,
shows that relations between them were still far from easy. Osterman
must have been aware of the future problems of sending this obstinate

young man to the very borders of revolutionary France, and the effects which his reports would have on an increasingly terrified Empress. Alexander did not hide his indignation:

I must admit to your Excellency, that in presenting true and fair observations of the present situation, which are perhaps new, and based on the characters of men of influence, I had expected approval rather than reproach. As for the delay in my return, your Excellency's reproaches would surely be well founded if I had not taken the precaution of informing your Excellency on several occasions, that I had been ill with a fever which laid me low for more than two months, and from which I have only just recovered, and that my wife having suffered from an extremely dangerous miscarriage, I had begged your Excellency to intercede on my behalf with her Imperial Majesty.

He signs himself off with the formal 'your humble and obedient servant', but the tone is unmistakably unrepentant.[13]

At last he was on his way. His natural curiosity and impulsiveness ensured that his travels were always adventurous, providing ample opportunities for dining out on his adventures, as his close friend Prince Viazemsky later recalled in his notebooks:

No one was more famed at the end of the last century and the begining of this one, for the liveliness of his talk and his abilities as a raconteur, than Prince Beloselsky. Here is his account of an adventure he had on his way to Turin. Having stopped in Lyons for the night, he set off for a walk that evening and got lost. He had, of course, forgotten the name of his hotel. After several hours of walking around the dark and empty streets he suddenly chanced upon a brightly lit house, from whence came the sound of music. Deciding to go in, he explained his situation to the host whereupon the Prince was very kindly received and invited to stay for the party. He accepted with pleasure, and spent a very agreeable evening dining, dancing and drinking toasts with his new friends, though he was a little surprised by a certain sombreness and reserve among the men and also by the fact that they were almost all unusually tall and heavily built. Towards the end of the evening the Prince's innkeeper appeared. Worried about the long absence of his distinguished guest he had searched the town, finding him only by chance. They must leave at once, he whispered anxiously to Alexander, who, greatly enjoying himself, was most unwilling to leave such a hospitable household. In a frightened whisper, the innkeeper informed the Prince that they were in the house of the chief executioner of Lyons, who was celebrating the marriage of his daughter to one of his colleagues. He pointed out several other 'Executioners of the Law', as he repectfully called them, among the burly guests, who had come from all the neighbouring towns.[14]

In April 1792 the Prince was at last installed in his embassy in Piedmont. In one of Turin's handsomest arcaded squares, the Piazza San Carlo, the embassy was housed in the splendid, seventeenth-century Palazzo del Borgo, which had been partly rebuilt some forty years earlier. Shortly after Alexander Beloselsky had arrived in Turin, Count Zappata de Ponchey, the Court Chamberlain, had this to say of the new Russian ambassador, in his report to King Victor Amadeus:

A short man, thirty-five years old. My information is that he is of mild disposition, with a love of the arts and sciences, and is the author of a short work on music. He is quite rich in his own right, married to a Tatishchev, who accompanies him on his missions, and who is heiress to 3000 serfs, which means an income of approximately 15 thousand roubles. He is of good family, since I hear that he is a nephew of both the Saltikovs and the Stroganovs, but he can be a little caustic. This is the portrait which I have the honour to present to you as it has come to me. One might add that there is no Russian with so little of the savage about him.[15]

Alexander Beloselsky was indeed far from the then traditional image of Russians as barbarians from the East. An outstanding example of the enlightened Russian nobleman, a man of deep culture, he was the personification of the values of eighteenth-century France, values which were about to undergo violent and radical change.

From Turin, Alexander sent out his almost daily despatches. He had his wish. His embassy was on the very borders of France, and the Revolution was about to spill over into the whole of Europe. In France, the Girondins (radical revolutionary deputies mainly from the Gironde, the country around Bordeaux) had just gained the upper hand in the Assembly. King Louis XVI and his Queen, Marie Antoinette, discredited after their unsuccessful flight the previous year, were rightly suspected of negotiating their rescue with the Queen's brother, the Emperor of Austria. As demands for war grew more insistent, Louis XVI was forced to give in. France declared war on Austria on 20 April 1792 and on Prussia in June of the same year. It was at this dramatic moment that Beloselsky began to send his daily and sometimes twice daily despatches over the next year giving a precise, lively and balanced account of events.

As the Revolution gathered strength, the Prince's despatches (of 19–30 June), made no attempt to hide the gravity of events in France. Emigré friends pouring into his house in Savoy and his correspondents in Paris made it clear to him that the Jacobins were growing in strength by the day:

Regicide is being plotted under the very windows of the palace and if circumstances do not change in favour of Their Majesties, one has every reason to fear acts of extreme fanaticism against the King and especially against the Queen [he predicts accurately]. The Jacobins around the King having been replaced by moderates, in their rage tried every trick to deprive the monarchists of this temporary victory. I say temporary, because Jacobin ideas have grown deep roots all over France. This is the inevitable consequence of the Constitution, that is to say, of political equality, of the People's sovereignty, of the wiping out of Royalty in the person of the King, who is now a simple functionary. I would further add that even if, as a result of measures taken by the Court at Vienna, the Jacobins were to be chased out of Paris and all France, their ideas, already rooted in the country, would create more believers. As long as the cause exists, they will continue to be active. – On the 21st of this month (June) the lowest rabble, armed with pikes, hatchets and pitchforks, broke down three doors to enter the King's apartments by force.

Beloselsky goes on to describe in detail how Louis was forced to put on the revolutionary red bonnet, and the terror of the Dauphin and the royal ladies as they huddled together, ending: 'It was in this terrible and ridiculous position that the deputies found the Royal Family.' While Beloselsky is clearly outraged himself, the effects of this kind of news on the nervous Empress and on the Russian court can only be imagined.[16]

In July, as diplomatic relations between Russia and France were broken off with the expulsion from St Petersburg of the French chargé Edmond Genet, Beloselsky betrays slight concern. Are his despatches on France welcome or should he confine himself to events in Savoy? He was aware that the Empress did not welcome bad news, and that this might mean trouble for the messenger. But his lively intelligence, curiosity and sense of duty always made it impossible for him to take the line of least resistance and tone down his reports.

The Revolution had given the Prince more personal reasons for concern. In September 1792 he was still anxiously awaiting the arrival of his wife, who because of revolutionary activity had been stuck for several months in Switzerland, unable to cross into Savoy. His letter to her in Geneva, in his rapid hand and idiosyncratic spelling, is full of love, concern for her safety and contradictory advice:

I cannot imagine my dearest friend why you have failed to write to me this time. It is too bad of you. Has it [the letter] been returned? Is it forgetfulness? Is it indifference? In any event you are at fault. That this should happen when I am trembling about your journey! The roads in Savoy are no longer safe. There are fears of a French insurrection. In the name of God do not set out lightly. It might be best to go through Vaud and come into Italy by way of the Tyrol? It would be longer but safer. If you are already in Geneva – Monsieur Saugis will give you good directions. I consign this letter to chance. I don't know whether it will find you. Come as soon as possible I beg you. We are all well here including little Mimi. Farewell my good and beautiful one, until the happiness of being able to embrace you tenderly. We shall come to meet you at Suza together with the Abbé and Zinaida. But you must let me know the day and time you intend to cross the Mont Cenis pass.[17]

Insurrections apart, the Prince was well justified in fearing the journey. Before Napoleon built the carriage road over the Mont Cenis pass, there was only a steep and narrow road overhanging many a sheer drop. Travel by carriage, at about six miles an hour, was slow and tiring. Even in the best-sprung coaches the passengers were horribly jolted. To cross the Alpine passes carriages were unloaded, the contents loaded on to pack mules, and the passengers carried in sedan chairs. If there was enough snow, the descent was by sledge, which would first be dragged by mules, the driver walking between the animal and the sledge and kicking snow into the passengers' faces. The sledge was then unhitched and down they would go.

The Princess, whose health was fragile, was finally able to join her husband but their happiness was short-lived. She died in Turin in November 1792, probably of consumption, and was buried there. She was only twenty-eight.

Alexander was devastated. He commissioned a chapel of white marble for his wife by the banks of the Po on land given to him by the King of Sardinia. With characteristic generosity, he also wished it to be a burial place for any of his fellow countrymen who might die in Piedmont.[18] Several years later when Turin was occupied by the French the Prince, worried about the fate of his first wife's resting place, sent a request to Talleyrand via the French ambassador in St Petersburg, Hédouville, with a request to the First Consul, Bonaparte, that he recognise the Prince's ownership of the monument. Napoleon, keen to promote his friendship with the Tsar, conveyed some high-minded phrases through his minister to the effect that respect for the dead was, for the living, a foretaste of a happy reunion in eternal life, and that when such sentiments were illuminated by religious feeling there could be nothing more worthy of the respect of foreign governments. In short, the Prince got his agreement.[19] His own family tragedy was followed in the New Year by news which horrified all the courts of Europe. Louis XVI was executed on 21 January 1793 and his wife, Marie Antoinette, later that year on 16 October. As soon as the news reached her, in February, the Empress Catherine annulled the Franco-Russian commercial treaty of 1787, recalled all Russian citizens from France and expelled all French citizens who were not willing to swear an oath of allegiance to the French monarchy.

At the end of that year, recalled for his 'ideological despatches' on the French Revolution, the Prince returned to Russia with his children.[20] The execution of the King and Queen had been the last straw for the Empress, who by then had had a bust of Voltaire removed from her presence, had closed Russian ports to French ships and had welcomed many émigrés to Russia. There was no way back for the Prince, who suffered the fate of many a herald of unwelcome news. With his diplomatic career at an end, he remained out of favour until Catherine's death in 1796.

Zinaida, just too young at the time of her mother's death to remember her, was five when the family left Turin, and had already been profoundly affected by her earliest memories of their house. Many years later, when returning to Italy in 1829, she visited the Russian Embassy, her old home in Turin. The visit brought back a flood of memories. This was the house which she associated with her earliest years and with her beloved father, before he had married again. It was here that her eyes were first opened to the wonders of art, and to the beauties of Italy. In a letter to her friend, the Egyptologist and Academician I. A. Gulianov, she described what the visit had meant to her:

I've been reading your letter, my dear Gulianov – can you guess where? In my father's house, under our familiar roof, where I grew up illuminated by Greek, Egyptian and Italian art, where my young eyes grew used to their ideal forms. Pictures, ancient bronzes, marbles – are all dear to me. They are like brothers – we were all a part of my father's family.[21]

On his return to Russia the Prince at first found solace in his writing and in the company of his three daughters, especially of his favourite, Zinaida. The Prince was an uncommonly warm and paternal man and the three motherless girls were lovingly cared for. Their mother's own wet-nurse, Sophia, looked after them until they were old enough to be put in the care of their French governess, Madame Bellay. Years later when Zinaida arranged her Alleé des Mémoires, these two friends of her childhood were lovingly remembered. Her nanny's inscription reads: 'I sat on her lap and stroked her white hair, but had not known the one [her mother] whom she had fed with her own milk,' while her governess's plaque states simply: 'To my old friend from her grateful pupils.' In another plaque – 'To my father's three faithful servants, Peter, Kolmar and Parmen' – Zinaida remembered other family retainers who had meant much to her. The three sisters grew up close to their maternal grandparents, Jacov Afanasievich and Maria Dimitrievna Tatishchev, who, as she inscribed on another plaque to their memory, 'transferred the tenderness they had felt for their beloved daughter to us.'

In 1795 the young widower, handsome, rich and universally loved, who was sought by the highest families in the land as an exceptional matrimonial prize, married again. His bride, Anna Grigorievna Kozitsky, though not of Alexander's social rank, was one of the greatest heiresses of her time. Her father, Empress Catherine's Secretary of State and professor of philosophy and rhetoric at the University of St Petersburg, had been rewarded with a fortune in land and mineral wealth in the Urals when he married the daughter of one of Russia's earliest pioneers. The new Princess Beloselsky brought the Prince the beautiful Kozitsky Palace on Moscow's Tversky Boulevard as part of her dowry,[22] in addition to several estates, mines and 10,000 souls, as serfs were often referred to in Russia. The Prince enlarged this palace to house part of his vast art collection as well as a fine library. His daughter Zinaida would one day reign there, as 'Queen of the Muses and of Beauty' as she was called by Pushkin, in the most famous literary and musical salon of her time. She was to be a true successor to her father, who, as a great patron of the arts, was affectionately known as the Moscow Apollo, his houses ever full of artists and writers, among them the poet Zhukovsky and the historian Karamzin.

The Prince continued to write, translating into French some of Russia's best-known writers, such as Lomonsov and Derzhavin. In 1796 he composed a comic opera, *Olinka or First Love*, causing a scandal at its first performance in Moscow. Performed by serf actors in Prince Stolypin's private theatre before an audience of all Moscow's grandees, the light-hearted opera with its frivolous language and feminist message so shocked the audience as to cause them to walk out, first the fathers, followed by the mammas, indignantly sweeping out their daughters. The play was about nothing more shocking than two young ladies who, deceived in love decide to do without men.

> Farewell, men, you will not forget us, for we will have nothing more to do with you. As for you, you can make as many promises and tell as many lies as you like and fall in love with the whole world, for all we care,

ran the refrain which had caused the furore. Reports of this soon reached the Emperor Paul, who demanded to see the manuscript at once. Amused and alarmed, Prince Alexander appealed to his friend Karamzin for help: 'Please do me the great favour of correcting all suspect passages. Clean up the play as best you can!' Karamzin must have done well. The play not only passed the Tsar's censorship but he even recommended it to the St Petersburg theatre, where it enjoyed some success during the next few years.[23]

One of Alexander's chief interests in the early years of his marriage was the supervision of the rebuilding of their palace in St Petersburg. Designed in classical style by his friend, the architect Thom de Thomon, the new palace stood on the Nevsky Prospect, on the corner of the Fontanka canal, near the Anichkov bridge. It was described as the finest house in St Petersburg, even boasting a private church.[24] Here the Prince displayed the magnificent collection of paintings, sculpture and books which he had brought back to Russia.

While St Petersburg society could easily forgive the Prince his good fortune, it was less kind to the new Princess. Jealous tongues spread rumours about the love of luxury, the ambition and the ignorance of the parvenue. It was said that when in Rome at a papal audience, the Princess had congratulated the Pope on his splendid palace, asking him for the name of his architect, so that she could bring him back to Russia. Another story had it that the Princess insisted on travelling to England by land, whatever the cost, apparently unaware that Britain was an island. But nothing marred the Princess's happiness. She adored her husband unreservedly: 'He has pierced my soul with light,' she wrote in her diary. 'He is a God to whom I bow and the light of my life.' Indeed, the Prince was loved by all her family. His brother-in-law Prince Laval described him as 'a wizard who warms whatever is frozen, restores the dead to life, enlivens the boring and makes the sad happy.'[25]

The Prince too seems to have been happy in his marriage. He was very much a family man and, although sometimes bitter about his ruined career, he was grateful for domestic happiness, and glad to have found a new mother for his children. In a poem, 'Épître à ma Femme', he tenderly thanked his wife for the love with which she had embellished his life.

> *Vivons pour nous, ma tendre amie,*
> *La fortune avec ses brillants*
> *Ne vaut pas un des sentiments*
> *Dont vous embellissez ma vie.*[26]

After a worrying few years of childlessness, three children were born of this marriage. His son Esper's birth in 1802 was noted in the Prince's journal: 'After two miscarriages, my friend Esper was born on 27 December at five o'clock in the afternoon.' Esper – the unusual name was a tribute to hopes fulfilled – was followed by two girls, Ekaterina and Elizaveta, Zinaida's much-loved sisters Kety and Betsy.

Zinaida may well have found it difficult to share her beloved Papa with his new wife, but she was only six at the time of his remarriage, and if her relationship with her stepmother lacked the warmth and closeness of that with her father, it was due to difference of temperament. Whatever her intellectual shortcomings, Zinaida's stepmother obviously had the ability to create a close and loving family circle. All the children seem to have been exceptionally close, and remained so all their lives. Zinaida grew up in this lively family, openly worshipping her father, whose firm favourite she always remained. She was a charming and beautiful child, her large blue eyes looking out inquisitively at the world, golden curls framing a delicate face. Intelligent and, like her father, richly gifted, she was a willing and able pupil, sharing all his tastes, composing verse in French from an early age and showing a special aptitude for music. She became an excellent musician, playing both the piano and the harp, while her clear and lovely voice was to develop a rich, velvety quality which some described as mezzo-soprano and others as contralto, and which was to enchant all Europe. She studied music with François Boieldieu, the French composer and conductor of the Imperial Opera in St Petersburg. Again like her father, she soon showed a great talent for acting, often performing in private theatricals in their own theatre and in those of their friends. Here she was helped and encouraged by her governess, Madame Bellay, who had, in her time, been an intimate of the renowned French actors Clairon and Dumesnil.[27] Zinaida was especially close to her elder sister Maria. Madeleine, as she was always called, had neither Zinaida's beauty nor her talent. Unlike her volatile and gifted sibling, she had a calm and equable temperament and infinite kindness. Zinaida relied on her from the start, while Madeleine, devoid of jealousy, worshipped her brilliant younger sister.

The Prince took personal charge of his children's education, particularly Zinaida's, teaching her Latin and Greek in addition to French, English and Italian which he knew particularly well. Father and daughter knew long passages from the plays of Corneille and Racine by heart, declaiming them with great feeling. They also enjoyed reciting Dante and Petrarch. French was, of course, Zinaida's dominant language, as it was for all patrician Russians. Like her father, she never properly mastered Russian although later she made a determined effort to do so.

The young Princess grew up in great wealth, in her parents' splendid palaces filled with works of art and surrounded by her father's many distinguished Russian and foreign friends. Sharing his love of beauty, she would be the first to admire any new addition to his collections. The art and architecture, the landscape and climate of Italy profoundly affected the sensitive young girl. Her exotic name, Zinaida, that of a Byzantine princess, was prophetic. She always stood out among her more traditionally named sisters, and throughout her life she was irresistibly drawn to the South. Perhaps there were already signs of the depressive illness which dogged her all her life. The signs of it were always there in a restlessness and a highly strung reaction to art and beauty. While her beloved father was alive, however, all was well with her world.

*　　*　　*

In 1803 the Prince bought the Krestosky Ostrov. This densely forested island was dissected by two roads in the shape of a cross, giving the island its name (*krest*, cross, *ostrov*, island). Lying to the north-west of St Petersburg and only about three miles from the Winter Palace, the island had originally been given by Peter the Great to his sister. The painter Elizabeth Vigée-Lebrun, who spent several years in Russia and had even been courted by Alexander Beloselsky, recalled: 'The far end of this island seemed to merge into the sea, large boats sailed past, and the whole aspect was one of calm and beauty.'[28]

An existing stone house was now much enlarged by the Prince. Built around a seven-door rotunda, the house was star-shaped, light and spacious, containing a rare collection of prints and a splendid library. It was here, close to the sea and surrounded by the northern forests, that the family spent their summers. Despite being so close to the capital, the island with its forests, stables and beautiful gardens had the atmosphere of a country estate. Soon, more houses and streets were added, the streets being named after members of the family. Canton-Joli, as the estate was called, was where the Beloselsky children and their large tribe of cousins spent their early years. Gradually, the island estate was embellished with beautiful gardens full of rare plants and trees. Around the gardens was untamed Russian forest, while along the shore the Beloselskys, their friends and members of the royal family were often to be seen fishing peacefully.

Zinaida particularly loved the long rides through the forest with her father. An accomplished horseman with a large stable of thorough-breds, the Prince taught all his children to ride himself. It was while they picked their way through the forest paths that Alexander would talk to them about his travels and teach them about Russia's history, particularly Peter the Great, whom the Prince greatly admired. Those early history lessons had a profound effect on the imaginative young girl. Later she took great pains to study her country's past, especially the early history of the Slavs. As she grew up Zinaida was obviously as much admired by her younger siblings as by her father, as was later vividly recalled by one of Zinaida's step-cousins, Catherine Laval, always known as Katasha, who was the same age as Zinaida's younger half-brother and sisters. Katasha remembered the huge gatherings of family and friends. The Beloselskys were extremely hospitable even by Russian standards, and lavish entertainments followed one another, interspersed with a constant round of simple family gatherings. On Saturday evenings throughout the summer there were children's parties. Katasha recalled the merry-go-rounds when the children, mounted on wooden horses and armed with lances, would attempt to thread as many hoops as they could on to them as they went round and round. On Sundays the Lavals would join the Beloselskys for Sunday Mass in the family church which would be followed by lunch. Often, as more and more people arrived, there would be hurried consultations with the cook whom her aunt, Zinaida's step mother Anna Grigorievna, would beg to make the soup stretch just a little further. Zinaida and Katasha's paths were to cross again later, when Katasha, her future husband, Prince Troubetskoy and Zinaida's future brother-in-law, Sergei Volkonsky would be exiled to Siberia for their part in the Decembrist revolt. Katasha's letters from Siberia always sent love to Zinaida. She was never to forget her childhood admiration for her beautiful older cousin, nor of how thrilled they had always been as children to be allowed to stay up to hear Zinaida sing, and how much they had longed to please her.[29]

While she loved summers at Canton-Joli, Zinaida never liked St Petersburg, with its long, freezing winters, when the lamps would be permanently lit against the endless, bitter, northern night. Her depressive nature yearned for and needed the sun. '*Dans le sein des frimats s'écoula mon enfance*' ('My childhood passed amidst the hoar frost'), she wrote in a poem to Madame de Staël, some years later.[30] Despite the rigours of the climate, the life of the aristocracy in Russia was so splendid that every traveller of the time remarked on it. Lavish entertainments, so beloved of the Russians, punctuated the year, beginning with the New Year celebrations when both the Winter Palace and the Hermitage were thrown open to all ranks of society. In the Salle du Concert of the Winter Palace, under the most magnificent chandeliers ever seen, weekly balls were held throughout the winter. Every night there was a ball at one of the great houses. All visitors, however grand, were astonished at the richness of court dress. At Peterhof, the Emperor and Empress and the entire court would attend chapel in gold and silver dresses embroidered with diamonds. One of the Grand Duchesses wore a dress trimmed all round with four rows of diamonds. To Madame de Staël, the Russians were really southerners condemned to live in the North, who did all in their power to fight a climate so ill-suited to their nature. The conservatories and orangeries of the palaces along the Neva were luxuriant with exotic fruit and flowers, while their reception rooms were full of treasures, opulent with colour and exuberant with rich gilding and the light of a thousand candles.

Madame de Staël thought St Petersburg one of the most beautiful cities in the world, 'as if', she wrote some years later, 'with a wave of his wand a magician had conjured up all the marvels of Europe and of Asia out of the desert.'[31] Pushkin too loved this city, a love incomparably expressed in the introduction to his poem *The Bronze Horseman*. He loved the winters, with the sleighs whizzing along the broad Neva, the girls' faces, 'brighter than roses', the brilliance, and the sparkling conversation at the balls and the bachelors' gatherings with foaming glasses and the blue-flamed punch.[32]

Then still only a hundred years old, the marble city grew out of the surrounding swamps around the River Neva, its clear waters flowing between granite quays. The river was the centre of life, but also an ever-present danger to the city, as prevailing westerly winds, together with a high tide, frequently threatened to flood Peter's city. In January, at the feast of the Epiphany, the Tsar and the Imperial family followed by the entire court would descend the Jordan staircase of the Winter Palace, to watch the blessing of the waters. Men in dress uniform and bejewelled ladies swathed in their winter furs, escorted by the assembled ranks of the horse guards and surrounded by the townspeople, would all gather at the water's edge. Finally, magnificent in his vestments, followed by acolytes swinging sensors, the Metropolitan would lower the cross into the icy, black waters of the Neva through a hole cut in the ice, by then three feet thick. After the blessing, the Emperor would be presented with the first glass of water drawn from the river, which he would solemnly drink. Only then could the townspeople come to draw some of the blessed water.

Winter would drag on into May. As the days began to lengthen and the air to warm up, a sudden drop in the temperature would signal the breaking up of the ice fields on Lake Lagoda. Alexander Pushkin described the sense of euphoria at the end of winter 'when having broken her dark blue ice, the Neva sweeps it to the sea, and scenting the days of spring, exults.'[33]

The whole city would turn out to watch the enormous ice floes, often dotted with black seals, as they rumbled down the Neva to the sea, making a terrible noise as they piled up on each other and ground against the ice breakers under the bridges. Suddenly the winter would give way to the short spring, the trees unfurling their leaves almost visibly, white blossom of bird cherry foaming over the countryside, wild flowers carpeting the meadows. Then the long, lilac-scented summer days would set in; the sun ever-present on the horizon, the light pearly against the clear waters lapping the reeds. Then the Neva, flowing full, smooth and clear, was

> enlivened by the gayest ten or twelve-oared boats half-covered with a canopy fringed with gold for the company, the rowers moving in perfect unison pausing gracefully after every stroke on the water and often singing hauntingly lovely songs.[34]

Pushkin recalled the transparent twilights and moonless brilliance of summer nights when he could read all night without a lamp, and when dawn followed dusk leaving but a half-hour for night.[35] The end of August would signal a short autumn when the forests would flash with the yellow of birch leaves and the earth would be carpeted in amber and gold before the first snows reclaimed this northern land.

2

At Court

'Of Alexander's days the beautiful beginning.'

A. S. PUSHKIN.

The twenty-four-year-old Alexander's accession to the throne in September 1801 was greeted with universal rejoicing. People danced in the streets, kissed his feet when he appeared among them and called him blessed. Liberal reformers hailed him as a guardian angel; the historian Karamzin greeted his coming as that of spring, after the dark fears of the winter, while his wife the Empress Elizabeth wrote to her mother that at last Russia would now be like the rest of Europe.[1]

Foreign observers were less optimistic. 'Alexander, as good as he is narrow minded, walked to his coronation (I have this from a letter from a woman in Moscow) preceded by his grandfather's murderers, surrounded by his father's and followed, perhaps, by his own,' the Prince de Ligne noted in his journal.[2]

Too young, at twelve, to attend the countless balls inaugurating the new reign, Zinaida was nevertheless caught up in the general rejoicing. The handsome young Tsar seemed to be the very embodiment of the values of the Enlightenment so ardently desired by educated Russians. To Zinaida he seemed like a fairy-tale prince. She never entirely lost that early impression of him, through the joys and sorrows of their close friendship over the next twenty years. The Beloselskys were now firmly back at the centre of court life. The new Tsar Alexander brought the former ambassador back as Councillor and Court Chamberlain, while the widowed Empress Dowager, Maria Feodorovna, remained a close friend of Alexander Beloselsky, with whom she shared many literary and musical friends.

The four-year reign of Catherine the Great's son, Paul I, had come to an abrupt end in March of that year. Unstable and capricious, Paul had hated his mother and began his reign by reversing as many of her decrees as he could. Soon, naturally suspicious of everyone and increasingly terrified of revolution himself, Paul began to impose a series of restrictions on his unfortunate subjects. He was obsessed with order, and one of his more absurd ukases obliged everyone to dine at one, at the same time as the Tsar himself. Similarly, all government officials were required to begin work at six o'clock in the morning, since that was when the Tsar would be at his desk. It was also decreed that men and women should get out of their carriages and bow or curtsey whenever the Emperor passed. A ban was imposed on the wearing of waistcoats, believed by Paul to have been one of the causes of the French Revolution, and on the wearing of round hats, a sign of Jacobinism. The waltz was banned on the grounds that it was French and therefore Jacobin. It was strictly forbidden to use the Russian word for 'snub nose', which Paul, the unhappy possessor of one, considered an affliction. More obviously revolutionary words such as 'citizen' and 'society' were also forbidden.[3] More importantly, foreign books were banned and printing presses closed down.

Paul had fortified his main residence at Gatchina, turning it into a military camp. He rose at dawn and, taking the Prussian army as his model, personally drilled a private army of 2000 troops whom he dressed in Prussian uniforms and wigs. On one occasion when inspecting the guards, Paul, displeased with the Preobrazhensky regiment, angrily bellowed out the order: 'Right turn, quick march to Siberia!' The entire regiment wheeled about and marched out of the square, down the streets of St Petersburg and out of the city eastwards in the direction of Siberia. It was stopped some days later somewhere near Novgorod by the Tsar's messenger bearing a royal pardon which returned the regiment to the capital.[4]

The young Crown Prince Alexander, brought up mainly by his grandmother the Empress Catherine, who had entrusted his education to the liberal Swiss republican Frédéric de La Harpe, found it increasingly difficult to please his unstable father. He was also horrified at what was happening in Russia. In a long and desperate letter to his tutor La Harpe in September 1797, he confided that the country was being reduced to a terrible state, and he himself to the most wretched of men.[5] It was not difficult for Count Peter Alexandrovich Pahlen, the governor of St Petersburg, to persuade Paul's heir that it would be an act of patriotism to get rid of the Tsar and save Russia. Alexander saw that the Tsar must be forced to abdicate, after which he could ascend the throne, having had nothing to do with the actual preparations for the *coup d'état*.

On 11 March, Pahlen and his fellow conspirators strangled Paul in his apartments, while Alexander waited uneasily for news of his father's abdication in his own quarters of the gloomy, recently finished Mikhailovsky Palace. When told of the murder, he was overcome with remorse, bursting into sobs in his wife's arms. 'That's enough childishness, now go and reign,' was Pahlen's cold advice. The official reason given for the Tsar's death was apoplexy. It had been used so often that, on hearing the news, Talleyrand remarked that the Russians really ought to invent a different illness to explain the sudden death of their emperors.

Simple in his manners, noble in his bearing, progressive and humane, the new Tsar immediately lifted the restrictions imposed by his father on dress, travel and foreign books. He abolished the secret police and the use of torture in investigation and recalled from exile thousands who had been persecuted by Paul. Alexander now set about trying to cure some of Russia's problems with the help of his liberal and idealistic young friends. Together they formed the so-called Secret Committee, which he jokingly referred to as the Committee of Public Safety, recalling the French Revolution. Its members were the Polish Prince Adam Czartoryski, Count Victor Kochubey and Count Paul Stroganov.

Alexander's hope was that this committee of his friends, really no more than a private discussion group, would become the nucleus of reform. Their first task would be nothing less than the abolition of the autocracy and of serfdom. However, the Committee soon came up against the practical problems associated with the proposed reforms, and lost heart. After two and a half years of talk, it ceased to exist, stalled by a combination of the Napoleonic wars and the Tsar's own character.

Alexander was a dreamer, a young man of romantic ideas, with the vague philanthropy which was then the mode, and constituted a sort of Northern Lights, or a cold glimmering reflection of that other, warmer philanthropy which was preached in those days in Paris,

Alexander Herzen wrote of him later.[6]

Full of idealism and committed to the democratic principles which had been drummed into him by La Harpe, the sensitive and charming Alexander was an autocrat when it came to any challenge to his own ideas. Intelligent, but also impressionable and stubborn in turn, equally moved by republicans or reactionaries, the Tsar liked to please but never committed himself fully, nor allowed anyone to know his mind. Brought up in his grandmother's court, Alexander had seen her abandon her former devotion to the ideas of the Enlightenment after the French Revolution. He had also experienced his father's rule. The need to accommodate himself to such polar differences reinforced a natural ambivalence of character. He never came to terms with himself or his own actions. Forever haunted by his part in his father's assassination – 'He hoped that the conspirators would kill his father, but not to death,' as Herzen wickedly put it – he eventually turned to religious mysticism. All three members of his Secret Committee came up against the Tsar's elusive and evasive temperament. 'His soul has not yet acquired a definite colour, it is all the colours of the rainbow, with a misty grey predominating,' wrote Czartoryski, while Stroganov wrote uneasily that he could not fail to notice how confused were the ideas of the young Emperor.[7]

Apart from these three friends, the most important of the reformers around Alexander was the brilliant, self-made, priest's son, Mikhail Speransky. He hoped by means of a series of proposals for constitutional and educational reforms to base a strong monarchy firmly on the rule of law, freeing it from corruption and arbitrary decisions. However, most of Speransky's proposals came to nothing.

The Tsar's principal preoccupation was the war against Bonaparte whom Alexander early considered a menace to peace. Should he now join in a coalition against him, or continue with the policy of neutrality, proclaimed after Paul's death? The thought of war tormented him. He told Bonaparte's ambassador Duroc that he wished only to contribute to the tranquillity of Europe. In 1804, however, the Tsar's mind was made up for him when a Bourbon prince, the Duc d'Enghien, accused of plotting against Napoleon, was kidnapped in the Grand Duchy of Baden and executed without trial.

Shocked by the murder of a member of the royal family, and by the absence of a trial, the furious Alexander ordered a week of mourning, writing to La Harpe that Bonaparte was one of the most infamous tyrants that history had ever produced. Alexander's fury was further roused by Talleyrand's public reply to Russia's official protest that Alexander had no right to meddle in the affairs of France, especially as no effort had been made to bring Paul's murderers to trial in Russia. The insult hit a particularly sensitive nerve.

Alexander ordered a funeral Mass to be held in the Roman Catholic church of St Petersburg. It was attended by all the Imperial family and the diplomatic corps. Together with her older sister Madeleine, the fifteen-year-old Zinaida may have just been allowed to attend the reception given by her father that evening, at which all guests arrived dressed in mourning. When the French ambassador's wife, Madame d'Hédouville, appeared in a coloured dress, all backs were turned on her.

While Alexander was grappling with affairs of state, Zinaida's life for the moment followed the pattern of Russia's great families. The happy summers of travel and at Canton-Joli would come to an end, and each autumn the family would return to spend the winters in St Petersburg and in Moscow, where their palaces were surrounded by great conservatories and orangeries filled with palms and tropical flowers, providing a warm and scented buffer against the white, icy world outside. Here there would be all the pleasures of the city, receptions and balls, concerts, theatres, opera and ballet as well as the private recitals and theatricals at which the young Princess was beginning to excel.

In 1807, to celebrate Zinaida's eighteenth birthday, her father composed a prose poem in her honour, based on the legendary Zinaida, Queen of the Cimmerian Bosporus (the area around the Straits of Kerch which connect the Black Sea with the Sea of Azov). In the absence of any biographical knowledge of this Queen, the Prince decided to make her a daughter of Emperor Andronicus Comnenus (1183–85), who was saved when her parents were massacred in a plot led by Constantine Gabras, Duke of Trebizond. The work was not intended for publication, and included many of the Prince's reflections on society.[8]

Zinaida had now grown to womanhood. In a portrait by Bruni, her large blue eyes, at once soulful and intelligent, look out above a small straight nose, a rosebud mouth and a dimpled chin. With her fair hair tied up in a fashionable topknot, Zinaida's rounded but slender figure was admirably suited to the flowing white muslin caught up beneath her bosom with a blue sash in the fashion of the Empire. Everyone remarked on her beauty.

Moving between the Beloselsky houses in St Petersburg and Moscow, their country estates and those of their friends and family, as well as the various European capitals, Zinaida's closest and most beloved friend remained her father. Her exceptionally lovely voice and musical talent had been well trained, and she would often perform with him. At other times, they would write and produce a play to celebrate some family festival together. Her charm and sincerity, her immediate sympathy for those in trouble, made the young Princess universally loved. Intelligent, artistically gifted, tender-hearted but strong-willed, Zinaida was also highly strung, with a deep streak of melancholy. Her life was to be dogged by bouts of deep depression. For the moment, though, it was unfolding in the bosom of one of the grandest of Russia's aristocratic families in the warmth of domestic happiness.

Among Alexander Beloselsky's closest friends were the Viazemskys and the Stroganovs. Prince Viazemsky, patron and collector, shared Alexander's love of the arts; his house was known as the Russian Parnassus while his son Peter Andreevich was to remain a lifelong friend, almost a brother, to Zinaida. The Stroganovs too were part of the background of Zinaida's girlhood. Fabulously rich, the family came to prominence under Catherine the Great. Madame de Staël, who visited their magnificent palace on Stroganov Island, full of ancient Greek sculptures and staffed by 600 serfs, described the Count's way of life:

> He kept open house every day of his life. Anyone who had been introduced, could return. He never invited people to dine with him on such and such a date. It was simply understood that once admitted to his circle, one was always welcome. Often he didn't know half the people who were dining at his table, but this luxurious hospitality pleased him like all other forms of magnificence.[9]

Stroganov's house, like those of several nobles, had its own theatre and serf orchestra. His son Paul was one of Tsar Alexander's closest friends. Paul's older cousin, Sergei Nicolaevich Stroganov, was married to Zinaida's aunt, Natalia Michailovna Beloselsky. Unlike his cousin, Sergei was part of a group of nobles who were worried by the Tsar's liberal young advisers. His house was full of émigrés, among them Count Xavier de Maistre and his better known older brother, the ultramontane, legitimist philosopher Joseph. Of the two, Joseph de Maistre had a much more profound effect on contemporary Russian thinking. He came to Russia in 1802, not as an émigré, but as ambassador of the kingdom of Sardinia. Joseph de Maistre, like Alexander Beloselsky, had experienced revolutionary Piedmont; and while Beloselsky was a liberal by nature and conviction and Joseph de Maistre the very opposite, both were men of the *ancien régime*, who had been profoundly shocked by the French Revolution and the beheading of Louis XVI and Marie Antoinette. A passionate, ideological opponent of the French Revolution and a fierce critic of all forms of liberalism, de Maistre preached salvation by faith and tradition, advocating the Roman Catholic Church as the only antidote to the godlessness of the Enlightenment and the nihilism of the Revolution. He became one of the most important influences on Tsar Alexander after 1805, as well as a key figure in Alexander's shift away from liberalism, playing a major role in the acceptance in Russia of the Jesuits, whom he considered to be the shock troops of the counter-revolution. De Maistre certainly had hopes of converting the Russians, beginning by launching a programme for the conversion of 'one dozen women of quality'.[10] It may be that the roots of Zinaida's later conversion to Catholicism stem from this period of her life.

Zinaida shone in the salons of Moscow and St Petersburg. Her many talents and her lively intelligence naturally drew her to artistic and intellectual circles. One of these was the so-called 'Stroganov Academy'. Presided over by her first cousin, Alexander Sergeevich Stroganov, son of her paternal aunt, Natalia, it was not an academy in a formal sense, but rather a literary and artistic salon. The young Zinaida was its life and soul, foreshadowing future salons where she would be the undisputed queen. Other members included her older sister Madeleine, now Princess Vlasova, her Saltikov aunt, Princess Dolgoruky, the court poet Yuri Neledinsky-Meletsky, and several émigrés, among them Xavier de Maistre and a former abbot, Antoine Spada, who had become a tutor in the Beloselsky household.

Modelling themselves on the salons of pre-revolutionary Paris, the Academy's members not only held literary and political discussions, but also composed and performed poetry and songs and held musical evenings, readings, charades and theatrical performances. When, on one occasion, Alexander Sergeevich suggested that they all choose a painting in his collection, and celebrate it in poetry or prose, Zinaida paid her cousin and host a graceful compliment by choosing as her subject a portrait of him painted by Madame Vigée-Lebrun, about which she composed her 'Vers au Président de L'Académie Strogonovienne'.[11] In another poem, the light-hearted 'Couplets à Spada', addressed to Antoine Spada, a former abbot from Piedmont and now her tutor, Zinaida rather self-consciously celebrates her love of books:

> *Gloire à ma Bibliotèque!*
> *Elle vaut un coffre-fort;*
> *Milton, Le Tasse et Sénèque*
> *Donnent le mépris de l'or.*
> *En effet que sert de vivre,*
> *Quand on n'a pas de bouquins? . . .*
> *Moi, j'aime mieux un seul livre,*
> *Que mille livres sterlings!*[12]

In 1808, Zinaida and Madeleine were appointed maids of honour to the Dowager Empress Maria Feodorovna. Zinaida loved her from the start, commemorating her many years later in her Roman garden with a column which bears the inscription:

> *Les jeunes filles dont*
> *elle était la protectrice*
> *répétaient en pleurant:*
> *Qui nous bénira dans notre entrée*
> *dans le monde.*

Born Sophia-Dorothea of Württemberg, the grand-niece of Frederick the Great, Maria Feodorovna, as she became on converting to the Orthodox faith, was as much loved as her husband Paul had been feared and hated. She, on the other hand, seemed to be the only person to have loved him, bearing him ten children while accepting his eccentricities and infidelities with loving calm. Madame Vigée-Lebrun, who painted her, recalled an occasion when the Empress was sitting for her portrait and the Emperor, with the young princes, came to join them:

> Paul began to caper about just like a monkey; he scratched away at the screen and pretended to climb over it. Alexander and his brother Constantine were visibly suffering while watching their father play such grotesque games in front of a stranger and even I felt embarrased for him.[13]

The Empress, however, remained unworried. When Zinaida first joined her household, the Empress was already in her fifties and had grown a little stout; yet she still had the most magnificent blonde hair which fell to her shoulders in thick curls, and was always described as looking fresh and elegant. Her warm smile, her kindness and her interest in everyone made her much loved in spite of her decided views and the old-fashioned ways which she liked to preserve at her beloved estate of Pavlovsk, which, named for her husband Paul, had been a gift from the Empress Catherine. Maria Feodorovna had been deeply affected by her husband's murder, but although, after his death, she remained faithful to his memory, keeping his bloodstained nightshirt in a casket at Pavlovsk, she nevertheless banished all the military marches and drills that Paul had insisted on. Now that she was free to follow her own interests, she turned Pavlovsk into a centre of intellectual, artistic and scientific life, just as she had already turned the palace itself into a treasure house of all that was best in furniture and the decorative arts and crafts, both in Russia and in Europe.

Adored by all her children, Maria Feodorovna was especially loved by Alexander who, after his father's death and suffering from abiding guilt, continued to give his mother precedence over even his own wife. She was an important influence on him, her forthright and determined character in marked contrast to his own. Whenever he was in residence at Tsarskoe Selo, Alexander would appear to visit his mother precisely at three o'oclock; and it was to Pavlovsk that he returned to celebrate his victory over Napoleon in June 1814. When in St Petersburg, the Tsar dined with his mother at least three times a week, often staying for the night.

Alexander's need to be universally loved and admired was especially evident in his relationships with women. At only sixteen years old he was married to the fourteen-year-old, angelically fair beauty, Princess Louise of Baden, who took the name of Elizabeth on her baptism into the Russian Orthodox Church. The Empress Catherine had described her grandson then as a superbly handsome, fine young man, comparing him to the Apollo Belvedere. Tall, fair-haired and blue-eyed, always immaculately dressed in the military uniforms he loved so much, he was the picture of a romantic hero. He genuinely loved to please women, enjoying hours of conversation with them and delighting in their company. Although his cold and detached nature required one conquest after another, he knew how to make each woman feel that she was the most important to him. He had had a long liaison with the dark-haired, voluptuous Polish beauty, Maria Narishkina, with whom he had several children, only one of whom survived childhood. While Zinaida had been admiring the Tsar from her schoolroom, Alexander had been paying court to most of the beauties that crossed his path. Among them was the famous French actress, Mademoiselle George, formerly Napoleon's lover, who was a great favourite in St Petersburg in 1808 and 1809. Zinaida, who had seen her performing, was stagestruck, expressing her admiration to the actress in a poem, her 'Vers à Mademoiselle George':

> *Quelle est cette beauté, qui des bords de la Seine,*
> *Pour enchanter nos choeurs arrive en ces climats?*[14]

Most of Alexander's relationships were platonic, however. What he loved most was the excitement of the chase, the flirtation, the dancing, the pleasure it gave to the lady. 'It was very seldom that the virtue of the ladies with whom Alexander was occupied was really in danger,' wrote his friend Prince Adam Czartoryski. The Prince had himself become the Empress Elizabeth's lover, and was probably the father of her daughter, born in 1799, who had survived barely a year.

Alexander's closest relationship, perhaps, was with his younger sister, the Grand Duchess Catherine. With a dazzling complexion, and 'the most beautiful hair in the world',[15] this wilful and intelligent young woman always exerted a powerful influence over her brother. His letters to her, however, reveal a relationship which seems to have gone somewhat beyond brotherly affection, even allowing for eighteenth-century hyperbole. Writing from Pulavy on 20 September probably in 1805, Alexander addresses her as 'Absurd little mad thing' and ends, 'Farewell light of my eyes, adored of my heart, polestar of the age, wonder of nature, or better than all these, Bisiam Bisiamovna [a personal nickname], with the snub nose'; and again, 'What is that dear nose doing, the nose I love to flatten and kiss? – If you are mad, you are the most delightful madwoman who ever existed. – I am mad about you. – I love you like a madman. – I rejoice like a maniac to be seeing you again. After having run like a man possessed, I hope to take delicious rest in your arms.' Whatever the true nature of their relationship, Alexander loved her perhaps more than any other human being and the bond between them remained unbroken until Catherine's tragically early death.[16]

The Empress Dowager took a close maternal interest in all her family and in her ladies-in-waiting and pages. To Zinaida, Maria Feodorovna was mother, friend and lifelong example. The younger woman shared with the old Empress two dominant characteristics: a deep love of music and a passionate desire to help those in need. Artists and writers were regularly invited to stay and work at Pavlovsk, among them all the members of Alexander Beloselsky's circle – the historian Karamzin, the poet Derzhavin and Ivan Kylov, Russia's 'Aesop', as well as, after 1815, the romantic poet Zhukovsky, who was to be a frequent guest at Zinaida's salon and later visited her in Rome. Zinaida bloomed in the congenial atmosphere of the Empress Dowager's court which was renowned for its elegance and gaiety. As well as being more amusing, Maria Feodorovna's court was much grander than Alexander's. All important visitors were received by the Empress Dowager, sometimes before they saw the Tsar himself. Zinaida would have certainly been in attendance at the Winter Palace in 1809 when Maria Feodorovna received the first ambassador of the United States to Russia, John Quincy Adams, on the first morning of his arrival in St Petersburg. Adams remained in Russia until 1814, returning to the United States to become, first, Secretary of State, and later, in 1825, President.[17]

All her life Maria Feodorovna was deeply interested in the welfare of her people, founding and supporting twenty-seven charitable institutions not only at Pavlovsk but also in Moscow and St Petersburg. Her warm-hearted sympathy for the poor and weak was always followed up with a practical act. Energetic, disciplined and active, she was up at six, supervising all her projects personally. She founded the Marinsky hospital in Pavlovsk which became a model for others. Orphanages, shelters for sick children, a school for the deaf (after a chance encounter with a deaf child in her park), schools for practical agriculture, weaving workshops, hospitals and homes for soldiers and their widows were among her foundations. Zinaida learned much from her and throughout her life always responded actively to any cry for help.

For Tsar Alexander, the years since his accession had not been easy. Bonaparte had crowned himself Emperor Napoleon in May 1804, in the presence of the Pope who had been dragged unwillingly to Paris for the occasion. In the same year Russia had signed a treaty of alliance with Austria, and in the following year with England and

Sweden. Prussia was still wavering about joining the third coalition against Napoleon, and in 1805 Alexander went to Berlin to secure Prussia'a alliance. He was received with full honours by the King and Queen Louise with whom, in a highly romantic gesture, he paid a visit to the tomb of Frederick the Great. Here, in the torchlit crypt, as the Tsar bent to kiss the tomb, the three sovereigns solemnly called on Frederick's help against Napoleon. They then travelled to Potsdam, where a treaty was duly signed on 3 November. Meanwhile Napoleon, who had spent a frustrating summer on the Channel coast, abandoned his plan to invade England and turned his attention instead to eastern Europe, in what became known as the campaign of Austerlitz. In his proclamation of a victory at Ulm, which had cost the Austrians 60,000 men, Napoleon added the ominous rider, 'We shall not stop there. That Russian army, which the gold of England has brought from the extremities of the earth, shall share the same fate.' To his wife Josephine he wrote. 'I have fulfilled my destiny. I have destroyed the Austrian army. I have lost only 1500 men.' By coincidence, that day Nelson defeated Admiral Villeneuve's fleet off Cape Trafalgar but the news, of course, had not yet reached Napoleon.

Nearly two months later, on 2 December, as a great red sun rose out of the thick mists near the village of Austerlitz in Moravia, Napoleon sent his troops into the attack. By dusk, with a light snow falling over the thousands of dead and wounded, Napoleon had won his most glorious victory, smashing the combined Russian and Austrian army commanded by the two Emperors. 'The Russian army is not only beaten, but destroyed,' he wrote to Josephine.[18] A deeply humiliated Alexander had narrowly escaped death by a cannon-ball and left General Kutuzov, who had been against the engagement all along, to lead the straggling remnants of his army home across the plains of Hungary. Napoleon imposed very severe terms on Austria and Prussia. Both Russia and Prussia suffered further defeats at Jena, Auerstadt and Eylau, and in June 1807 Alexander saw Russian troops suffer another crushing defeat at the battle of Friedland where he lost almost a third of his men. With his army demoralised and in a state of complete disorganisation, Alexander was forced to negotiate. An armistice was duly signed, followed by a meeting of the Emperors of Russia and France, on a raft theatrically anchored in the middle of the River Nieman. Alexander was aware that Napoleon wished to neutralise Russia in order to tackle England. The two Emperors could then divide the world up between them. An agreement was signed in Tilsit in 1807. Napoleon left believing that he was now free to turn his attention elsewhere. For the moment Alexander hoped only to gain time.

In Russia, Alexander's popularity was waning. Little had been achieved at home, while the Tsar himself seemed to be constantly wavering between his advisers. Russia had been prepared to forgive him for Austerlitz and the Friedland defeat, but the Treaty of Tilsit, which precluded trade with England, was seriously damaging to Russia's economy. Discontent seethed on all sides. When relations between Russia and France were again strained by differences between them over Poland, Alexander agreed to another meeting with Napoleon in the autumn of 1808 at Ehrfurt, provoking anger from many of his courtiers and a warning from his mother who urged him to turn back and abandon Prussia. Alexander ignored all warnings. He had made up his mind that war with Napoleon was unavoidable and believed that now the most important thing was to gain time.

That same year, Napoleon decided to consolidate his power by forming a dynastic marriage. Proposing to repudiate Josephine and prepared to abandon his Polish mistress, the beautiful Marie Walewska, Napoleon asked for the hand of the Grand Duchess Catherine. A hastily arranged betrothal to a minor German prince, the Duke of Oldenburg, saved Alexander's beloved sister from the 'Corsican ogre', and the Tsar from his mother's wrath. A subsequent offer for the hand of the Grand Duchess Anna, Alexander's next sister, was stalled on the grounds of her age; she was barely fifteen.

In January 1809, St Petersburg was in festive mood, preparing to celebrate the marriage of the Grand Duchess Catherine to the Duke of Oldenburg. Among the many foreign guests, the King and Queen of Prussia were especially honoured. Queen Louise, feeling unwell in the early stages of pregnancy and miserable that it had taken a slight toll of her looks, was longing to resume her flirtation with the Tsar. Alexander, however, was visibly irritated by the coquettish Queen's bare shoulders and daring décolletages. At the Dolgoruky ball she had appeared covered in jewels from head to foot, in stark contrast to Alexander's mistress Maria Narishkina, dressed in one of her usual simple Grecian white gowns which were such a perfect foil to her dark beauty. Alexander was probably bored with both. At ball after ball his eyes kept turning to a slender young woman, one of his mother's ladies-in-waiting, who had been chosen to attend on the Queen of Prussia during her visit.

The Tsar had often seen Zinaida before, during his frequent visits to his mother's court. Now he realised that the young Princess was not only beautiful, but intelligent and cultivated. Furthermore, she sang like an angel and looked like one too, always preferring a simple style of dress unlike many of the other diamond-encrusted ladies of the court. Charmed by her youth and freshness, touched by her adoration, interested in her conversation, Alexander now gave her his full attention. To the romantic Zinaida the Tsar was literally a knight in shining armour. Young and idealistic, she saw a man of the West whose enlightened views must change Russia for ever, a man of ideas, and one moreover who was as handsome as he was good. Zinaida fell in love with the Tsar as he did with her. She must have known of the Tsar's romantic involvements, and probably neither expected nor wanted more than a romantic friendship. The Tsar too would have been unlikely to take further a strong attraction for an unmarried girl of his own circle, particularly one who was lady-in-waiting to his mother. However, the relationship developed. They thought alike and the uncommonly well-educated Zinaida could take an intelligent interest in his preoccupations. Thus began a friendship based on mutual trust which would outlast their love affair, and indeed endure until Alexander's death.

At the end of that year, on 26 December, Zinaida suffered the most crushing blow of her life. Just as Alexander entered her life so the man she loved most left it. Prince Beloselsky, her beloved father, friend and mentor, died unexpectedly in St Petersburg of a stroke. He was only fifty-seven. His death was mourned by all who knew him. The Spanish ambassador, General Pardu, wrote that one of the columns of Russian civilisation had fallen. He was buried at the Lavra of Alexander Nevsky. The Prince's journal, his *Vademecum*, begun so many years before in Italy, ends with a silhouette of him. Beneath it, in Italian, his wife has written: 'I weep for his death and for my life.'

Devastated by her father's death, alone and miserable, Zinaida was grateful for Alexander's friendship and the two were increasingly seen together. The Tsar's attentions to a beautiful and unmarried girl, 'the loveliest decoration of my court' as he called her, inevitably became a matter of concern to Zinaida's stepmother and her family. The problem was apparent to the Empress Dowager, who felt a sense of responsibility as well as affection for her unhappy young lady-in-waiting. The Princess was almost twenty-one and it was time she was settled. Marriage was the obvious answer. What better match than to one of the Tsar's aides-de-camp, and the son of her closest friend, the formidable Mistress of the Robes. Whatever the relationship between the Tsar and Zinaida after her marriage, it would be far more easily tolerated than an affair with a vulnerable young woman of high birth.

Zinaida's marriage to Prince Nikita Grigorievich Volkonsky took place on 3 February 1811. It had been arranged by her stepmother, Anna Grigorievna, with the support and connivance of the Empress Dowager and the groom's mother, Princess Volkonsky. In worldly terms it was an excellent match. The Prince was the second son of one of the greatest families in the land. Descended from the ninth-century Prince Rurik, the family's history was woven into that of Russia. Extremely rich and very powerful, the Volkonskys had a long tradition of service to the state, enjoying great independence even from the Tsars. At the time of Zinaida's marriage, there were four Volkonsky aides-de-camp to the Tsar: Nikita, his two brothers, and Prince Peter Mikhailovich Volkonsky, one of Alexander's most trusted friends, who was head of the senior branch of the family and married to Prince Nikita's sister, Princess Sophia. Prince Peter, who had joined the Semenovsky regiment as a boy, became Alexander's aide-de-camp when Alexander was heir presumptive, remaining his friend and loyal servant for the whole of the Tsar's life, and probably saving Alexander's life at Austerlitz. He distinguished himself in every campaign during the Napoleonic wars and was the most highly decorated officer in the land, rising to the highest ranks. After Kutuzov's death in 1813, he became Chief of the General Staff. A brilliant mind and a calm and agreeable manner were allied to exceptional organisational talents and an unswerving loyalty to his country and his sovereign.

Prince Nikita, alas, was not in the same mould. Born in 1782, in St Petersburg, he was the second of three surviving sons of Prince Grigory Semeonovich, governor of the province of Orenburg, and of his wife, Princess Alexandra Nicolaevna Repnin. Zinaida knew her formidable mother-in-law well. The old Princess was the Empress Dowager's closest confidante and her Mistress of the Robes, and, as such, the first non-royal lady of the Empire. They were, however, very different. As her descendant later wrote, Princess Volkonsky was a courtier to the marrow of her bones; a cold and forbidding woman whose life was dedicated to the court, for whom duty, discipline and form had replaced feelings and natural impulses. Alexandra Nicolaevna rarely visited her husband in his far-away post, remaining at the family palace on the Moika canal in St Petersburg, the very same palace in which Pushkin was to live and die. After her husband's death in 1824, she moved to apartments in the Winter Palace with her faithful French companion Josephine, leaving the palace to her children. A family portrait shows the Princess seated at a round table at the Winter Palace, a bonnet with large satin ribbons and bows on her large unattractive head with its red, fleshy face, small hooked nose and large protuberant eyes, bent over one of her endless games of patience.[19]

Nikita's father was a charming and eccentric character who had, since 1803, retired to live among the Kirgiz and Bashkir natives in the wild and far-flung province at the foot of the Ural mountains, of which he was military governor. A soldier himself, he had served under Suvorov who had commended him for his energy and industry. Always attracted to the exotic, he had hoped to be Russia's ambassador to Constantinople. He revelled in life on the Asian frontier, in the arrivals of vassal khans, of camel caravans with their loads of treasures from the Asian steppe, in the colourful bazaars and majestic scenery of his province. Quite unconcerned about what others thought of him, the Prince would go to market in his coach, returning home with his liveried manservants festooned with geese and legs of ham which he would distribute to the poor. Deeply religious, he would sometimes stop his coach and kneel beside it in the mud, praying. Frequently, the people of Orenburg would be treated to the sight of their military governor wandering the streets of the town in his dressing-gown, all his orders blazing on his chest. In this dress he would wander quite some distance, perhaps returning on the back of a passing farm cart.[20] It was a great pity that he was never to know his daughter-in-law Zinaida. Their unconventional temperaments and passion for Italian music would have made them natural friends. The old Prince would have enjoyed listening to her singing the operas of his favourite, Paisiello, so beautifully. But he never saw her. St Petersburg and Moscow were both too far away.

Indulged and easy-going, Nikita had inherited the Volkonsky aristo-cratic, blue-eyed looks but not much else. He seems to have been his mother's favourite and remained under her thumb, to Zinaida's dismay and irritation. He was outshone by his grandee older brother Prince Repnin (who, in the absence of male heirs in his mother's family, had taken his maternal grandfather's title) and by his dashing younger brother Sergei, who was already a decorated war hero, having been wounded during the battle of Eylau when only eighteen. Nikita had first become an officer in the Ismailovsky regiment, serving as aide-de-camp to his grandfather, Field-Marshal N. V. Repnin. Later he served under Mikhelson in the Turkish campaign of 1806, before becoming aide-de-camp to the Tsar. In this capacity he was entrusted with a diplomatic mission which had a comic sequel. In 1808 Alex-ander sent him with a letter to Napoleon. The Prince was graciously received by the Emperor, and duly delivered his letter. On the way out, General Duroc caught up with him, handing him a small box: 'Please accept this remembrance from His Majesty, Prince.'

On opening the box Nikita found a ring with a rather small diamond in it. Finding the gift unworthy of an ambassador of the Emperor of Russia, he casually tossed it to the gendarme who had escorted him, telling him to 'keep this in remembrance of a Russian officer'. The gendarme couldn't resist boasting of the incident. Soon the story reached Napoleon. Corsican pride was quite the equal of Russian. The furious Emperor instructed his ambassador in St Petersburg to lodge a formal complaint. The Tsar called in his aide-de-camp. Had anything been left out of his account of the journey?

'No, Sire, I have told you everything,' replied the puzzled Prince. Then, remembering the ring, he confessed the story.

'*Il paraît que vous avez manqué me brouiller avec Napoléon. C'est une imprudence de votre part. Après tout vous n'avez pas eu tout-à-fait tort dans cette affaire. N'en parlons plus,*' the Tsar said as he dismissed him, not altogether displeased. ('It would seem that you have almost made me quarrel with Napoleon. It was careless of you. Still you weren't altogether wrong. Let us say no more about it.')[21] On this occasion the Tsar was disposed to forgive his young emissary's *faux pas*. However, he did not like Nikita, whose post had probably been arranged by his mother. His letters to Zinaida later reveal a growing contempt for her weak and lazy husband.

Zinaida's marriage was unhappy from the outset. She had married while still grieving for her father, the one person who had satisfied both mind and heart. Her courtship by the Tsar did not make for an auspicious start. Pregnant almost at once, she was much alone, with plenty of time for brooding. Her husband was away most of the time on his official duties and about his private pleasures. Zinaida's expectations of marriage were gravely disappointed, while Nikita's infidelities threw her into panic. The birth of her son on 11 November 1811, exactly nine months after her marriage, gave new meaning to Zinaida's life. She called him Alexander, her father's name and that of the Tsar. In December he was christened with great ceremony in the private chapel of the Winter Palace with the Tsar standing godfather. With all the Volkonskys gathered around the font and the chapel full of Russia's greatest families, Zinaida must have felt proud and happy as she looked at the Tsar with her son in his arms.

Although Zinaida adored her son, she plunged into deep depression after his birth, and by the summer was suffering from a serious nervous breakdown. The weight of the past two years and the profound changes in her life had caught up with her emotionally fragile nature. The young Princess had everything to make her happy and yet she was overwhelmed with despair. Idealistic and talented, Zinaida felt trapped in her marriage and guilty at her inability to come to terms with her life. Her despair and her fits of hysterical weeping, which were known to all her circle, greatly worried her family. Post-natal depression was then unknown, and many of her friends thought she was suffering from some sort of madness. Princess Lanskaya, writing to a friend, expressed the fear that she 'might go mad like Zinaida but for my faith in God.'[22] Zinaida, who may well have thought so herself, was desperately searching for some sort of answer. Many years later she confessed that she had experienced a strong religious call at this time, but 'the call of the world had been too strong then'.[23] During one hysterical fit, perhaps brought on by her husband's infidelity which in the first years of her marriage seemed to strike at the very heart of her insecurity, Zinaida bit through her upper lip. The resulting scar remained with her all her life. It was noticed three years later by the Comtesse de Boigne, a friend of Nikita's, when the Volkonskys were in Paris with the Tsar. She too believed that the Princess had bitten through her lip in a jealous fit:

> Princess Volkonsky suffered from an altogether oriental type of jealousy; she did not allow her husband to even look at a woman. Some months before, in an excess of jealous rage, she had bitten off a sizeable piece of her lip. There was still a livid scar and it spoiled her beauty which was none-the-less real.[24]

Zinaida was still recovering from her breakdown in August 1812, when she unexpectedly received a letter and a present from Madame de Staël – a copy of her novel *Corinne ou L'Italie*. Zinaida had always been fascinated by Madame de Staël and had already read the book. The romantic tragedy, which included an account of Madame de Staël's travels in Italy, had gone straight to her heart. The story of the beautiful Corinne, whose exceptional talents and intelligence allow her, for a time, to lead an independent existence, was a theme Madame de Staël had already explored. Her earlier novel, *Delphine*, marked the beginning of the debate about women's role in society, and their right to an independent existence as artists and writers. Both novels end tragically. Madame de Staël's aim was to show that, in spite of the Revolution, those rights were far from won; that women were only accepted by society if they were submissive. She was also defending the artist's right to freedom of expression at a time when that right was under serious threat.

Always well informed, Madame de Staël was aware of Zinaida's closeness to the Tsar, and besides, she was curious to see this young woman of enlightened views, who was being compared to the heroine of her book – Zinaida was already being called the Northern Corinna by her friends. Prince Nikita had visited Madame de Staël at Coppet before his marriage, probably in 1808 after he had completed the Tsar's diplomatic mission to Napoleon. Madame de Staël also knew Zinaida's aunt Princess Laval; it was probably through her that she had learned of her illness.

Zinaida, longing to meet the famous writer but unwilling to allow Madame de Staël to see her when she was still weak, and probably embarrassed to be seen when still carrying the scars of an hysterical illness, nevertheless wrote at once to thank her for *Corinne*, sending an engraving of Coppet, and a poem, 'A Madame de Staël en Lui Renvoyant Corinne'. In it, Zinaida praises the author's powers of imagination, goes on to salute 'lovely Italy, clothed in all of nature's gifts' and then, turning to the novel's heroine Corinne, follows her:

> through the sombre ruins at the feet of volcanoes boiling with fury. – My childhood was spent among the frosts of a land where the lute is without harmony, while the mid-winter flower gasps for the breath of life.

Her poem ends with a plea to the poet, 'you whose genius soars in full flight under a free sky,' to go on singing.[25]

Delighted by the poem and the present, Madame de Staël was more than ever anxious to persuade Zinaida to see her. She knew that Zinaida had been seriously ill, and immediately guessed that a young beauty might be anxious about her altered appearance. A warm letter of thanks to the Princess was quickly despatched:

Princess!
Your letter and your present have made such a strong and profound impression that I cannot bear not to see you. Everyone tells me you're an angel, and now I know it better than anyone. Could you

not receive me for a few moments? I know that you are pale and that your charming face is a little altered, but consider: I will love you even more, because you will evoke tenderness in me as well as charming me. You are sick in spirit – who knows but that I might find words which will comfort you? I don't wish to press you but a moment of your time would be a great favour. I saw your husband the Prince at my Coppet retreat which you recalled to me so vividly. He has since then become the happiest of men: preserve the one he loves for him. Consider that the God of all goodness, who has given you so many reasons to be loved, wishes you to enjoy the gifts of life in peace. I feel that you will soon be cured: so many good people are close to you! So many prayers have been sent up for you that they must be answered! As for me, I am one who will understand you and wish you so much good. I should like to lay some of those good wishes at your feet myself and tell you that you will ever be in my thoughts.

My most tender wishes to you and also to Princess Beloselsky,
Necker de Staël Holstein.[26]

Soon, Madame de Staël was presented to the Empress Elizabeth. During the audience, Alexander came in unannounced. She was overwhelmed with admiration. Everything about the Tsar pleased her: his manner, his modesty, his intelligence and his learning.

The Tsar was at this time working with his Minister of the Interior, Mikhail Speransky, on a proposal to improve the lot of the serfs who represented nine-tenths of the Russian population. Although not in the strictest sense slaves, they had no civil rights at all. Landowners could sell them with the land, marry them off at will, send them off for years of military service and, with the exception of the death penalty, punish them as they liked. Male serfs, known as 'souls', had actually been a taxable unit since the time of Peter the Great and successive sovereigns had distributed them, together with the land they worked, as gifts, their labour a basic guarantee of wealth. Alexander rightly saw this as the most important of his reforms if Russia were to consider herself a civilised country. When the Tsar spoke to Madame de Staël of his intentions, she exclaimed: 'Sire, your character is the constitution of your Empire and your conscience its guarantee,' later writing, 'I doubt that he could find a minister in his Empire more capable of judging or directing affairs than himself.' Surely, she thought, such a man would rid Europe of Napoleon.[27]

Napoleon had always been wary of this brilliant woman. Born in Paris where her father, the Swiss banker and financial expert Jacques Necker, was Louis XVI's reforming and influential minister, and her mother held one of the great literary salons of her day, Germaine married Eric de Staël, the Swedish ambassador, who was, his twenty-year-old wife declared, 'of all the men I could never love the one that I like best.'[28] Soon, her 'Thursdays' at the Swedish Embassy became the centre of political, intellectual and artistic life in Paris. Many of the most influential men of her day, men like Louis de Narbonne, Lafayette, Talleyrand, André Chénier and Benjamin Constant, were or would become her lovers. During the Directory she was eager to welcome Bonaparte, but he always held her in suspicion and she soon saw the dictator behind the brilliant young soldier. He, for all the might of his sword, feared her pen and her tongue, exiling her to her Swiss estate of Coppet in 1802 after the publication of *Delphine*, which he pronounced immoral. This was a severe punishment for a woman who later wrote: 'For me, true pleasure can be found only in love, in Paris, or in power.'[29] Napoleon's contempt for women and for intellectuals soon turned Madame de Staël into his implacable enemy, and Coppet into a centre of European liberal resistance. Neither of them ever underestimated the other, however. Napoleon kept *cette véritable peste*, as he called her, under constant surveillance while she feared not only his power but also his ability to spread slander. 'A Senator once said to me,' she wrote, 'that Napoleon was the best journalist he knew. If the art of slandering individuals and countries could be considered as such, then he was indeed.'[30]

No mean propagandist herself, Madame de Staël was now in St Petersburg in order to incite the Tsar against Napoleon. Tired of her Swiss exile, she was on her way to England, taking the long way around via Austria, Russia and Sweden. She arrived in Russia on 14 July 1812, struck by the coincidence of the date with that of the beginning of the French Revolution, a revolution she believed had been so comprehensively betrayed by Napoleon. She was obliged to go the long way via Kiev and Moscow, and was impressed by the hospitality of the Russians, at a time when their territory had already been occupied by the French and she might well have been considered an enemy. Fêted wherever she went, she loved the Russians in return. 'I can only retain the noblest and sweetest impressions of this Russian Empire, so wrongfully called barbarian,' she wrote later. 'May my gratitude bring down more blessings on these people and on their sovereign.' She was not blind to their faults however:

> Their nature has not changed as a result of Peter I's rapid modernis- ation: for the present it has only changed their manners: luckily for them they remain what we think of as 'barbarian', that is led by their instincts which are often generous, always involuntary. In so far as they reflect, it is usually on the choice of means, never to examine the ends. I say luckily for them not because I applaud barbarians; what I mean by that word is a certain kind of primitive energy, which for nations, is the only thing that can act as a substi- tute for the concentrated force of freedom.[31]

In St Petersburg, where she arrived at the beginning of August, Madame de Staël was overwhelmed with invitations. Interested and charmed by the Russians, she saw them nevertheless with her custom- ary clear-sightedness. Their conversation was limited because:

> The Russian character is too passionate for them to love abstract thought, and in any case ideas of any significance are always more or less dangerous at a court where there was a great deal of envy and watchfulness.[32]

Standing on the threshold of the golden age of Russian literature, although of course she could not know that, she had a low opinion of much of the writing of the time, considering most of it derivative. However, without any knowledge of Russian she guessed from its sound that it might be a marvellous language for poetry.

> The Russians are mistaken in imitating French literature. It seems to me that they would do better to turn to the Greeks for inspiration than to the Latins. The letters of the Russian alphabet are similar

to the Greek, the traditional links between the Russians and the Byzantine empire, their future destiny . . . all this should turn them towards the study of Greek.[33]

Madame de Staël was not alone in her views. In Pushkin's *The Queen of Spades*, written two decades later but set at the beginning of the nineteenth century, when asked by her grandson if she would like to read a Russian novel the old Countess replies: 'I had no idea that there were such things as Russian novels. Do please send me some, my dear boy, I'd like to see them.'

But Pushkin, who was to change all that, was then still a schoolboy, his first poem two years away, an event which coincided with the birth of another of Russia's greatest poets and writers, Michail Lermontov. Gogol was a little boy of three, while the next fifteen years would see the birth of Turgenev, Herzen, Dostoevsky and Tolstoy — and with them the arrival of a great body of literature as universal as it was Russian.

3

War: 'Our Knight and Angel'

'I have but one desire: it is to be even a little like the being you describe and to whom you give my name.'

EMPEROR ALEXANDER TO PRINCESS ZINAIDA VOLKONSKY

Zinaida saw little of the Tsar during the first half of 1812. She had been so ill and depressed in the previous year that even her music had ceased to cheer her. Now, although a little thin and pale, the scar on her lip a constant reminder of her terrifying nervous breakdown, she gradually regained her spirits and her health. The baby Alexander, her Sachon, was her great joy. The political situation was now very tense and Zinaida, at the centre of events, was naturally caught up in the general preoccupation with the war. She knew how testing the coming year would be for the Tsar and for Russia.

Gossip about the Tsar's attentions to her, though muted, had hurt her, and she avoided the social life of the court. In her search for answers and for protection, she turned to religion. Brought up in a completely Western tradition, and surrounded by French émigrés, Zinaida was powerfully drawn to the Catholic Church. But, as she herself wrote later, the time was not yet ripe. As she recovered her health, life with all its pleasures drew her back. Torn between hope and fear, for the moment she could only wait. In a thoughtful and poetic piece, 'Pensée Détachée', she reflects on this state of mind:

Is Expectation not the same as Hope? Yes, but Hope smiles like an angel from heaven, and heaven smiles back: Expectation is dreamlike, anxious, like the Peri [a benign fallen angel from Persian mythology in the shape of a beautiful wingèd woman] who seeks on earth the key to the gates of happiness. Her ear is tuned to every shadow, every sound. Hope listens untiring and watches untroubled: Expectation is passion; Hope is rest. Both are wingèd. But the wings of Expectation are heavy with illusion, fears, disquieting images weighing heavily on the shoulders, and the air around them is full of clouds, whereas Hope spreads its light and shining wings in air which is pure and free.[1]

There seemed no end to Napoleon's ambition. After defeating the Austrians at the battle of Wagram in July 1809, Napoleon had captured Vienna, setting himself up in great splendour at the Hapsburg Palace of Schönbrunn, just outside the city. By the end of the year he had asked for the hand of the young Austrian Princess Marie-Louise, whom he married in the following spring. In March 1811, Marie-Louise had produced the longed-for heir, Napoleon II, who was named King of Rome. Most of Europe was now Napoleon's, or allied to him, with only the Iberian peninsula and Russia outside the economic blockade against his one remaining enemy, England. The progressive destruction of Russia's trade had turned the tide of public opinion once more towards the Tsar as anti-French sentiment swelled.

Alexander had been preparing for war for some time. The last months of 1811 had been so tense that he felt unable to leave the capital. 'Hostilities could break out at any moment ... We are on continual alert,' he wrote to his sister, the Grand Duchess Catherine.[2]

The Tsar was constantly engaged in diplomatic negotiations. He was particularly concerned about Austria which, since Napoleon's marriage to Princess Marie-Louise, was committed to the French side. The best he could now hope for was that Austria would remain passive. For her part, Prussia, as her king put it, 'had to yield to irresistible necessity', but the friendship between Alexander and Frederick William III would continue to unite them. In Sweden, Bernadotte, a former Marshal of the Grande Armée but now Napoleon's bitter enemy, had been happy to sign an offensive and defensive alliance with Russia. In April 1812, Kutuzov's victory over the Turks, with whom Russia had been at war since 1806, liberated the troops that would be needed in the coming struggle against Napoleon. The army had been reorganised and prepared, and intensive mobilisation was now under way.

Alexander informed Napoleon that he was prepared to return to the Treaty of Tilsit (under the terms of which Russia had promised to join the Continental blockade against England in return for a free hand for Russia in the Balkans, the Dardanelles and Asia Minor), on condition that the French withdraw from Prussia, Swedish Pomerania and the territories they now occupied beyond the Elbe. He did not expect Napoleon to accept the terms but wished to put the responsibility for the coming war squarely on him. Napoleon was not deceived, suspecting the Tsar of having a hidden agenda.

'He is weak and false,' he said to Caulaincourt (the French ambassador to Russia),

> he has a Greek nature; he is false. – Alexander is ambitious; he has one aim which he hides in opting for war; and he wants war I tell you, since he has refused all my proposals. He must have a secret motive: have you not been able to find out what it is?[3]

The Tsar awaited the inevitable with a heavy heart. To Caulaincourt, whom Napoleon was always accusing of being far too pro-Russian, Alexander was for once unequivocal:

> If the war was to go against me I would retreat to Kamchatka rather than give up provinces or sign treaties in my capital that were mere truces. Your Frenchman is a good soldier but long-term shortages and a harsh climate will try him and discourage him. Our climate, our winter will fight for us. You have worked miracles, but only when the Emperor was present, and he cannot be everywhere nor can he be absent from Paris for years.[4]

In April 1812, determined to take personal command of his troops, Alexander left St Petersburg for Vilna in Lithuania. He was accompanied by a great retinue of advisers and generals: his Chief of Staff, Prince Peter Volkonsky (Zinaida's brother-in-law), Count Nikolai Tolstoy, Arakhcheev, Admiral Shishkov and General Balashov. As one of his aides-de-camp, Nikita Volkonsky went too. At this difficult moment the attitude of the Poles was critical. Determined to win them over to his side, the Tsar exempted Polish nobles from tax, distributed rewards and danced with their wives and daughters at countless balls, charming them so thoroughly that one lady, the future Comtesse de Choiseul-Gouffier, wrote in her memoirs that he was 'an angel in human shape – with eyes the colour of a cloudless sky – with a serene and open look' and more in that vein.[5]

It was during one such festivity at Zakret, General Beningsen's estate not far from Vilna, while dancing a mazurka with one of the Polish beauties on 24 June 1812, that Alexander heard that the Grande Armée had crossed the Niemen. There had been no formal declaration of war. Napoleon had mobilised the largest army in history, of which less than half were Frenchmen. His troops were not equipped for winter. Napoleon expected the campaign to be over by mid-July.

From Sventsiani, the new headquarters east of the Niemen, to which he had withdrawn, Alexander wrote a final letter to Napoleon, warning him that no peace was possible so long as a single French soldier remained on Russian soil:

> *Monsieur mon frère*, yesterday I learned that in spite of the good faith with which I have kept my word to Your Majesty, his troops have crossed the borders of Russia. – If Your Majesty agrees to withdraw his troops from Russian territory, I shall consider the matter as not having occurred and we could still come to terms. If not, then Your Majesty will force me to think of him henceforth only as an enemy.[6]

Napoleon had already made his intentions clear to Caulaincourt:

> Alexander takes me for a fool. – Does he think that I've come to Vilna to negotiate trading treaties? I've come to put an end once and for all to that northern barbarian colossus. The sword has been drawn. We must pack them off back to their ice, so that they aren't inclined to meddle in the affairs of civilised Europe for at least twenty-five years. We must take this opportunity to give the

Russians a distaste for meddling in what goes on in Germany. Let them receive the English in Archangel by all means, I accept that, but the Baltic must be closed to them.[7]

The letter which Balashov carried back to the Tsar nevertheless implied that Napoleon might still be open to peace if the Tsar would come to his senses.

Should Your Majesty wish to end hostilities, you will find me willing to do so. And even if, despite hostilities, Your Majesty wishes to maintain direct communications with me that too could be arranged and regulated by agreement. My private feelings for you remain unaffected by these events.[8]

The armies were on the march, however. There was a period of prolonged, violent, cold rain that June. Chaos reigned as the Grande Armée with men from all over Europe, ill-equipped, without stores or rations, marched through already impoverished countryside. The horses, for which there was no fodder, fed with wheat cut in the field, were dying like flies, the rivers clogged with their carcasses. Men driven by hunger were shot daily for desertion. Napoleon's army marched on, capturing Vitebsk, but failed to engage with the Russians. By the end of July the French had lost some 100,000 men through starvation, desertion and disease.

After several days of torrential rain, during an unusually changeable summer, 12 July 1812 promised to be another hot day in Moscow. The previous day had been scorching. In the early morning sunshine, as street hawkers set up their stalls, people began to gather, streaming towards the Kremlin. For the past month there had been talk of war. Napoleon had crossed the Niemen. Now, after several days of rumour, the Tsar was to address the people. Crowds gathered at every gate, filling the Kremlin's square, pressing around the Cathedral of the Assumption, growing by the hour. It was impossible for the carriages of the nobility and the rich merchants to get anywhere near the Kremlin. Preceded by liveried footmen who cleared a way for them, old dowagers and young women in light muslins, their faces framed in poke bonnets, picked their way carefully towards the specially reserved places, escorted by younger sons and old men. Most men of military age had been called up, though some were now in Moscow with the Tsar. Uniforms of every colour – the red of the Hussars, the orange of the Uhlans, the green of the Preobrazhensky Guard – vied with the splendour of the merchants in their full-skirted blue and green coats accompanied by their wives, their faces painted like china dolls, their rich satins covered in jewels. The sun gleamed on the helmets and breastplates of the cuirassiers, sparkled on the epaulettes and gold frogging of the dragoons. Cossacks and Kalmuks on splendid horses rode past the crowds of peasants in their bright shawls. The weather grew sultry. The last six months of expectation and anxiety were nearly over. Now the Emperor of Russia would speak to his people, and he would speak of war.

From the top of the Kremlin's staircase of honour the Tsar looked down on a sea of faces. In a surging wave of national feeling, which was almost religious, a million voices roared as one; 'Little Father! Angel! Hurrah!' – Holy Russia must be saved, he was their father, he must lead them to victory. The Tsar descended the steps and moved towards the cathedral on the long strip of red carpet which the militia were desperately trying to keep clear. Thousands of hands reached out to him, people weeping, trying to kiss the hem of his coat, blessing him, pledging themselves to win or die. As the cathedral bells rang out, the ancient Metropolitan of Moscow intoned: 'Moscow receives Alexander, Her Christ, as a mother would her daughters full of zeal, and sings Hosanna! Blessed be the one who comes among us.'[9]

Two days later, there was a meeting of nobles and merchants in the Slobodsky Palace. Everyone was in uniform. Merchants pledged enormous sums, while nobles promised to levy more men. 'The young Count Momonov had promised a whole regiment, but wished to serve only as a second lieutenant,' wrote Madame de Staël, who had arrived in Moscow that same week. She found that the talk was only about the war and the sacrifices that were required. Many of the noble families who would have been away at their summer estates by now stayed on in Moscow and St Petersburg. Balls and receptions went on as usual. Madame de Staël was received by Count Rostopchin, the governor of Moscow, who gave a splendid banquet in her honour at which she met all the most enlightened society of Moscow. Nobody seemed to worry about what they had already lost or might yet lose. Most of all she was impressed by ladies such as Countess Orlov, who, 'agreeable and orientally rich, was offering a quarter of her revenues'. Another had offered a thousand men to the state. 'I found it hard to use the expression to give men; but the peasants were offering themselves with ardour,' she recounts; 'in this war their masters were merely interpreting their wishes.'[10]

After the formal announcement of war to the Russian people in Moscow on his return from the front, the Tsar returned to St Petersburg. In Moscow, he had been astonished and moved by the strength of his people's faith in him and their love of their country. St Petersburg too was in a patriotic fever. This soon turned to panic, however, when the city came under serious threat from a detachment of the Grande Armée led by Oudinot. Grand Duchess Catherine, now pregnant, fled the city. As the Empress Dowager and many others prepared to leave too, news came that the French advance had been halted by General Wittgenstein.

St Petersburg was safe for the moment, but the enemy was marching steadfastly on Moscow. In this electric atmosphere, Alexander went to Abo (Turku) in Finland to obtain guarantees from Prince Bernadotte of Sweden which would enable him to bring his troops in Finland back to Russia. There, he heard that Smolensk, the last great city before Moscow, had been taken by the French. The road to Moscow was now open. As the French advanced, the ladies of St Petersburg, led by Princess Dolgoruki and Countess Stroganov, spent their days rolling lint bandages in a fever of patriotism, pledging large parts of their fortunes, careless of the losses of their estates. Yet social life continued as before. Caught up in the general enthusiasm, keen to help, Zinaida recovered her spirits. When Alexander returned, she was once again dancing at the many balls, and busy helping to prepare for whatever was in store. She had regained her beauty with her spirits, the small scar on her lip the only reminder of an unhappy year.

As the Russian retreat continued, and despite his personal reservations, Alexander appointed the immensely popular old hero, Marshal Kutuzov, to overall command of the Russian forces. Blind in one eye, fat, lazy, careless about dress, fond of women and food, he affected an earthy populism which offended Alexander's delicate sensibility. On the other hand, he delighted the Russian people. He was, they felt, one of them, a true Russian and an Orthodox Christian, one who could speak to soldiers in their own language. The war, they believed, had gone badly mainly because all those foreign generals had been competing with each other. Kutuzov, however, could also speak elegant French and German, as Madame de Staël discovered when she met him on the eve of his departure from St Petersburg, just six days before the great battle of Borodino. She found an old man with graceful manners and a lively face, who had lost an eye among the dozen wounds he had received in the course of a fifty-year military career. 'I was moved when I left the illustrious Marshal Kutuzov,' she wrote, 'I did not know whether I was embracing a conqueror or a martyr, but I saw that he was fully aware of the greatness of the cause which was now in his hands.' Before leaving for the front, the old Marshal went to pray at the Cathedral of Our Lady of Kazan. He was followed by a huge, adoring crowd shouting, 'Save Holy Russia.'[11]

In September, some eighty miles outside Moscow the Russian army knelt to the icon of the Holy Virgin of Smolensk as it was paraded before it. Old Marshal Kutuzov struggled to get up from his knees to kiss the image of the miraculous Black Virgin. The next day his forces would face the Grande Armée. On his side the Emperor Napoleon prepared to engage at last with the enemy who had evaded him at Smolensk. His army was greatly reduced and exhausted, but as he rode up and down the lines the soldiers nevertheless shouted, '*Vive l'Empereur*,' their voices carrying across to the encamped Russians. Forty-eight hours later, the legendary battle of Borodino was over. Eighty thousand men from both sides lay dead. Both sides claimed the victory.

Kutuzov, refusing to sacrifice more men, now ordered a retreat. In so doing he knew he was saving the Russian army but abandoning Moscow to its fate. Soon the streets were clogged with endless processions of coaches and carts loaded with baggage as people began to flee the city. Before long only about 15,000 people were left of a population of 250,000. Ivan Yakovlev, a member of an ancient family, remained in his large and gloomy house on the Arbat together with the seventeen-year-old Luiza Haag, his German 'wife' whom he had never properly married, and their baby son, refusing to leave. The baby was Alexander Herzen, who never took his father's name. It was Yakovlev who, a few weeks later, in return for a safe conduct out of the city, took Napoleon's message to Alexander. Before long Moscow was in flames, although there are doubts to this day as to whether the wooden city was deliberately put to the torch. Robert Wilson, a British general attached to the Russian army, was an eyewitness to the deliberate setting on fire of his own palace by Count Rostopchin as the French approached.[12] Napoleon later compared him to Marat. Madame de Staël, who obviously believed the story, remarked indignantly that Marat had burned other people's houses while Rostopchin had sacrificed his own. The French now had the terrible problem of finding shelter and supplies. Winter would not be long in coming.

Zinaida was in St Petersburg and joined in the general rejoicing about the victory of Borodino, but when the news that Moscow had been abandoned reached them, there was anger and dismay. Perhaps St Petersburg would be next? Foreign commentators also understood the gravity of the situation. 'Moscow has been taken,' wrote Joseph de Maistre; 'but for a miracle, Russia will be no more.' When he heard the news, the Austrian Chancellor Metternich declared that Russia had ceased to exist as a European power. 'So long as I live I shall never forget the moment when we ascended the steps of the cathedral, between two ranks of common people who uttered not a single cheer,' wrote one of the Empress's ladies-in-waiting, Mademoiselle Sturdza, as Alexander prepared to celebrate the anniversary of his coronation.[13] Two of Zinaida's young friends thought differently. Perhaps with the optimism of youth, Alexander Turgenev wrote prophetically to his friend Peter Viazemsky:

Moscow will rise again from her ashes, and the desire for vengeance will be the source of our glory and our greatness. Her ruins will be the pledge of our moral and political regeneration. Sooner or later, the glow of the Moscow fire will light our way to Paris.[14]

Alexander left the cathedral a different man. All doubts were now cast aside. If the Russian people and foreign observers were downcast, he was not. Rejecting the advice of his courtiers he knew that whatever happened there could be no negotiations with Napoleon 'so long as one enemy soldier remained on Russian soil'. A message went out to Kutuzov who was encamped at Tarutino, south-west of Moscow: 'Tell all my subjects that when I have not one soldier left, placing myself at the head of my dear nobles, of my good peasants, I shall fight to the last man in my Empire. Now it is Napoleon or I, I or he; we can no longer reign together.'

Encamped in a burnt-out Moscow, Napoleon at first refused to believe that he was no longer in control of events. Five weeks later in early November, with the Tsar still refusing to talk peace and the first snows beginning to fall, he ordered his army to retreat. Kutuzov's forces had cut off any chance of marching south, so the terrible trek home, shadowed by the Russian army, had to cross the devastated lands and the scorched earth of the original march from Smolensk, which the tattered remains of the Grande Armée, just over 40,000 strong, reached in mid-November. Collapsing from exhaustion, starvation and frost-bite, the French were attacked by packs of wolves and constantly harried by troops of Cossacks who would suddenly appear out of the winter forests. At the end of the month, on the Beresina River, in a fierce battle which was to be Kutuzov's last, the French lost another 20,000–30,000 men.

In early December, before they recrossed the fateful Niemen, Napoleon abandoned what remained of his exhausted, frost-bitten army to speed to Paris where he hoped to rally public support and raise fresh troops. The Russian campaign had cost him half a million men. He travelled incognito with Duroc and Caulaincourt. Though shaken by his losses, he was as yet unaware that, for him, time was running out.

Kutuzov entered Vilna that November, soon to be joined by the Tsar who decorated the old Marshal, recently created Prince of Smolensk, and received from him the captured enemy flags. Kutuzov was very unwilling to send his battle-weary troops beyond the border. They had liberated Russia. It was more than enough. Alexander, however, was now determined to crush Napoleon once and for all.

The time of indecision was behind him. The peace could only be signed in Paris.

On Christmas Day 1812, all the church bells of Russia rang out in jubilation. The enemy was gone from its soil, Holy Russia was free once again. The Tsar was the hero of the hour, inspiring joy and enthusiasm. The people mobbed him, 'tearing his handkerchief out of his hands so that each could keep a shred', as Zinaida recalled after the Tsar's death.[15] As for Alexander, under the influence of his close friend Prince Alexander Golitsyn, he had increasingly looked to the Bible for guidance. Throughout his struggle with Napoleon, Alexander had been consulting the scriptures daily, and was now convinced that with God's help he would liberate Europe. He had stood firm against Napoleon. It was surely God's hand that had prevailed, Alexander was but his instrument.

The Tsar had remained in St Petersburg throughout the weeks of Napoleon's retreat, where he resumed his close friendship with Zinaida who was now fully recovered after the birth of her child and her nervous breakdown. Her husband had been in the Tsar's entourage since the campaign began in June 1812. As the military situation improved in the spring of 1813, the Tsar moved his headquarters to Kalitsch and, always liking feminine company, invited some of the wives of the members of his staff to accompany them. What more natural than to invite Princess Volkonsky? It was well known that the Tsar 'liked to relax from his military and political duties in her company'.[16] Here was a perfect opportunity to keep Zinaida at his side.

The prospect of joining the Imperial suite at such a momentous time was thrilling. Zinaida would be at the very centre of events, close to Russia's hero, and to hers. She could see the Tsar as much as she liked with perfect propriety, away from the eyes of court gossips. She would be accompanied not only by her husband but also by her two sisters-in-law. She had always relished travel; the prospect of it now, after the confinement of the past two years and at such a time, was particularly thrilling.

Zinaida was the first to arrive at Alexander's headquarters in Kalitsch, accompanied by her baby son, from whom she was never parted, and Nikita's sister, Princess Sophia. Soon, the arrival of their older sister-in-law, Princess Repnin, wife of Nikita's elder brother Nikolai, as well as Countess Osterman, the two Princesses Turkestanov and Kutuzov's granddaughter, who was married to General Sadan, completed the little circle of the ladies of the Imperial suite. Not long after, at a dinner given by Field Marshal Prince Kutuzov, a sparkling Zinaida was seated next to her host. Clearly she charmed the old man. 'Zinaida Volkonsky whose manner I like very much is here,' he wrote to his daughter.[17] Kutuzov was now seriously ill, but determined to stuggle on. A few weeks later, his condition worsened and he had to remain at Breslau.

The Imperial suite's journey through a newly liberated Saxony towards Dresden, Zinaida's birthplace, was made in an atmosphere of carnival. Delirious crowds cheered the Tsar wherever they stopped. It was also a time of great personal happiness for Zinaida and the Tsar. Away from watchful eyes, they saw each other often. 'On the way, at each stop the Tsar would come and see the ladies,' but he often visited Zinaida alone.[18] He was finding that with her he could share all his hopes and thoughts. Sympathetic and intelligent, as well as beautiful and accomplished, she was a pleasure to be with. Her open admiration of him, a romantic liking for chivalry and a mutual tendency to mysticism served to reinforce the Tsar's growing belief that he had been specially chosen by God in his struggle against Napoleon. Zinaida too, lonely and neglected, basked in the approval and admiration of 'her knight and angel'. Her husband was proving less complaisant than Alexander would have wished, and was constantly sent here and there on the Tsar's business.

If her sister-in-law Sophia wondered about Zinaida's growing closeness to the Tsar, she said nothing – they had become firm friends. Dark-haired and wilful, Sophia was a perfect foil to Zinaida. Although less beautiful, she was a spirited and attractive young woman, with a witty turn of phrase, a robust sense of fun and a lively imagination. A portrait of her, painted by Isabey during the Congress of Vienna in 1815, some two years after she set out together with Zinaida in the Imperial suite, shows 'Sofia Grigorievna's good-looking energetic head, set above a white satin dress tied with a sash below the bosom. Her flashing, dark eyes look out in a three-quarter pose. In her dark hair, below her right temple, there is a bunch of poppies and small ears of wheat, all under a cloud of gauze blown by a wind which always seems to blow in Isabey's portraits of women.'[19] In sharp contrast to her own mother, but very like Zinaida, Sophia was often impatient with formality and social niceties. Zinaida, always more comfortable among fellow artists enjoyed her sister-in-law's lively company and uninhibited love of life. Sophia's passion for travel was, if anything, even greater than her own.

Zinaida and Sophia often entertained the company with music. None of the ladies could compete with Zinaida's singing, but Sophia was proud of her arms which she enjoyed showing off when playing the harp. 'I was never a great beauty, but I played the harp quite well, and my arms from the shoulder to their fingertips might have been carved. My eyes too had an indefinable something which men found attractive,' she would recall many years later.[20] They continued to produce amateur theatricals and all the salon entertainments of St Petersburg. Together, the two young women decided to surprise the Tsar with a specially written play which they commissioned Admiral Shishkov, the Tsar's Secretary of State, to write for them. A few days later he brought them an outline, entitled 'A small celebration or a token of thanks to the Russian warriors in the presence of their Commander-in-Chief'. It seems that the young women were pleased with his efforts, keeping it for a few days, the Admiral wrote, but for some reason the Tsar, who saw it, did not like it and the plan was abandoned. Very possibly Zinaida and Sophia had used the Tsar's name in vain to save the Admiral's feelings, since the play was awful. Upset perhaps by this slight, Shishkov grumbled in his memoirs that Zinaida was 'one of those people who, though intellectually gifted, talk like children when they assert that there could be no enlightenment in Russia without the theatre and a French education!'[21]

At the end of April, Field Marshal Prince Kutuzov, now sixty-eight, died at Bunzlau, in Prussian Silesia. He was deeply mourned by his armies and by all Russia. His body was transported back to St Petersburg, where he was given a hero's funeral and buried in the crypt of the Cathedral of Our Lady of Kazan. On the same day Alexander, who had arrived with his suite in Teplitz, about seven miles from Dresden, was writing to his sister, the Grand Duchess

Catherine, who, recently widowed and always keen to be at the centre of things, had just arrived in Prague. 'I learn of your arrival at Prague,' he wrote. 'The hope of seeing you again gives rise to emotions that cannot be described.'[22]

Napoleon meanwhile, having accomplished prodigious feats of rearmament – he had mustered a new army in record time – was already across the Rhine. His plan was to push the Allies back over the Elbe and then march on Berlin. By the end of April he was at Weimar, by early May in Dresden. The clash with Napoleon which Alexander had been waiting for took place at Lutzen. After a fierce battle the Russians suffered a defeat, followed on 21 May by another at Bautzen, just outside Dresden.

On 17 April 1813 the great German poet Goethe left for Teplitz, having been persuaded to leave Dresden, recording that frightening month in his journal. Before he left, he had removed his literary archive and manuscripts from the house, burying them for safe-keeping. It was not a day too soon for, on 18 April, Napoleon's arrival in Dresden was heralded by cannon fire all over the town and fighting in the streets. Goethe's diary for 1 May also records a court reception in Teplitz: 'In the evening I was at his Highness's. Von Alopeus, Countesse Nesselrode and the Princesses Volkonsky [were there]. Prince Baryatinsky [the Russian ambassador] came later. News of the death of Kutuzov.'[23] Zinaida visited Goethe at his house later that month, but they were not to meet again until 1829.

On 8 May, Goethe noted that Teplitz was filling up with Russian wounded. Alexander himself ordered the retreat to Reichenbach where he reappointed Barclay de Tolly Commander-in-Chief. In spite of his victory, a crippling shortage of cavalry forced Napoleon to accept an armistice brokered by Metternich, which was gratefully accepted by the Allies. The Reichenbach Armistice lasted for about two months and was followed by a conference in Prague at which Austria changed sides, joining the alliance against Napoleon.

Throughout the campaign of 1813, whenever the military situation permitted, the Tsar contrived to spend time with Zinaida, and when they were apart they wrote to each other. Of the Tsar's letters to survive from this period, six were later published in censored form by Zinaida's son Alexander after his mother's death. It is probable that other letters were destroyed by the Prince, who was determined to protect her honour. Fifteen letters from the Tsar to Zinaida, covering the years 1813 until his death in 1825, still exist.[24]

Whatever the true nature of their love affair, it clearly meant considerably more to them both than the usual court flirtation which Alexander had enjoyed with so many women. The Tsar's first letter from Jauer, where he had gone to be near the front, was probably brought to Zinaida, then in Teplitz, by her husband. The tone is affectionate and romantic. The letter, dated 14 May, is clearly in answer to one from Zinaida:

> If good intentions alone ever deserved a reward, I certainly had the one which gives me the greatest pleasure while I am far from you, Princess, in the charming letter which they brought me from you. I cannot adequately express how much I was touched by all that you said to me. Please believe that I know how to value your words. The bearer of this letter will describe to you the manner in which our troops distinguished themselves, and if the final result was not quite as successful as we might have wished, the events which took place are no less glorious for our brave army. When times are hard, only perseverance brings a successful outcome. Let us hope that Divine Providence will bless our efforts. We are all in the best possible spirits. To all the hopes which I have for our military success I must add most sincere ones for the happiness of seeing you at the earliest opportunity. In the meantime, please keep a place for me in your thoughts, so dear to me, and kindly remember me to Princess Sophie. I beg you to accept these wishes as a mark of an affection as respectful as it is sincere.

His letter showed that, in spite of recent setbacks, Alexander was reasonably optimistic. He already knew that Metternich would bring Austria over to Russia's side and was about to deliver an ultimatum to Napoleon. Alexander's allusions to Divine Providence were no mere pieties. He was by this time convinced that he had been elected by God to be the instrument of Napoleon's downfall.

Zinaida, still in Teplitz at Imperial headquarters, was basking in the Tsar's attention. In the previous year he had been preoccupied and she had been ill, but now circumstances had altered. Marriage had changed her and put their relationship on a different footing. She was no longer the carefree young court beauty who had first caught his eye, but a married woman and a mother. She did not love her husband, but her loving and kind nature made her unwilling to hurt his feelings or his pride. She loved the Tsar, but, as he made it clear that their relationship was important to him and that he wanted it to grow closer still, she was afraid. He was not only the Tsar, he was the man on whom all hopes were pinned, the great hero, soon to be 'the saviour of Europe'. He was also, she knew, a practised Don Juan. She was intelligent enough to know that she could not hope to keep him exclusively. Yet the great affinity between them, the friendship that was the bedrock of their love affair, drew her inexorably closer to him. She was honoured and delighted by his interest, excited, guilty and uneasy. She needed and wanted to love and to be loved. Her artistic and spiritual nature craved the understanding and complicity that had ended with her father's death. Now twenty-three and in love, she could hide her feelings no longer. His letter, she now wrote, had reached her heart, but she was unsure about what he had meant by 'reward' in his previous letter. Alexander was at the time staying in the castle of Peterswaldau, not far from Reichenbach, where he was engaged in diplomatic as well as military negotiations. His previous letter to Zinaida (which has not survived) must have contained a declaration of his feelings. Aware of her fears, he wrote at once to reassure her:

Peterswaldau, 28th May
You seem to have been surprised, Princess, by my use of the word 'reward', when I spoke of your penultimate letter. What other word could I use to describe the effect your letters have had on me, especially the last? To say that I felt I had been rewarded is to say little – Indeed what could be at once more kind, more soulful, as well as more flattering to me? – You cannot remain unconvinced of how much I have always treasured anything that came from you. I treasure it all the more since you allowed me to approach you. I could hope for nothing more than a little of your good will, but your delightful letter has fulfilled all my wishes.

I have often said that I was afraid of disturbing you when I expressed my sentiments to you, and while I was certain from the bottom of my heart as to the purity of these sentiments, I wanted to be sure that you yourself were sure too and had not misunderstood. Your letter calmed all my fears and gave me the sweetest joy. The kindness with which you treated me fulfilled the one desire to which I felt I had a right – You say that my letter reached your heart and was accepted. May I place yours at the same address? – it is so dear to me. It is my heart which now dictates these words to you, and which in revealing the closest interest in you, and the most sincere affection, believes that it has nothing with which to reproach itself. Far from it, I would confess these sentiments before the world and even before your husband himself. – Your man [this is how the Tsar sometimes referred to her husband Nikita] will carry these lines to you, and I have no fear that they would fail to pass his censure if need be. Forgive me, please, for the involuntary impetuousness of my pen. I needed to express my feelings to you. I do not believe them to be unworthy.

Alexander's letter, while romantic, contains all the escape clauses which are an inevitable part of a true philanderer's armoury, but Zinaida was still too young and inexperienced to know that.

The Tsar goes on to thank her for 'the very warm interest which you show in our military affairs', explaining that they are resting because the French had offered an armistice after the battle of Bautzen, which was gratefully accepted by the Allies and had just been signed. The Allies spent the next six weeks rearming and enlarging their forces. 'You will know that the *expected hundred thousand bayonets* are almost equipped; they have been maddeningly slow,' the Tsar goes on. 'It has meant a delay of some weeks more, and therefore an armistice. This is why we are resting while preparing ourselves to return ever more strongly to the attack.' On the diplomatic front, a crucial agreement had just been concluded whereby the Allies were given £2,000,000 by England, to carry on with the war, and Austria, £500,000 to enter it.

In the same letter the Tsar again refers to Nikita, whom he frequently used to deliver his letters to Zinaida, calling him the courier or postman, sometimes even 'the ordinary or surface post', always with a note of irony: 'Your commands have been carried out to the letter, the feverish postman swallowed everything that was prescribed, and is now in a fit state to rejoin you, the fever having left him some days ago,' Alexander continues, referring to Nikita who had been laid low with a fever. Zinaida's 'commands', were her frequent requests on behalf of her husband and others. Perhaps guilt towards Nikita made her redouble her efforts to persuade the Tsar to promote him in the army (he was a lieutenant-general) and to offer him a post in the diplomatic service. Alexander also refers to two others on whose behalf the Princess had interceded. One he calls '*l'amoureux*'; the other, 'young Gérambe', who was the son of an Austrian general who had fought against Napoleon and was imprisoned by the French. His son now wished to serve under the Tsar and, Zinaida having interceded on his behalf, this request was granted.

After sending his best wishes to Princess Sophie, Alexander concludes very tenderly:

> I must, at least for form's sake, present my excuses for the length of this letter, but I would rather crave your angelic indulgence, and beg you to believe that I await the moment of our meeting with the most lively impatience, without alas, knowing when I might hope to see you again.
>
> In the meantime do not quite forget me, and believe me to be for ever yours, heart and soul. A.

A few days after writing this letter, Alexander left Peterswaldau for his headquarters at Teplitz, where Zinaida was waiting for him.

> I am impatient, Princess, to be at your feet. I had hoped for this happiness yesterday, but Heaven, or rather Prince Schwarzenburg with General Radetsky, decreed otherwise, since they remained with me until 11 o'clock. May I come to you between 7 and 8 o'clock? – in the meantime my respectful best wishes.

The Tsar's inconsiderate visitors were Austrian commanders engaged in strategic planning for their country's entry into the war.

The Tsar's confidence that Metternich would bring Austria in against Napoleon was vindicated when, in August, Napoleon rejected the coalition's peace terms, which were to return France to her 'natural frontiers', and Austria duly declared war on France. Bernadotte of Sweden also joined the coalition. At the end of August, Alexander's troops beat General Vandamme's at Kulm. The Tsar, soaked to the skin by the torrential rain, remained in the field for two days without rest during this battle. He was becoming a seasoned warrior. Zinaida's letters must have expressed her fervent admiration. Three days after the battle of Kulm, as soon as he was back at headquarters in Teplitz, Alexander wrote to Zinaida, who had withdrawn to the safety of Prague:

It is impossible for me, Princess, to await the departure of the *ordinary post* [Nikita] to express to you my boundless gratitude for your charming letter and for all the very kind things you say. I have but one desire: to be even a little like the person you describe and call by my name, a being, however, I am still very far from resembling. It is you alone who have that rare talent of making all those around you more lovable, since you yourself are full of that inborn and indulgent kindness which puts each person at ease, and it is a true joy to spend hours in your company. Your wishes have been fulfilled. Our army, especially the Guards, covered themselves with immortal glory on the 17th & 18th. Vandamme's corps has been entirely destroyed; – the Generals, the Staff, also 12,000 prisoners, 81 cannon and all the supplies were captured. At the same time the Silesian army performed miracles of real worth, depriving the enemy of 103 pieces of artillery and took more than 18,000 prisoners. The Crown Prince of Sweden took 42 cannon and between six and seven thousand prisoners. As you see, thanks to the Almighty, things aren't going at all badly. Please continue, I beg you, to take an interest in us warriors, and be sure in advance that we will bring you tributes of gratitude. At the very first opportunity I shall dispatch the *ordinary post* to Vienna and he will therefore have to go through Prague both ways. Please accept my grateful thanks for the tea. As it is you who send it, I cannot give it away and prefer to keep it for myself.

Please believe in the sincere attachment which I have sworn to you for life. A thousand compliments to Princess Sophie.

During the next month, despite his heavy commitments, Alexander saw Zinaida at every possible opportunity. A note from him at the beginning of October, in response to something she had written, sheds a fascinating light on their complex relationship:

> The note which I have just received from you, Princess, touched me very greatly. Only discretion prevented me from coming to say farewell to you in person last night since I did not wish to interrupt the few moments left to you with your husband. I should like, however, to take advantage of this opportunity to stress how grateful I am for all the indulgence with which you received me.
>
> These moments will never be erased from my mind. May your wishes come true, Princess; my only ambition is to give the world a stable peace. All your commands will be fulfilled to the letter. As for your husband, the friendship which I bear him will be added to the care with which I will endeavour to fulfil your wishes.
>
> My compliments to Princess Sophie. With what impatience I await the moment which will give me, once again, the happiness of being able to tell you in person that which my pen expresses so inadequately. Please keep me in your thoughts a little, and believe in the assurance of my respectful devotion for ever.

Unusually this brief note makes no reference to the confrontation with Napoleon for which the Allies were mobilising. On 7 October, Napoleon moved towards Leipzig, leaving two of his strongest corps in Dresden. A few days later the Allies cornered him outside Leipzig. His troops, though ill fed and outnumbered, fought hard for two days. By nightfall on the 18th, in what came to be called the Battle of the Nations, the battle of Leipzig was over with a conclusive and devastating defeat for Napoleon. 'Towards the end of the second day,' wrote Chateaubriand, 'the Saxons and the Württembergers, going over from Napoleon's to Bernadotte's camp, decided the result of the action, – a victory stained by treason.'[25] 'Napoleon's soldiers were in such a state of starvation by then that they were trying to exchange ear-rings from their ears, and whatever else they could for bits of bread, but to no avail.'[26]

In spite of his many military and strategic preoccupations, the Tsar found time to write a long letter to Zinaida after this battle. His previous reunion with her had been happy enough for him to have written that it would never be erased from his memory. Her genuine and informed interest in the course of the war made her a natural confidante. She was the first person to whom the Tsar would write not only of his triumphs but also of his hopes. Alexander was by this time utterly convinced of the necessity for the total defeat of Napoleon in spite of the fact that in the opinion of many Russians the continuation of the war was not in their interest. His letters to Zinaida speak constantly of his growing conviction of being an instrument of God:

Leipzig, 10/22 October 1813.

It was in the midst of great strategic movements, Princess, that I received your delightful letter, undated, brought to me from Prague by your man [Nikita], but which he had given to the brother-in-law [Prince Peter Volkonsky] and which, as is his noble habit, hung around for two days in the pockets of his numberless wardrobe before I could have it, he making the excuse that he had left it in a third coat, though he was already wearing two.

Before I continue, allow me to give you a brief account of the enormous numbers [of arms and men] which we have won with the help of Divine Providence during those memorable days of the 4th, 5th, 6th and 7th, when Napoleon in person, having united all his forces, was utterly beaten outside Leipzig. 300 Cannon, 23 generals and 37,000 prisoners were the fruits of our brave armies' exploits. It is the Supreme Being alone who guided everything, and to Whom we owe this amazing success. I have no doubt of your reactions, Princess, and I am anxious to send off the *ordinary post* to reassure you as to his safety, and to enable him to have his *reward* since I was very pleased.

To return to your dear letter – it would be completely adorable as I said to you, if it had not ended with a blasphemy: *Have you forgotten me* you ask! How could such an idea have even entered your thoughts, is this not an injustice on your part which I had a right to be spared? But I admit that I may have seemed to be in the wrong – this is what happened. When on the previous occasion I sent my letter to your man, he had already left, so the letter remained with me. Finding it rather gloomy I did not hurry to send it to you, and would have destroyed it, had it not contained an answer to something you had asked. I enclose it herewith.

Please accept my boundless gratitude for your very kind – your enchanting congratulations on the subject of my Order of the Garter. [Alexander had been invested with the Order of the Garter in Teplitz, which had been awarded to him in London, in July.] While not believing myself to be entirely worthy, I absolutely share your sentiments on chivalry, and have always preferred these principles. If one of its requirements is to feel passionately about everything that comes from a beautiful and charming woman, then I dare to hope that I am faithful to it. More than ever believe me yours for life, body and soul, and I would add *Hony soit qui mal y pense.* All my respects to Princess Sophie.

Though couched in the romantic imagery and the language of chivalry which they both loved, Alexander's letters reveal a deep and tender affection. However, the intimacy of their relationship was about to be challenged by the Tsar's powerful and demanding sister Catherine, who had now reappeared in his life. She had been bombarding Alexander with letters from Prague complaining of his neglect. Although clearly exasperated, he was never quite able to slip from her hold on him. He wrote back crossly, complaining of being falsely accused, but nevertheless gives her the reassurances she sought: 'Now, after having preached to you a bit, I will tell you, dear, that I love you none the less madly, though you are a little mad yourself sometimes.'[27] Soon, together with their younger sister Marie, Princess of Weimar, the two were reunited. Jealous of Zinaida's relationship with the Tsar, Catherine had decided to put an end to it. From then on the Grand Duchess remained close to her brother.

It is possible that Alexander was beginning to tire of his entanglement with Zinaida. She was becoming more demanding both in her need for constant reassurances – his letters often allude to her complaints of being neglected – and also in her unceasing requests on behalf of her friends and her husband. The passion which had been fuelled by the heady atmosphere of the campaign could not be sustained. The Tsar, never very steady in his romantic attachments may have grown slightly bored and also alarmed at Zinaida's growing expectations. Catherine's arrival may well have provided him with a welcome diversion from an affair that had become too complicated.

After the battle of Leipzig Alexander was anxious to make all possible haste to Frankfurt where he was to be joined by his Allies. Their intention was to remain in Frankfurt long enough to plan the continuing campaign against Napoleon, who had made all speed back to Paris with the remains of his army.

No language can describe the horrible devastation these French have left behind them. – Every bridge blown up, every village burnt or pulled down, fields completely devastated, orchards all turned up. – None of the country people will bury them or their horses, so they remain lying all over the fields and roads with millions of crows feasting – we passed quantities, bones of all kinds, hats, shoes, epaulettes, a surprising quantity of rags and linen,

wrote Wellington's twenty-year-old niece, Priscilla Burghersh, as she travelled along the line of the French retreat, accompanying her husband on his posting as military attaché to the headquarters of the Austrian army in Germany.[28]

In Frankfurt the conquerors met to plan their next move and to celebrate the liberation of the German lands. There were military parades, ambassadorial dinners and balls. With few women present, those who were there found themselves greatly in demand. On 6 December (25 November old style, the feast of St Catherine) the Grand Duchess Catherine gave a great ball to celebrate her name day. The assembly rooms were beautifully decorated with orange trees and the splendour of the occasion was enhanced by the variety and magnificence of the military uniforms. The Tsar opened the ball with a polonaise, 'a sort of walking to music', according to his partner Lady Burghersh. She did not think him at all handsome, though later she agreed that 'his countenance was pleasing. He has certainly fine shoulders, but beyond that he is horridly ill made. He holds himself bent quite forward [Alexander's well-known habit of leaning forward was partly due to being deaf in one ear] – for which reason all his court imitate him and bend too, and gird in their waists like women!'[29]

The Allied camp now moved to Freiburg where they were to set up their headquarters. From here Alexander was able to visit his sister who was staying at Schaffhausen, for a few days at the end of December. During this time their relationship returned to its former closeness and when Catherine had to leave for Stuttgart she was clearly very unhappy at the parting. Recently widowed, she was contemplating marriage to the Crown Prince of Württemberg but wrote miserably to her brother:

> As I have told you, if I could devote my life to you I should be content, but how can that be, and what can I do more prudent than espouse a man whose character pleases me? My health is feeling [the absence of] Schaffhausen, I am not well; the happy days spent together were all too few to heal me.[30]

The Volkonskys too were at Schaffhausen, where at last Zinaida received a letter from Alexander, written some five days after his arrival. It is obvious from the Tsar's letter that Zinaida had written several to him which had remained unanswered. With the last of these she had sent a New Year gift, a print engraved in Leipzig, representing the Temptation of Adam. Where previously Alexander had found time to write to her even in the midst of battles, now there were only excuses:

> December 30th/January 11th, 1814. Schaffhouse. For some time, Princess, fate has been against me each time I received your letters. This time too, your last letter arrived on the day before the eve of my departure, when I was more than usually occupied and truly had not a moment. While I hope to be able to pay my respects to you in person today, I would not deprive myself of the pleasure of expressing my gratitude in these few lines, for your letter and your felicitations. Please accept my sincere good wishes for your lasting happiness, which I have never ceased to wish for, nor do I need to wait for the renewal of the year to wish

you every possible happiness. I hope that you are aware of the longstanding, true and respectful attachment which I have vowed to you.

Zinaida, probably wishing to make the Tsar a little jealous, had light-heartedly threatened to throw herself into the Rhine if her husband wasn't restored to her. Alexander answers with a play on words:

I am delighted to have been able to prevent another two falls into the Rhine Falls [for which Schaffhausen was famous]; – that of the two Princesses Volkonsky, who were threatening to throw themselves in if their husbands failed to arrive. One, will be with you already, hanging on to your skirt [another dig at poor Nikita and Zinaida's efforts to secure Alexander's patronage for him], while the other apparently thinking that his lady is not quite so impetuous, will probably arrive a day later [Prince Peter].

Thanking her for her present, which he will keep as a memento of her goodness to him, he goes on:

I admired the beauty of the print less than that of the drawing and I thought your reflections on the Devil – very true. But I must admit that I was shocked by the coolness of Father Adam at a moment such as the one represented in the picture. If indeed things took place in such a calm way, then you must admit that it was even more inexcusable of Papa Adam to have infringed the ban which had been imposed on him.

The rest of Alexander's letter deals very affectionately with Zinaida's many requests on behalf of friends, who included Antoine Spada who had been a tutor in the Beloselsky household, Madame Aufresne, the widow of an actor and friend of Zinaida's, and two others:

You ask God's forgiveness for your suspicions, but it is you of whom I ask forgiveness for mine. You have very charmingly quoted La Fontaine's fable to me, making me fear that my promises to you should also be fables. I shall do everything I can to prove that they are real, beginning with an express message to Golitzine and Gourief, since they were responsible for carrying out my orders regarding Spada. All correspondence is dealt with in Petersbourg, and then sent on to me for signature, since here we have neither time nor the necessary staff to deal with it. Will you permit me to present myself at six o'clock after dinner? I shall await the moment of presenting my respects in person, with impatience.

Alexander's letter, while friendly and full of the repartee which they had always enjoyed, sends her ominous good wishes for her lasting happiness; a sure signal of the end of love.

The Tsar visited the Princess that evening, perhaps for the last time in their romantic relationship. He left Basle five days later. He had been kind and charming as always, but their romance, intensified by war, had run its course. Zinaida knew of the return of the Grand Duchess Catherine, and had no illusions about her hold on Alexander. She fully understood that Alexander was standing at the peak of his influence, the push to Paris now uppermost in his mind. Perhaps she recognised too that the Tsar's temperament, like hers, was more romantic than passionate. Her own constant and tiresome demands had undoubtedly helped to cool his ardour. It was probable that the break with the Tsar had not come as a complete surprise. Though undoubtedly sad that the romantic dream was over, Zinaida could take comfort in the enduring strength of their friendship. Alexander had shared his thoughts and plans with her. She believed, as he did, that it was his destiny to be the saviour of Europe. Zinaida would remain with the Imperial suite until the Tsar's return to Russia, but for more than two years there were to be no more letters from him.

The Volkonskys returned to Basle a little in advance of the Tsar. With his usual mixture of religion and superstition, Alexander had decided that the Russian New Year's Day, 13 January 1814, was the most propitious for his army to cross into France. Zinaida joined the other members of the Imperial suite to watch the Tsar's troops parade through the town. Priscilla Burghersh, also present as part of the Austrian suite, described the scene in a letter to her sister:

The Russian army with a great part of the Prussian, all in their best accoutrements, passed the Rhine and defiled in town before the two Emperors and King etc. It is impossible to see a finer sight or a more interesting one, than to see these men and recollect what they had done since last year, and now in such perfect order, the horses in such excellent condition, and the men (especially the Russian) so clean. Soldiers will tell you it is ridiculous but there is a *recherche* and *coquetterie* in most of the Russian regiments which makes them a sight too magnificent to be described! The extreme care and cleanliness of their dress is quite beautiful. The Cossacks of the Guard and the Emperor's footguard are all picked men, the handsomest of the empire. The latter are all gigantic; they are composed of the tallest men to be found in Russia; their coats are all padded to stuff out their chests and widen their shoulders, and therefore they really look like statues for fine make.[31]

Alexander stood hatless and coatless in driving sleet and snow at the Basle bridge – the weather had suddenly turned very cold – watching his troops as they crossed the Rhine. Three days later he left for Langres, their next headquarters.

Napoleon's end was now imminent. In Basle the Allies argued over the future of France. Should the Bourbons be restored or should there be a regency until Napoleon's son reached his majority or perhaps someone else should fill the vacant throne of France? In London Lord Castlereagh, the Foreign Secretary, had been so much disturbed by his ambassadors' reports that he decided to journey to Basle himself. It was essential for him to see Metternich who, it was reported, was at loggerheads with the Tsar.

Castlereagh's foreign policy, learned from Pitt, was based pragmatically on the principle of non-interference in the affairs of the Continent on condition that no single power was dominant since that would have constituted a serious threat to British trading interests. Napoleon had shattered the balance of power. Consequently, but for a brief truce, England had been at war with France continuously since 1793. Pitt's treaty of alliance with Russia in 1805 was designed to ensure the defeat of Napoleon. In 1807, after Alexander and Napoleon signed an offensive and defensive alliance at Tilsit, Britain once more stood alone. When he became Foreign Secretary in 1812, after Napoleon's defeat in Russia, Castlereagh had revived Pitt's plan. It soon became obvious, however, that Russia had territorial ambitions of her own in Europe.

Castlereagh's meeting with Metternich confirmed this view and, more importantly, opened his eyes to the realities and importance of Europe. The rapport with Metternich was instant and mutual, the latter writing:

> I found Lord Castlereagh not quite thoroughly informed of the real state of affairs on the Continent. His straightforward feeling, free from all prejudice and prepossession, and his justice and benevolence gave him a quick insight into the truth of things. I soon saw that his ideas about the reconstruction of France in a manner compatible with the general interests of Europe did not materially differ from mine.[32]

Metternich and Castlereagh left Basle on 23 January, travelling together in Metternich's coach and arriving at Langres on the 25th. The position of the town on the heights of the Vosges overlooking the plains of France and the Ardennes made it suitable for the next stage of operations. On the 26th they called together on the Emperor Alexander. They found him in an exalted mood. There was much talk of the Divine will. Alexander may have been unclear about who should succeed Napoleon, but he was absolutely clear about his refusal to negotiate until the final capitulation of 'the tyrant'.

On the same day, the 'tyrant' himself handed over the government to a Council of Regency, leaving Paris undefended, to take over personal military control. From the Rhine to the Marne, the towns of eastern France had offered no resistance to the advancing Allied commanders. In the first half of February, and with all the odds against him, Napoleon fought as brilliantly as he had ever done. During the campaign of France, as it came to be known, he beat the Prussians three times in the space of six days, at Champaubert,

Montmirail and Vauchamps, throwing the Austrians back across the Seine at Montereau.

It was bitterly cold at Langres. The journey from Basle had been difficult. Beggars, almost always women and children, followed them wherever they stopped to change horses fighting like animals over anything they were given. All the men including boys had been conscripted for Napoleon's last stand. Wolves howled outside the town. The Russians, used to being greeted as liberators in Germany, now found that they were seen as a savage enemy, and not without reason. The Cossack troops, so much admired when on parade, would swoop down daily, robbing and plundering the villages in spite of strict orders to the contrary. Filled with hatred for the French, the Prussian troops, too, behaved savagely.

Castlereagh came away from his meeting with Alexander with an austere man's distaste for Alexander's mystical pronouncements but an accurate evaluation of his state of mind. In a hurried despatch to the Prime Minister, Lord Liverpool, a few days later he wrote:

> I think our greatest danger at present is the *chevaleresque* tone in which the Emperor Alexander is disposed to push the war. He has a *personal* feeling about Paris, distinct from all political or military combinations. He seems to seek for the occasion of entering with his magnificent guards the enemy's capital, probably to display, in his clemency and forbearance, a contrast to that desolation to which his own was devoted. The idea that a rapid negotiation might disappoint this hope added to his impatience.[33]

The 'rapid negotiation' to which Castlereagh was referring was the conference at Chatillon which opened on 3 February. In spite of Alexander's impatience and his daily consultations with the 'All-Powerful' it had been agreed, in the Langres Protocol, to accept Napoleon as ruler of France so long as the French accepted him as such. Caulaincourt, in charge of the negotiations as Foreign Minister of France, had warned Napoleon time and again not to underestimate the Tsar. Alexander may appear weak, he warned, but 'underneath his appearance of goodwill, frankness and natural loyalty, there is a core of dissimulation which is the mark of an obstinacy which nothing can move.' Alexander's obstinacy was matched by Napoleon's. In vain did poor Caulaincourt urge him to make the necessary sacrifices and accept the Allies' terms while there was still time. Napoleon too wanted a final showdown. His spectacular military victories at Montmirail and Montereau had increased his confidence.

Those same victories helped to concentrate the minds of the Allied sovereigns who signed a treaty at Chaumont on 1 March. That this treaty was signed was thanks largely to the patience, tireless work and considerable diplomatic skills of Castlereagh, to whom one of his ambassadors to the Allied sovereigns, Lord Aberdeen, paid tribute:

> The enemy is, in my view, a source of danger much less to be dreaded than what arises among ourselves. The seeming agreement at Langres covered distrust and hate. A little success will cement them again; but if they are to be severely tried in adversity, their dissolution is certain. Your presence has done much, and, I have no doubt, would continue to sustain them in misfortune, but without it they could not exist.[34]

'My treaty', as Castlereagh called it, established a Quadruple Alliance of Britain, Russia, Austria and Prussia whereby the signatories promised not to treat with Napoleon separately and 'to concert together on the conclusion of a peace with France' for twenty years after the cessation of hostilities. Peace terms based on allowing France to keep her 1792 frontiers were rejected by Napoleon in spite of Caulaincourt's best efforts. The Allies now called on France to reject Napoleon. It was agreed that henceforth the war would be pursued until his unconditional surrender.

4

Peace: Paris and London

'Do you really wish to see Cossacks in the rue Racine?'

MADAME DE STAËL, letter to Benjamin Constant

As the Allies prepared for the last act against 'the Corsican ogre' in March 1814, Zinaida could look back on the most momentous year of her life. She was no longer the young woman who had left St Petersburg to join the Tsar at Kalitsch the previous spring. As a member of the Imperial entourage during that long campaign she had seen the effects of war, the devastation of the countries they had travelled through, the destruction of people's lives. She had lived at close quarters with the Tsar, as well as with her husband, and she knew both men better now. She realised that she could only be a small part of the Tsar's life. As for her husband Nikita, she knew that he could not be relied upon and would always need her support. From now on she would have to take charge of her own life. Nikita was not a bad man, but he was weak-willed. She did not love him but accepted him as her husband, as the father of her child, their adored Sachon, now over two years old. Also, she was once again pregnant.

Zinaida respected her husband's family and his name and had succeeded in obtaining promotion for him to the rank of general. He was not a bad soldier, and had distinguished himself sufficiently during the campaigns of 1813 and 1814 to be awarded the George Cross and a sword with diamonds.[1] They were still uneasy together as the campaign came to its end, but there was no time to think about anything except Paris, and the glorious reception awaiting Alexander there.

By the end of March they were installed in the Imperial head-quarters at the Château de Bondy, just to the north-east of Paris. The Tsar was preoccupied with his entry into the capital. As one of his aides-de-camp, Nikita had been asked to accompany Pasquier, the chief of police in Paris, and the prefect, Monsieur de Chabrol, back to the city after their visit to the Tsar at Bondy. He was also charged with the immediate task of preparing lodgings in Paris for the Tsar and the Imperial suite.

Alexander, who did not much admire the Bourbons, was determined not to impose their restoration on the French unless they genuinely wanted it. He had considered replacing Napoleon with Bernadotte, and even with a regency for Napoleon's son, the infant King of Rome. To this end he had therefore charged all his entourage with the important task of sounding out their own friends in Paris, personally consulting as many people as they could.

So it was that on the morning of Wednesday, 31 March 1814, the fashionable young countess Adèle de Boigne, looking out of the mezzanine window of her parents' house near Montmartre, saw a Russian officer approaching on horseback, escorted by some Cossacks. She recognised with relief that it was Nikita Volkonsky, an old acquaintance. Leaving his Cossacks in the courtyard, with two posted at the door, the Prince explained that he had been sent by Count Nesselrode, the Russian Foreign Minister and an old friend of her father's, 'to assure us of their protection and our safety', and to discover from her father what were the wishes of his friends regarding the future. The Emperor Alexander, he said, would soon be arriving. He had taken no decision as yet. Madame de Boigne sent for her father. As Nikita posed the question of the restoration, her young cousin, Charles d'Osmond, bounded into the room showing them his hat decorated with the white rosette of the Bourbons.

'I could not give you a better answer, Prince [her father said].

You can see the love, the zeal and the passion which these colours inspire.'

'You are quite right, Monsieur le Marquis,' replied Nikita. 'I will report this, and I hope that on my way this will be confirmed by everyone.'[2]

By 'everyone', Nikita of course meant the aristocratic families personally known to the Russians around the Tsar.

The spring of 1814 in Paris was one of the most beautiful that anyone could remember. Exhausted by war, her citizens were in a strangely fatalistic mood as they awaited the end of the Empire. All the signs were unmistakably there, though no one knew what was going on on the battle fronts. The government-controlled press, once full of Napoleon's victories, was now silent. In the previous weeks Napoleon's military strategy had indeed shown all his former genius, provoking an admiring 'Excellent, quite excellent' from the Duke of Wellington, who, studying it in later years, added that had Napoleon continued his system for a little longer he would have saved Paris. Rumours circulated around the salons. The streets were full of hungry and tired young conscripts, some of them hardly more than children, for whom no provision had been made. Nothing, wrote Madame de Boigne, neither battles nor occupations nor risings nor any kind of trouble, could have stopped the Parisiennes from enjoying their elegant toilettes.[3] Lady Burghersh, on the other hand, thought the fashions hideous:

> It is the rage now in France to have everything enormous. Never was anything so frightful as the French fashions – everything *outré* to a degree of monstrosity. The hats get worse and worse; they make them now with very narrow, small pokes, and crowns two feet high, and the front covered with enormous bows and bunches of flowers – and these are worn by every creature.[4]

On the Sunday before Prince Nikita's arrival, a gaily dressed crowd – young women in the amazingly high-crowned hats and dresses with exaggeratedly large stripes – had watched as a magnificent regiment of cuirassiers, newly arrived from Spain, clattered through Paris on their way to join the Emperor's troops. The next day they were back, men and horses more or less badly wounded as they trickled through the barricades one by one, their long white coats covered in blood.[5]

Faithful to Napoleon's instructions, the Empress Marie Louise, with her son and members of the Council of Regency, left Paris for Blois, on the Loire, on 29 March. As a member of that council, Talleyrand should have accompanied the Empress, but Napoleon's former Foreign Minister had other plans and no intention of being out of Paris while the future of France was being decided. He therefore pretended to attempt to leave Paris in his carriage which, by arrangement with his friend Monsieur de Rémusat, a captain in the National Guard, would be intercepted and sent back. When Paris capitulated to the Allies at 2 a.m. on 31 March Talleyrand was at his house in the rue St Florentin. While he was still dressing later that morning, Count Nesselrode, the Russian Foreign Minister and an old acquaintance, was announced. The Emperor Alexander had been warned that it was unsafe for him to stay at the Elysée because the palace was said to be mined, Nesselrode explained to Talleyrand. He had therefore decided to stay at the house of Monsieur de Talleyrand. It was said that, wishing to keep the Tsar where he could best influence him, Talleyrand had himself been the author of the note about the mining of the palace. Now he would have his revenge on Napoleon, who had brought his beloved France to this pass.

Charles Maurice de Talleyrand-Périgord, former Bishop of Autun and, since 1806, Prince of Benevento, was the most important political figure in France after Napoleon. Born in 1754, he had forfeited his rights of primogeniture as a result of a fall in infancy which left him permanently crippled, and entered the Church. Banned by the Pope in 1791 for voting for the civil constitution of the clergy, he was out of France until 1795. He helped Napoleon in the coup of Brumaire and was rewarded with the post of Foreign Minister, which he held until 1807. An aristocrat in a world of parvenus, Talleyrand's exquisite dress, languid manners and brilliant conversation hid a mind as sharp as it was supple. He never ceased to believe in monarchical government and did not discourage Napoleon in his dynastic ambitions. His chief aim was to reconcile the old France with the new, and to establish peace in France and in Europe. He had no scruples in enriching himself significantly in the process. When, after the crushing defeat of Prussia, Talleyrand realised that he had no hope of dissuading Napoleon from imposing on that country terms so harsh as to turn

Prussia henceforth into an implacable enemy, or from mounting a blockade of Britain, or from turning Poland into a French protectorate, he did not hesitate to betray him.

Alexander had first met Talleyrand in 1808. Talleyrand had understood him perfectly then:

> Sire, it is in your power to save Europe, and you will do so only by refusing to give in to Napoleon. The French people are civilised; their sovereign is not. The sovereign of Russia is civilised, his people are not: therefore the sovereign of Russia should be the ally of the French people.

Alexander had trusted him then and he trusted him now.

The Tsar's determination to advance had been reinforced by a message from Talleyrand some weeks before, when the Allies, rattled by Napoleon's military successes, were doubtful about their course of action: 'You are groping about like children; you ought to stride forward on stilts. You are in a position to achieve anything you wish.'[6] Now Talleyrand was to have his reward. Dismounting outside Talleyrand's house after his triumphal entry into Paris, Alexander said:

> Well, here we are in Paris! It is you who has brought us here, Monsieur de Talleyrand. There are three possible solutions now: to negotiate with the Emperor Napoleon, to establish a regency or to call back the Bourbons.[7]

At Fontainebleau, meanwhile, Napoleon had shut himself up in his study with Caulaincourt. He could not hide his utter dejection from the man who had stood by him, and with whom he had travelled from Moscow. Outwardly, however, he continued to plan a new offensive to relieve Paris.

No one would forget that day. By early afternoon, on 31 March 1814, groups of young men sporting the white rosette of the Bourbons began to appear in the streets and shouts of '*Vive le Roi*!' were heard here and there. When the Allies had first entered Paris that morning they had been met by a silent, stupefied population not sure whether they were in the presence of conquerors or liberators. As the procession rode up to the Place Vendôme, the shouts intensified. '*Vive Alexandre!*', '*Vivent les Alliés!*', '*Vive le Roi!*' rose from all sides as white rosettes were pulled from pockets and hurriedly pinned to hats.[8]

Preceded by his own regiment of the Tsar's Red Cossacks, followed by the hussars and cuirassiers of the Prussian Royal Guard and the dragoons and hussars of the Russian Imperial Guard, Alexander entered Paris flanked by the King of Prussia, and Prince Schwarzenburg representing the Emperor of Austria. Behind them rode ranks of generals and ministers, Barclay de Tolly and Blücher among them. Mounted on his horse Eclipse (by a curious twist of fate, a present from Napoleon), Alexander wore the uniform of the chevaliers-guards. Across his chest lay the blue order of St Andrew, while a wide black belt clasped his waist. Under his plumed bicorne hat his pale, gentle face looked at once solemn and joyful.

At the entrance to the Champs-Elysées the Allied sovereigns stopped to review the troops. The crowds roared with delight as for almost five hours regiment after regiment marched past; they were particularly thrilled by the exotic Cossack and Kalmuk regiments, 20,000 strong.

In the crowd, Chateaubriand too would never forget that day. Earlier he had watched the approach of the Russians in the distance feeling, he wrote, 'like an ancient Roman might have done at the sight of Alaric's Goths'. Now he was 'stupefied and utterly vanquished, as if my name of Frenchman had been torn from me to be substituted by a number by which I would be known henceforth as a prisoner in the Siberian mines. At the same time I felt a mounting exasperation against this man whose desire for glory had reduced us to this shame.' He noted that it must have been the most ordered and disciplined entrance by a conquering army in history, attributing the impeccable behaviour of the Russians to Alexander's magnanimity and modesty.[9]

Alexander had been absolutely determined that he would come as liberator. The Russians continued to behave well, from the Cossacks camped on the Champs-Elysées, mending their clothes and harness in the spring sunshine, to the officers, who, wrote Madame de Boigne, did all they could to raise our own circumstances in our eyes. They had nothing but words of praise and admiration for our brave army. Not one comment escaped them which might have offended or hurt a Frenchman, whatever his views. This was their master's will and it was followed to the letter without any seeming difficulty.[10]

Indeed during those two months in Paris, Alexander, the great hero of the hour, could do no wrong. Undoubtedly his example and the strictest orders to his army kept the troops in line. While the Russians had suffered greatly at the hands of the French, for the Tsar and for all the officers Paris was in a sense their city too. Many had spent years here. Their education and culture had been as French as that of their willing or unwilling hosts. It was not too difficult to think of Napoleon as their common enemy. Paris, to whose glories Napoleon had greatly added, filled the Russians with admiration, indeed with almost a sense of reverence.

The French harboured mixed feelings. There was overwhelming relief that the war was over, for many relief too that Napoleon who had ruled ever more despotically was gone. They felt shame at the state to which France had been reduced, of which the sight of foreigners occupying their city, as well as the numbers of wounded French soldiers, were a constant reminder. There was also curiosity and uncertainty about the future and, for many, doubt about the return of the Bourbons. A large number of the young hotheads roaming Paris that day were royalists, unable to resist grand gestures, like one of Zinaida's close friends, young Sosthène de La Rochefoucauld who had met Nikita in the city that morning and with whom he had accompanied the Tsar to Talleyrand's house. To make his views about a restoration quite clear he had climbed up to put a rope around the statue of Napoleon on top of his column in the Place Vendôme intending to drag it down. He was restrained by officers of the Semionovsky regiment, horrified at such *lèse-majesté*.[11] Looking up at the statue later, Alexander was heard to remark, 'Had I stood so high I would have been afraid of my head turning dizzy.'[12] Above all, the French had had a bellyful of '*la gloire*' and longed for peace.

No one suffered greater anguish than Germaine de Staël, who had been living in England since May 1813. The French defeats, the very thought of foreign troops in her beloved Paris, caused her intense pain. She longed for 'two arms, one to repel the enemy and the other to overturn tyranny.'[13] Because Napoleon was identified with France and with liberty, she had ardently hoped that he would be killed in battle but victorious. Furious with her friend and former lover Benjamin Constant for what she saw as an anti-French attitude, she wrote:

> So you think Bonaparte unworthy of taking part in an assembly of Princes! Forty battles are also a badge of nobility. I loathe the man, but I blame the circumstances which force me at present to wish him success. Do you wish to see France brought to her knees? I will do nothing against France; I will not turn against her in her misfortune, I will use neither my fame which I owe to her, nor my father's name which she had loved. You are not French, Benjamin. All your memories are not linked to that land, that is where the differences between us lie: but can you really wish to see Cossacks in the rue Racine?[14]

Britain, which more than any other country had brought about the downfall of Napoleon, was unrepresented at the triumphant entry into Paris though there would be victory celebrations in London in due course. Castlereagh was still at Dijon where he had remained with his new friend Metternich. Although the Prince Regent, the Cabinet and public opinion favoured the restoration of the Bourbons, Castlereagh did not wish to be too closely associated with it.

Talleyrand, meanwhile, was preparing to preside over a dinner that night in his magnificent mansion, cooked by his peerless chef, Carême. He had every reason to be well pleased with himself. The Tsar was his guest and had asked him to decide the future of France. Alexander had told him in their preliminary talks that he had no wish to impose a restoration of the Bourbons on the French people. Might they favour a regency, or a republic? Measuring his words carefully, Talleyrand replied that, while he had little affection or respect for the Bourbons, France needed stability which only the legitimate monarchy could give her at the moment. A regency for the King of Rome was much too dangerous and certain to be exploited by Napoleon. Alexander had been impressed.

Zinaida, as part of the Tsar's suite, would have been one of the beauties at the banquet, presided over by Talleyrand's mistress, the Duchess of Courland, and her beautiful daughter Dorothea, Comtesse de Talleyrand-Périgord, Talleyrand's niece by marriage. As they left Talleyrand's house after dinner for a gala at the Opéra, the Tsar was again cheered by the crowds and they were met by more cheering on arrival. Inside, the opera house had been magnificently decorated with the white lilies of the Bourbons, while the ladies had garlanded their heads with the same. The crowd rose as one, cheering Alexander as he took his place in his box.

Sure of the Tsar's support, Talleyrand wasted no time. The following day, 1 April, he called a meeting of the Senate and persuaded them to appoint a provisional government. The day after, the Senate proclaimed the deposition of Napoleon and formally invited Louis XVIII to return to the throne of France. Writing to Castlereagh on 4 April, his half-brother and ambassador to the Allied sovereigns, Sir Charles Stewart, deeply regretted that he had not been in Paris to counteract the Tsar's influence.

It is deeply to be lamented that His Majesty's Secretary of State for Foreign Affairs, by accidental occurrences, has been thrown out of the way of affording that incalculable benefit which his presence would not fail of producing here at this moment. Napoleon managed everything by his immense military power and the satellites appertaining to it. I hope Talleyrand, who is equally ambitious, is not endeavouring to become another absolute ruler, by chicane and political manoeuvring.[15]

By the time Castlereagh arrived in Paris on 10 April, it had been decided to send Napoleon to Elba. Caulaincourt was still rushing back and forth between the Hôtel Talleyrand and Napoleon in Fontainebleau who, deeply depressed, had attempted suicide by drinking poison, which he had long carried around with him. He failed: the poison was so old that it had lost its potency.

The Orthodox Easter that year fell on Sunday, 10 April. Zinaida with the Volkonskys and all the other members of the Imperial retinue watched as a solemn Te Deum was celebrated according to the rites of the Orthodox Church before the Emperor of Russia and his assembled army, on the recently renamed Place Louis XVI.[16] An altar had been set up on a dais, on the very spot where Louis XVI had been executed. Afterwards they entertained their guests who were watching the ceremony from the windows of the Admiralty, where the Volkonskys had their apartments. The weather continued to be warm and all the chestnuts were now in leaf along the Champs-Elysées. From her balcony at the Admiralty, Madame de Boigne, who was a guest of the Volkonskys, looked down at the strange Eastern rites as Talleyrand did from his house at another corner of the square. Half of Paris seemed to have turned out to watch the exotic spectacle. Madame de Boigne recalled that she had not minded while there was noise and movement in the square, but when, at the most solemn point of the Mass, silence fell and the strange chanting of the Ortho-dox priests was heard blessing 'those strangers who had come to triumph over us', she had felt a strong pang of patriotic revulsion. She noticed, however, that after the service the rooms of the Admiralty were crowded with more Frenchwomen than Russians, all sporting the Bourbon lilies. She decided to see less of the foreigners from now on.[17]

While Madame de Boigne had her Russian coterie, she did not like Zinaida, much preferring Nikita, whom perhaps she found attractive. It may be that she did not much care for women generally, because she was also scathing about Madame de Nesselrode, whom she described as 'cold and stiff' and, while 'she had quite a lot of wit, she was determined to preserve the complete domination which she had always exercised over her husband and was jealous of any possible influence on him'. Nesselrode was nevertheless a constant visitor at Madame de Boigne's, as were Nikita and Count Pozzo di Borgo, the Russians' charming, Corsican-born ambassador to Paris and later to London, known to all as Pozzo. Nikita was obviously a close friend; it was to him that Madame de Boigne turned for protection. He offered her Cossack soldiers to guard her country house outside Paris. Madame de Boigne, while admitting Zinaida's considerable beauty, nevertheless thought it had been spoiled by the scar on her lip, which she attributed to jealousy. Zinaida, she said, had locked herself up since their arrival in Paris: 'I don't know why I found favour with her, and she allowed poor Nikita to come to visit me. All Europe since then has echoed with the quarrels and follies of this eccentric couple.'[18]

The next two months were a whirlwind of balls and receptions. Zinaida was probably only too pleased to be rid of Nikita. Far from locking herself up, she was delighted to be back in one of her favourite cities, resuming many old friendships and making interesting new ones. She was a welcome guest at many of the capital's most illustrious salons. Zinaida and Sophia were close friends of Mademoiselle Louise de Cochelet, who was the confidante of Queen Hortense of Holland, Napoleon's stepdaughter. The charming Queen was a great favourite of the Tsar who had persuaded Louis XVIII to create her Duchesse de Saint-Leu, as well as securing titles and revenues for Josephine's son Eugène. Once again, Zinaida and the Tsar met frequently at the Empress Josephine's house at Malmaison, although Josephine remained staunchly loyal to Napoleon. When, while walking with the Tsar in the garden after a ball, Josephine caught a chill as a result of which she died a few days later, Alexander attended the funeral, ordering a detachment of his guard to pay military honours to Napoleon's former Empress.[19]

Zinaida's step-aunt Princess Laval, to whom she was very close, was also in Paris and through her, and their friend Sosthène de La Rochefoucauld, she also knew the legitimist circles. Zinaida's pregnancy was not yet obvious and she took full advantage of all that Paris had to offer. Apart from the carnival atmosphere and the many entertainments, Paris looked beautiful. The recently restored Louvre was crammed with the treasures which Napoleon had looted from all over Europe. There was music every night. The great Talma performed at the Comédie Française, while the beautiful Grassini, once Napoleon's mistress and soon to be Wellington's, sang at the Opéra.

Napoleon himself left France for Elba at the end of April after the signing of the Treaty of Fontainebleau, whereby he and his family were granted quite generous terms. On 3 May Louis XVIII returned to France with his niece, the Duchesse d'Angoulême, the last surviving child of Louis XVI. He was fat and gouty while her stiff manners and English clothes shocked the Parisians as much as, if not more than, French fashions had shocked Priscilla Burghersh. The King and his niece made a poor impression. Louis had also succeeded in offending both Talleyrand and Alexander to whom he owed his throne, showing, the Tsar felt, no gratitude at all. Louis had received the Tsar at Compiègne, where he stopped on his way to Paris. The reception had been so offhand that Alexander later wrote indignantly: 'One would have thought it was he who put me back on my throne. The reception he gave me made the same impression as a bucket of ice thrown over my head. We northern barbarians have better manners in our country.'[20] Madame de Lieven, wife of the Russian ambassador in London, also noted that Alexander 'had not found the King of France as grateful or as polite as he had a right to expect'.[21]

Wellington, who had just been created Duke, arrived in Paris the next day. Castlereagh had offered him the Paris Embassy. Writing his acceptance on 21 April, Wellington was 'very much obliged and flattered', and while protesting that he felt himself unqualified to be ambassador, he was nevertheless 'ready to serve in any situation in which it was thought that I could be of service.'[22] That night at a grand ball given by Sir Charles Stewart, to which the Emperor and all the Russians were invited, Paris society had its first sight of the Duke, with his niece Priscilla Burghersh on his arm. Everyone was anxious to meet the great military hero. However, the evening was spoilt when, after the Tsar's departure, his brother the Grand Duke Constantine asked for a waltz, countermanding a request for a quadrille which Sir Charles Stewart had just made to please Lady Burghersh. The conductor hesitated, looked at the Grand Duke and struck up a waltz.

'Who has dared insist on the waltz?' asked the furious Sir Charles, to which the Grand Duke replied that he had done so.

'I alone give orders in my house, Monseigneur,' said Sir Charles. Turning to the conductor he said, 'Pray continue with the quadrille,' whereupon the Grand Duke stormed out in a fury, followed by all the Russians.[23]

In spite of this and other contretemps between the Allies, the first Peace of Paris was signed on 30 May 1814. The Allies were keen to prop up the Bourbons and avoid a revival of Bonapartism, which a punitive settlement might have provoked. France would give up Napoleon's conquests and go back to her 1792 frontiers, but with some important additions. No reparations would be demanded, nor would there be an army of occupation. The Emperor Alexander was now free to travel to London. The real negotiations would take place at a congress which was to take place in the autumn, in Vienna.

'The Emperor's fame has now reached its greatest splendour. Never had monarch owned a more wondrous reputation for greatness and personal glory, and the whole English nation awaited his coming with passionate impatience and enthusiasm,' wrote Dorothea, Countess Lieven, wife of the Russian ambassador to the court of St James.[24] She was scarcely an objective observer, of course, but on this occasion it was the truth.

Alexander had enjoyed his fame and glory in Paris, but he was spiritually exhausted, disappointed in the king he had helped to restore, disappointed too in his friend Talleyrand, whose capacities for intrigue outmatched his own. To Chateaubriand, the Tsar had appeared both calm and sad: 'He seemed astonished by his triumphs. Awareness of the hand of destiny, of changing fortune, which was shared by both ordinary people and kings, could not but make a profound impression on a mind as religious as his.'[25]

The Tsar now prepared for his visit to London. Having wrested a promise from Louis that the charter guaranteeing the French people a constitution would be passed on 4 June, he wrote to the person he most longed to see, the person with whom he could be himself, his sister Catherine:

At last I see light about our departure, and I can tell you definitely that I shall get under way on Friday 3 June. I shall be at Boulogne and perhaps the same day at Dover on Sunday 5th. For Heaven's sake make them believe I shall not be in London till Tuesday 7th. I cannot convey the bliss I feel at the thought of seeing you again, and pressing you to my heart.[26]

Zinaida left Paris just ahead of the Tsar accompanied by Sophia and by her husband who, as usual, had to see to the many practical arrangements for the Tsar's visit to London. They were astonished by the festive atmosphere of London. At night the capital was illuminated as never before. Not only were all the public buildings blazing with the light of thousands of lamps, but even private houses were all lit up. The Bank of England was traced in light, a huge transparency in the centre depicting 'the genius of France reviving'. Smaller transparencies could be bought, with pictures of scenes and heroes. At night, lit from behind, they decorated the windows of many London houses. Carlton House, the Prince Regent's London residence, was alight with red and yellow torches, placed between pots of palms. All of London seemed to be perpetually in the streets. The Volkonskys had never seen such crowds. At the Lievens' – the Russian Embassy in London – the talk was all about the Tsar's visit. It had been planned as one of pleasure; there would be time for work at the Vienna Congress in the autumn. Now the two Princes who had liberated Europe from Napoleon would at last have a chance to meet.

The Tsar was accompanied to London by the King of Prussia and Marshal Blücher. 'The Tsar has the greatest merit and must be held high, but ought to be grouped and not made the sole feature for admiration,' Castlereagh had warned the Prince Regent, worried by the special attention given to Alexander. Castlereagh hoped to settle many of the outstanding political questions in London, ahead of the Vienna Congress, the hectic pace of social life in Paris having made it almost impossible to work. London, however, was to prove even worse. Writing to thank Louise de Cochelet for a coat which Queen Hortense had sent for the Tsar, Count Nicholai Tolstoy, one of Alexander's entourage, excuses himself for not writing sooner: 'it is because of the whirlwind in which we have been caught up since our arrival in London'.[27]

Alexander's reception in London was as ecstatic as it had been in Paris. He was met at Dover by the Russian ambassador, Count Lieven, with whom he travelled to London, arriving almost incognito to the fury of the crowds, many of whom had paid money for places in the stands which had been erected along the way. The Tsar had annoyed the Prince Regent by declining the quarters he had been offered at St James's Palace in favour of the Pulteney Hotel, where his sister, the Grand Duchess Catherine, had been staying for the past three months. Unwilling to go back to Russia, Catherine had spent some time in Holland but had decided as early as February that she wished to visit England.[28] In London, the Grand Duchess almost at once fell out with the Regent, his ministers and the Russian ambassador, cultivating instead the society of all those opposed to the Regent, which included his daughter.

By the time of the Tsar's arrival, her relations with the Prince Regent had deteriorated to the point where there was nothing she would not do to annoy him. Wilful and imperious, Catherine had much of her grandmother and namesake in her nature. More importantly, her influence over the Tsar was undiminished.

She was a very remarkable person in all repects [Countess Lieven recalled in her memoirs]. The Grand Duchess had an excessive thirst for authority and a very high opinion of herself, which perhaps exceeds her deserts. I never saw a woman so given over to the need-stirring acting, coming to the fore and effacing others. She was very seductive in glance and manners, an assured gait, a look proud but gracious, features but scantily classic, but a dazzling brilliance and freshness of complexion, a bright eye, and the most beautiful hair in the world. Her mind was cultivated, brilliant and daring; her character resolute and imperious. She startled and astonished the English more than she pleased them.[29]

The first meeting between the Regent and the Grand Duchess had been a disaster, and a nightmare for the poor Lievens. As he left, the Prince Regent had hissed to Countess Lieven, 'Your Grand Duchess is not good-looking,' while Catherine's verdict was that the Regent was ill-bred. That evening, at a dinner at Carlton House, Catherine, who was still in mourning for her husband, talked readily of her grief, whereupon the Regent not only cast doubt on the sincerity of her feelings but suggested coarsely that she would soon find consolation. An outraged silence and a haughty stare had greeted this sally, after which the Grand Duchess demanded that the Italian musicians be sent away since music made her ill!

'From that evening she and the Regent hated each other mutually, and the feeling remained to the end,' wrote the sorely tried ambassadress. The Grand Duchess now embarked on serious Regent-baiting,

ignoring his mistress the Marchioness of Hertford, and openly entertaining all those on the Carlton House black list, particularly the Whig
members of the opposition, and, of course, the Regent's despised
wife, the Princess of Wales. Since Catherine insisted on controlling
the ambassador's guest lists, she was soon in more or less permanent
combat with Lieven, who was prevented from entertaining government ministers and people close to the court. 'Every dinner led to a
small dispute between her and my husband,' wrote Dorothea Lieven,
'to the point where Catherine refused to speak to him for almost two
months before the arrival of the Tsar.'

As soon as the Regent heard that Alexander had arrived at the
Pulteney, he sent word that he would come to visit him there. The
Regent then kept the Tsar waiting for three hours, while the crowd
grew denser, shouting for Alexander, who eventually appeared on the
balcony several times to their delighted roars of 'Hurrah!' At length,
a note arrived from the Prince Regent: 'His Royal Highness has been
threatened with annoyance in the streets if he shows himself: it is
therefore impossible for him to come to see the Emperor.'

'That's what he's like,' said the Grand Duchess triumphantly, greatly
satisfied with the way the Regent had played into her hands. She
continued to do all she could to prejudice her brother against him.
Alexander was nevertheless obliged to get into the ambassador's carriage and go to Carlton House. 'A poor Prince,' he remarked to
Lieven on their return, to which Lieven replied, 'Who helped you to
wage a glorious war and a peace to match.'[30] After that it was all
downhill. Nor were matters helped by the fact that the Regent was
very unpopular at the time. Although he had a good mind and was
a great collector of art and a passionate lover of architecture, he was
so gross in his personal habits and appearance that to be excluded
from invitations to Carlton House had become '*bon ton*'. Writing in
the radical weekly, *The Examiner*, Leigh Hunt described him as:

a libertine over head and ears in debt and disgrace, a despiser of
domestic ties, the companion of gamblers and demireps, a man
who has just closed half a century without one single claim on the
gratitude of his country or the respect of posterity.[31]

Alexander, meanwhile, was drawing adoring crowds wherever he went. There were never fewer than 10,000 people watching out for him around the Pulteney. He was mobbed by people wishing to shake his hand whenever he got in or out of his carriage. His unfailing good humour delighted everyone. However, in spite of the best efforts of his ambassador and members of his suite, Alexander behaved with an extraordinary lack of tact towards the Regent. Both the Tsar and his sister befriended the Princess of Wales, the Regent's estranged wife.

Born Caroline of Brunswick, the Princess was if anything more coarse of habit and person than her husband, but his unkindness to her had made her a sympathetic figure in the eyes of the people. Their marriage had lasted a year. On first seeing his prospective bride the Prince had called for a glass of brandy, declaring that he was unwell. He was drunk on his wedding night, spending the night 'under the grate, where he fell and where I left him', the bride later recorded.[32] The marriage had nevertheless produced a daughter, Charlotte, whose forthcoming marriage to the Dutch Prince William of Orange was very much desired by the Regent and his government, but not by the Princess herself. Much political capital was made of this by the Whigs. At the time of the sovereigns' visit to London, the Princess of Wales was *persona non grata* at court, and forbidden to attend any official functions, the Regent having declared that he did not wish to see her in private or in public. The press and the political parties were divided – Tories for the Regent, Whigs and Radicals for Caroline. The Grand Duchess Catherine's open adoption of the Princess's cause and her siding with Charlotte looked to the Tory government like a Russian plot to wreck Charlotte's prospective marriage and with it Anglo-Dutch understanding.

On 16 June, the Princess broke off her engagement. Relations between the two Princes now went from bad to worse. At the Marquis of Cholmondely's ball, Lieven suggested that Alexander say a few words to Lady Hertford, the Prince Regent's mistress, who was standing near him hoping to be noticed. 'She is mighty old,' the Tsar commented unhelpfully as he moved away.

Considerable differences between Alexander and George IV, then Prince Regent, often placed me in a difficult position. Being kindly regarded by both princes and a confidant of their daily and personal troubles, my efforts were necessarily directed to prevent their mutual irritation from growing into serious dissension,

wrote Metternich mendaciously.[33] The truth was that a vastly amused Metternich had spared no effort to stir up further trouble between them, greatly enjoying the process while he plotted behind the scenes with Castlereagh. Part of the result of this was a secret treaty against Russia signed at Vienna by Austria, France and England.

During the Tsar's fortnight in London, Zinaida only saw him at an endless round of parties, balls and dinners. 'Never have I seen the chief [Alexander] so gay, so keen to dance as here,' Sophia Volkonsky wrote to a friend in Paris.[34] Lords Liverpool and Castlereagh gave balls, so did the Marquises of Hertford, Salisbury and Cholmondely. White's Club gave a great reception at Burlington House.

On the night of 11 June, Zinaida would have particularly enjoyed a gala performance at the King's Theatre, home of the Italian opera. While Madame Grassini and Madame Tramizzami were singing a special hymn of welcome during the interval, the Princess of Wales entered her box, directly opposite the royal one. As she sat down amid a buzz of recognition and pleasure from the public, she bowed her head to the Tsar. Alexander at once stood up and gallantly bowed to her, followed by the King of Prussia. The Regent, despite his loathing for his estranged wife, was obliged to follow suit. The house then burst into spontaneous applause, which enraged the Regent. He got his own back the next day, at a review of troops in Hyde Park, when he kept the Imperial party waiting for an hour. The Tsar trumped this a few days later by arriving very late at a court reception, explaining that he had been detained at the house of Lord Grey, the Regent's most notable Whig opponent.

On 18 June, Zinaida was present at the famous banquet at the Guildhall given by the Lord Mayor. Famous because disastrous. Although by tradition it was for men only, the Grand Duchess had insisted on going, so some of the ladies were included. As they assembled in the anteroom, Alexander, dressed in scarlet and gold, gave his arm to the Duchesss of York, the King of Prussia to the Grand Duchess Catherine, followed by the Prince Regent with Countess Lieven on his arm. Alexander, seeing the two Whig leaders, the Lords Holland and Grey, paused to talk to them, forcing the fuming Regent to wait. During the banquet, 'as sumptuous as expense and skill could make it', at which the Prince refused to address a word to either the Tsar or his sister, the Grand Duchess further infuriated him by complaining again about the Italian musicians, repeating that music made her ill and only grudgingly accepting 'God Save the King'. Lord Liverpool was incensed: 'When folk don't know how to behave they would do better to stay at home, and your Duchess has chosen, against all usage, to go to men's dinners,' he complained furiously to Countess Lieven as they left the table.

All the great Whig houses vied to entertain the Tsar, who attended balls given by the Duke of Devonshire and Lord Grey, as well as one given by the famous Whig hostess, Lady Jersey, the Regent's former mistress. The Regent would not attend any of them. He attempted to foil the Tsar's plans to go to Lady Jersey's ball by arranging a heavy programme in Oxford on the same day. Returning to London at two in the morning, however, the Tsar changed his clothes and went straight to Lady Jersey's where he danced reels till five. Here, as usual, he flirted with all the pretty women especially the younger ones, most of whom were delighted with him. He was a graceful and enthusiastic dancer and loved the waltz. Zinaida herself, no longer hurt or surprised by the Tsar's dalliances, was probably as amused as everyone else by a piece of gossip that flew around London just before they left. It was recorded by Countess Lieven:

Lady Jersey believed genuinely that the Emperor was in love with her. On the eve of the Emperor's departure, there was a ball at the Marchioness of Devonshire's. My husband had not accepted the invitation she sent him for the Emperor, thinking he would not take it, since he was to be off the next day at such an early hour. The Emperor, not thinking himself asked, could not go, but he knew Lady Jersey was there, and he took it into his head at one in the morning to send his cousin the Prince of Oldenburg there, asking Lady Jersey to leave the ball and come to him to say good-bye. Lady Jersey, flattered and alarmed, talked over with her friends there, not whether it was proper to pay the visit at such an hour, but as to what she should do if the Emperor became too pressing. She foresaw all the utmost possibilities, and asked if one might refuse an Emperor. Her friends told her it would be very uncivil, and she must go and trust herself to the keeping of Heaven. It appears that the Emperor, on his part, had thought of precautions against her, for he had made his Imperial sister get up, and the Duchess was present at the meeting, which ended at three in the morning. Lady Jersey, who had curious visitors next day, told them with downcast eyes that the Emperor had only asked to kiss her arm above the elbow.[35]

A visit designed to give pleasure, and to provide the opportunity for the two sovereigns who had brought down Napoleon to meet, began with antipathy and hardened to contempt and dislike on both sides. 'All agree', the Whig MP and gossip Thomas Creevey wrote gleefully, 'that Prinny will die or go mad; he is worn out with fuss, fatigue and *rage*.'[36]

Speculation about the the Volkonskys' troubled marriage had followed them to London. Madame de Boigne had written of their quarrels and of Zinaida's jealousy. Gossip was further fuelled when a baby boy was left on the pavement outside their house. Zinaida decided that there was no question of abandoning him. She determined there and then to keep him, bringing him up with her own son and the new baby she was expecting. She called the child Vladimir Pavey, since he was found on the pavement. Wicked tongues put it about that the child was an illegitimate offspring of Nikita's. Zinaida ignored them. It hardly mattered anyway, the baby needed care and she would see that he had it. As soon as she could, she had little Vladimir received into the Orthodox Church at the Russian chapel in Welbeck Street. Vladimir Pavey was brought up alongside Zinaida's son though he was not adopted as her son. He remained devoted to her for the rest of her life.[37]

Extraordinarily, the baby was hardly mentioned by anyone in Zinaida's circle. Writing to her friend (and Zinaida's) Louise de Cochelet on 25 June, just before their departure from London, Sophia rattles on about everything but – although it must have been a shock to them all – never refers to this unexpected new addition to the family.[38] Zinaida herself never mentions the boy, or, if she did, the relevant correspondence might have been destroyed later by her vigilant son. It is only as a grown man, years later in Rome, that we hear again of Vladimir Pavey. The utter silence on the subject suggests that perhaps the story of his being a by-blow of Nikita's was true, as the Volkonskys seemed to believe. If one compares the portrait of Vladimir Pavey as a young man, painted by one of Zinaida's artist friends, O. Kiprensky, when they were living in Rome, with that of Nikita Volkonsky at about the same age, there is indeed a striking resemblance. The shape of the face, nose, chin, even the look are similar. If the baby were indeed Nikita's then Zinaida's behaviour was even more exemplary. However little she may have loved her husband, she must have been dismayed and upset by the gossip, particularly if she believed or knew it to be true. And yet the needs of the baby left on her doorstep came first. Tender-hearted and idealistic, Zinaida was also very maternal. Her young son and the baby she was expecting must have made her especially receptive to the plight of the unknown child.

On Wednesday, 23 June, Zinaida left London with the Tsar's party. The Prince Regent and the Tsar were to review the fleet at Portsmouth. The Tsar was in a gloomy mood, while the Grand Duchess was in a petulant rage because of her mother's refusal to countenance her marriage to the Crown Prince of Württemburg with whom she had fallen in love. From Portsmouth they were to go to Dover, stopping on the way at Petworth where they were received by their host, Lord Egremont, who had already been joined by the Volkonskys. After a formal reception, later the subject of a painting,[39] and an early dinner at Petworth, the Regent took leave of his guests with no regret. The Imperial party too were aware that the visit, which had begun with the Tsar as the idol of the crowds, had ended on a much lower note. Even the Whigs, whom the Tsar had liked to flatter, had been offended by what they saw as a lack of respect to the state. Lord Grey described Alexander to Creevey as a 'a vain, silly fellow'.[40] To Metternich he had confided that he had been baffled by Alexander's request to produce a blueprint for the formation of an opposition in Russia. Did the Emperor truly intend to introduce a parliament into his country? 'If he really means to do so – and I should take good care not to advise it – he need not concern himself about an opposition, it would certainly not be wanting,' he added.[41] The Tsar's visit convinced both the government and the opposition that the future security of Britain and her Empire lay not with the Tsar but in a European balance of power.

On 27 June, the Emperor's party boarded the *Royal Charlotte*. The weather was cold and windy as it had been when they arrived. They cast anchor to the sound of guns. It had been decided that the Congress of Vienna would open formally on 1 October, to give the Tsar time to return to Russia. First, though, he would go to Baden to meet his wife, the Empress Elizabeth, whom he had not seen for eighteen months.

Zinaida, now more obviously pregnant, left London for Paris with her two babies, two-and-a-half-year-old Alexander who was her great joy, and the new foundling, Vladimir. She would again be parted from her husband, who was to accompany the Tsar, but Sophia would be with her. Sophia wrote to Mademoiselle de Cochelet that they were both looking forward to seeing her in Paris, 'where we will stop for 5 to 6 days, then going on to Vienna. The master [the Tsar] will join us in September. My sister will give birth in Vienna; I am thrilled.'[42] After a week in Paris, the two Volkonsky ladies travelled slowly to Vienna where they would once again be expected to join the social whirl. Zinaida, however, was preparing herself for a far more important event – the birth of her second child.

5

A New Europe: At the Congress of Vienna

'The Congress dances but does not advance.'

PRINCE DE LIGNE

In July 1814, after a much-needed rest in Paris, Zinaida and Sophia arrived in Vienna well ahead of the opening of the Congress. The weather was hot and sultry, making Zinaida's pregnancy even more uncomfortable. Sophia had already decided that she would go to Carlsbad to drink the waters for five weeks and then on to Égia, where she intended 'to fortify myself for ten days, after which I shall hurry to Vienna,' as she wrote to Louise de Cochelet. Her husband Prince Peter was to accompany the Tsar to Russia. 'How happy the Empress Mother will be to see her son. He will be in St Petersburg for his mother's nameday.'[1]

The Tsar returned home weary of pomp and ceremony and suffering from a mounting sense of anticlimax. He had rejected all preparations for a hero's welcome in St Petersburg, writing to the governor that 'the Almighty alone was the source of the glorious events that have put an end to the bloody fighting in Europe' and that he should inform everyone that the Tsar would not tolerate any demonstration of welcome or any receptions when he returned. However, he was unable to refuse his mother the pleasure of giving him a hero's welcome at Pavlovsk, which Maria Feodorovna had worked on so meticulously with her incomparable Italian theatre designer Gonzaga.

On 12 July, Alexander's departure from Tsarskoe Selo to Pavlovsk had been marked by the roar of cannon. As his mother waited anxiously, the first horseman appeared in the distance, signalling the Emperor's arrival. That afternoon, at a grand pageant, hymns and cantatas specially written by the poet laureate were sung to the 'liberator' before a march past of the Tsar's regiments. Later, the Tsar and Empress Dowager together opened a magnificent ball, followed by fireworks, hot air balloons and a supper in a specially constructed pavilion.[2]

When Zinaida arrived in Vienna it was already humming with preparations for the Congress. Houses were being refurbished, façades repainted, furniture and decorations regilded. Every square inch of lettable space in the city would be needed. The citizens of Vienna were keen to take part in the greatest event in living memory. While the sons of the aristocracy were being engaged as equerries and pages, workers were being turned into coachmen, footmen and valets. A whole army of spies had been recruited by the Austrian government and were being trained before taking up their positions in the various missions.[3] Uniforms of every kind were needed, and tailors and dressmakers prepared for the busiest time of their lives. The city was already filling up with a variety of entertainers: actors, actresses, acrobats, singers and ladies of the night, although the latter's professional services would meet serious competition from the enthusiastic amateurs among the flower of the European aristocracy.[4]

At the Hofburg, the enormous complex of buildings in the old heart of the city which was the Imperial Residence, the unfortunate Emperor Francis, known for his dislike of social life, was enjoying his last month of peace before the onslaught of Royal Highnesses. His beautiful Empress, the Italian-born Maria Ludovica, presided over a special festivities committee which the Emperor had appointed to devise entertainment for his foreign guests. The Empress could count on the advice of Metternich himself, while young Prince Trauttmansdorff, Marshal of the Court and Master of the Horse, would be in charge of the arrangements for the royal visitors at the Hofburg. The stables had had to be completely reorganised to accommodate the 1400 horses needed to ferry the guests. The

Emperor could at least take pleasure in the sight of the 300 carriages, newly painted a gleaming dark green with the Hapsburg coat of arms emblazoned in yellow on their doors, and the dozens of coachmen and grooms in their smart new yellow liveries. Much less cheering was the thought of the forty tables which would be laid every night for dinner, to entertain the foreign royals and their suites. Fortunately for the Emperor he, like everyone else, was unaware that the Congress, which was expected to be over by Christmas 1814, would last until the following June. The artistic Empress, meanwhile, was happily engaged with her decorators, planning the arrangement of rooms, the regilding of rococo cherubs, and the rehanging of curtains. Weekly balls were to be held at the Hofburg, the first of which was already arranged for 2 October. It was to be masked, and the palace's reception rooms would be decorated in red and gold. The Empress spent hours with Prince Trauttmansdorff poring over guest lists and tables of precedence. The intricacies of protocol inevitably turned out to be even more tiresome in reality than they had been in the planning. The minor royals caused endless headaches in their struggle for precedence.

Besides the Emperor and Empress of Russia, Vienna was expecting four kings, one queen, two hereditary princes, three grand duchesses and three princes of the blood, not to mention their chamberlains, ladies-in-waiting, equerries and attendant suites. There were also more than 200 German princelings who had been dispossessed by Napoleon's Confederation of the Rhine, in addition to sundry other princes, dukes and lesser members of the European aristocracy, all attracted to Vienna by the promise of a glittering social season.[5]

Accompanied by the Empress Elizabeth, Alexander arrived in Vienna on 23 September and took up residence at the Hofburg. The Volkonskys were once again reunited under the same roof. Although Zinaida met the Tsar frequently there was little warmth between them at this period. Alexander had returned to Russia in a mood of depression and irritability. He had been in a state of nervous exhaustion. Ahead of him lay not only the task of establishing a lasting peace in Europe, but also Russia's domestic problems.

From the moment of his arrival in Vienna, however, he kept the Emperor Francis's spies busy reporting on his love life. Princess

Esterhazy, the Countesses Szechenyi and Zichy, and the Princesses Auersperg and Liechtenstein were amongst the names they recorded. The 'platonic Don Juan' loved the atmosphere of romance and chivalry. Determined to enjoy himself, he would rub his face daily with a block of ice to tighten up the skin, before setting off in his closely fitting white knee breeches and embroidered high-collared uniforms to dance till dawn, charming so many of the young beauties that they began to doubt his sincerity. However, his temper, so sunny in his youth, had become unpredictable, as Sergei Volkonsky noticed.

> The position of our Russians was fairly sensitive in Vienna during the Congress. Our Emperor, while he was endlessly and particularly charming to all foreigners, was not the same towards us, giving the impression that our manners were well behind those of the Europeans. Full of respect towards any ensign not in Russian uniform, he was curt with us, so that we began willy nilly to refuse court invitations and those of the higher circles, living a rather noisy life more among our countrymen, but not one that might bring shame to national honour.[6]

Alexander was also publicly unpleasant to his wife, and his already difficult relations with Metternich were further complicated by rivalry over the affections of the beautiful Duchess of Sagan.

Zinaida was enjoying Vienna in her own way. Among the first people she saw, of her many acquaintances there, were her father's old friends, the Prince de Ligne and the Russian ambassador to Austria Count Andrei Razumovsky, whose daughter was Zinaida's sister-in-law, Princess Repnin. Charles Joseph, Prince de Ligne, who was born in Brabant (now Belgium) in 1735, had been a friend of the Empress Catherine and the Emperor Joseph and was a marshal of both the Russian and Austrian Empires. An invitation to his modest house on the Mölkerbastei, where he had lived since the French Revolution deprived him of his fortune and his vast estates, was much sought after. He was a famous and much-quoted wit, a prolific writer, a liberal spirit and a great lover of women. He had been a friend of Casanova as well as of Fredrick the Great; the lover of Madame du Barry and confidant of Marie Antoinette. He was adored by Madame de Staël, who had written a brilliant preface to a collection of his letters and thoughts. Zinaida loved him and became a habituée of his salon, and he of hers. His house became her refuge and a meeting place of just the sort of company she craved: people of talent and intellect, among them Chateaubriand and Benjamin Constant, Prince Eugène, Viceroy of Italy (Josephine's son and Napoleon's stepson) and the painter Isabey who had been brought to Vienna by Talleyrand to paint the official picture of the Congress.[7]

Although Zinaida was heavily pregnant, with the help of strong lacing and the high-waisted, loose dresses then in fashion she was able largely to disguise her condition and enjoy the social life. There was a welcome new addition to her close circle, in the tall and handsome form of Sergei Volkonsky, her youngest brother-in-law. Drawn by the fun and excitement, Sergei took leave of absence from the army and set off for Vienna. 'Monsieur Serge', as the Tsar, who was fond of him, always called him, was adored by his sister Sophia and a great favourite of Zinaida. He was her senior by exactly a year (born 8 December 1788) and although only twenty-seven was one of the most decorated officers in the Russian army, several times wounded in action. Kind-hearted and incurably generous, Sergei was idealistic and famously scatterbrained. A voracious reader, he was hardly ever seen without a book in his hand. Although he was an excellent raconteur and enjoyed company, reading and writing were always his favourite occupations along with music in which he also delighted. 'Only in his books and in his letters and notebooks did he exhibit any sense of order, in everything else chaos and disorder reigned,' his grandson wrote affectionately many years later.[8] Although Sergei was staying at Princess Bagration's, one of the leading hostesses of the Congress and an intimate of the Tsar, he was much more a part of Zinaida's circle, where he soon formed a close friendship with Prince Eugène of whom he wrote: 'What a wonderful man he was! What modesty, and with it a true warmth of character.' He was less sure about the old Prince de Ligne however:

I used to see the Prince de Ligne often at Zinaida's née Beloselsky, my brother's wife, but in spite of his fame as a wit, I had not found him that entertaining before nor did I do so then – he was, I thought, simply a chatterbox, and an overworked one at that.[9]

The Prince de Ligne had been delighted to welcome the daughter of his old friend. Zinaida was young, beautiful and intelligent. Her conversation was interesting and informed. As a front-line witness of the German and French campaigns, the arrival of the Russians in Paris and the celebrations in London, she had much to tell. She was also a member of the Tsar's inner circle. Her lovely voice was more in demand than ever at the many musical soirées. Disappointed in love, Zinaida began to take her talents more seriously. In a society which seemed increasingly shallow, this at least was something she could count on and it gave great joy and fulfilment to her artistic nature.

Zinaida and Sergei were often to be found at Count Andrei Razumovsky's, Russia's ambassador to Austria. The grandest of grandees as a result of a huge inheritance, he had used his wealth to turn his palatial embassy on the Landstrasse into a treasure house. Razumovsky had been a close friend of Zinaida's father, with whom he had much in common. Both diplomats, they shared a passion for art and music. The Count was a noted collector of paintings and furniture, a patron of artists and musicians, and a talented amateur musician himself. He was well known and loved in Vienna as the patron of Mozart, Haydn and especially Beethoven.

Razumovsky established one of the period's finest string quartets, to whose members he gave life contracts. Beethoven dedicated the three Opus 59 quartets to him. Zinaida would almost certainly have met Beethoven at Razumovsky's embassy where he was a frequent visitor. As Beethoven lived not far from the Prince de Ligne's apartments on the Mölkerbastei, Zinaida may well have seen him walking about the streets, a characteristic and famous figure in his distinctive blue frock-coat, with his pockmarked face, wild hair covered by an out-of-shape hat, his pockets stuffed with his ear trumpet and his music notebooks.[10]

Among the earliest arrivals in Vienna was a man who became one of Zinaida's dearest friends and was perhaps the strongest influence on her future conversion to the Roman Catholic faith, Cardinal Ettore

Consalvi, Secretary of State to the Vatican. Zinaida had no doubt already met him in London where the Volkonskys and the Cardinal had many friends in common, among them Madame de Boigne who greatly admired him. Consalvi had been sent to London by Pope Pius VII to promote the interests of the Papal States and had been particularly anxious to get an audience with the Tsar, to whom he wished to deliver a message from the Pope.

Aristocratic, charming and intelligent, the handsome Cardinal had been a great success with London society. He had been the beloved pupil and protégé of Cardinal the Duke of York, a son of James II, and was the first cardinal to visit England for 200 years. He was soon adopted by the Duchess of Devonshire who remained a lifelong friend and admirer. Indeed, he had been so successful in overcoming traditional English hostility towards the Vatican that he was dubbed the 'cardinal seducer' by the Prince Regent.[11] Consalvi was much more than a skilled diplomat; he had negotiated the Concordat of 1801 with Napoleon, who, impressed by the sincerity of his religious faith as much as by his negotiating skills, shrewdly observed: 'He is a person who does not like to be taken for a priest, but he is indeed one, and more so than all the others.'[12]

Zinaida was singing at a soirée at the Razumovskys' where she saw the Cardinal again, on the day after his arrival in Vienna, accompanied by the Marchese di San Mazzano, the ambassador of Piedmont, who noted it in his diary: 'Cardinal Consalvi came to see me, Castelafar dined with us. After dinner we went to Razumovsky; Princess Volkonsky was singing.'[13]

The Cardinal was very anxious to make close political contacts among the Russians. His task in Vienna was to re-establish the Vatican as a state as well as resolving several other issues. To this end he had to deal with the four leading powers, Russia, Prussia, Austria and England. Metternich was opposed to him and he was not invited to attend the official meetings of the Congress which made it all the more important for the Cardinal to strengthen his position with the Russians. There is no doubt that the Princess's closeness to the Tsar and his circle would have made her important to the Cardinal but their mutual love of art and music made them congenial friends anyway. More than that, Consalvi, with his long experience of human nature, must have seen the sometimes unhappy and lonely young woman behind Zinaida's outward liveliness and gaiety, and recognised a questing spirit in the worldly Princess.

Zinaida was more estranged than ever from her husband. No direct record of their personal relationship survives but the infidelities, hers as well as his, together with gossip about them, always painful to the highly strung and sensitive Princess – not to mention the possibility that Vladimir Pavey was indeed his child – and now his total neglect of her in Vienna, when she was pregnant, were enough in themselves to explain the breakdown of their relationship. The brilliant Zinaida was almost certainly a threatening presence to her husband. For the moment they went their own ways although living under the same roof. Zinaida had begun to have serious doubts about the purpose of her life and to search for a way to give meaning to her existence. What more natural than to turn to a priest, and through him to the Catholic Church? She was always happiest among Italians. Consalvi, brought up in eighteenth-century aristocratic circles, was very much at ease with women. He was an older friend who offered uncomplicated warmth and understanding, spiritual guidance and the pleasures of shared tastes and habits. Although the Cardinal was extremely busy throughout his ten-month stay in Vienna, they met often, sometimes at the Prince de Ligne's house, sometimes at the embassy, sharing the same circle of friends.[14] The Cardinal was received by the Tsar on 3 November 1814, at which time Consalvi repeated the invitation first extended in London, that Alexander visit Rome. The Tsar accepted.[15]

Vienna, meanwhile, had filled up with the most brilliant society in Europe. In the evenings, the ladies of the Viennese and foreign aristocracy competed to entertain the European grandees. None were more successful than the four daughters of the Duchess of Courland, herself Talleyrand's mistress for many years. The eldest, the beautiful and clever Wilhelmina, Duchess of Sagan, and Metternich's adored but unfaithful mistress, was one of the undisputed queens. At Talleyrand's house, her youngest sister, the dark-eyed twenty-one-year old Dorothea de Talleyrand-Périgord, was renowned as much for her acute intelligence and sparkling wit as for her ravishing looks. She had not yet supplanted her mother as Talleyrand's mistress, but it was in

Vienna as his hostess that she was to become indispensable to him. The chief rival to the Courland sisters, particularly to the Duchess of Sagan, was Princess Bagration. A blonde widow with a racy reputation, the Princess was delighted to have captured the Tsar at her salon. Catherine Bagration had also been Metternich's mistress and had had a child by him. The Tsar, after spending a night with Princess Bagration, was next seen coming out of her rival the Duchess of Sagan's apartments. His attentions to Wilhelmina de Sagan, with whom Metternich was very much in love, provoked Metternich's fury so that the two men, already enemies in the conference room, now had personal reasons for mutual dislike. Soon the return of Wilhelmina's former lover, Prince Alfred Windischgratz, added to Metternich's unhappiness. His inability to concentrate on affairs of state as he wrote desperate notes to his faithless love during meetings was noticed by several officials, among them an exasperated Edward Cooke, senior adviser to Castlereagh. 'Metternich is most intolerably loose and giddy with women,' he wrote severely.[16]

The Hofburg continued to provide Baron Hager, the Austrian Minister of Police, with endless material. Prince Volkonsky, it was reported, was receiving at his home every evening a young actress by the name of Josephine Wolters, often dressed as a man.[17] Zinaida had come to terms with her husband's infidelities. She had made her own life and continued to frequent the more interesting salons until the birth of her baby in December.

While the sovereigns had been put up at the Hofburg, the diplomatic missions had to fend for themselves. Arriving in Vienna on 23 September, Talleyrand took over the Kaunitz Palace. Not far from the Hofburg, in the lovely Minoritzenplatz, were the magnificent apartments of Britain's Foreign Secretary, Lord Castlereagh, who arrived in the middle of September.[18] It was a measure of the importance of social life that the shy and serious-minded Castlereagh had thought it necessary to take dancing lessons, earnestly practising the waltz with a chair when his wife Emily was unavailable. Thereafter the Foreign Minister became an enthusiastic waltzer, although most parties at his house began with an Irish jig. Although some laughed at his ineptitude on the dance floor, his tall, austerely dressed figure and handsome face were much admired by the ladies – Priscilla

Burghersh had described him as 'an absolute beauty'. He, on the other hand, had eyes only for his 'dearest Em' to whom he was devoted, although her silliness as well as her rotund shape and taste in clothes were much criticised.[19]

The work of the Congress continued meanwhile. Negotiations between the big four, Austria, England, Russia and Prussia, took place in the early afternoon at Metternich's chancellery and sometimes at the British legation. Personal difficulties between the Tsar and Metternich – at one point the Tsar actually threatened Metternich with a duel, after which he refused to speak to him – had reached such a pass that Castlereagh was obliged to take over all negotiations.

The two main issues to be settled at the Congress were Poland and Saxony. It was becoming clear that Alexander intended to create an expanded Grand Duchy of Warsaw, to include the territories which had been given to Prussia and Austria at the time of the last partition, with himself as king. In this way Poland would preserve geographical but not political autonomy. The two countries would be united under one sovereign and Russia would gain a buffer zone against any future invasion. Alexander, still influenced by the liberal teaching of La Harpe and his friend Prince Czartoryski, intended that Poland should have a liberal constitution. Only two months previously he had consulted the English liberal philosopher, Jeremy Bentham, on the subject. In exchange for giving up their parts of Poland, Austria would receive the north of Italy and Prussia a large piece of Saxony. The King of Saxony, who had sided with Napoleon, was to be excluded from the Congress while the Allies carved up his country.

This plan was strongly opposed by Metternich, Castlereagh and Talleyrand, who also feared the influence which the Tsar had over the weak King of Prussia. The dangers of a Russian-Prussian alliance were all too obvious to the three statesmen. For different reasons, all three were strongly opposed to any one country being in a position to dominate Europe. Prussia wanted Saxony and the Rhineland in compensation for her Polish provinces which she was prepared to cede to Russia. This had been agreed between Russia and Prussia by the terms of the Treaty of Kalitsch signed in 1813, and it greatly

Zinaida Volkonsky by Louis Berger 1829

Prince Grigory Volkonsky, Zinaida's father-in-law, by M. Bororikovsky

Prince Alexander Mikhailovich Beloselsky-Belozersky, Zinaida's father

Prince Nikita Volkonsky, Zinaida's husband, by F. Bruni

Vladimir Pavey, Zinaida's adopted son, by O. Kiprensky

Zinaida in Rome
about 1850,
by Emilio Rossi

Zinaida Volkonsky
by Pannemarker,
in Rome in the
1830's

Bust of Tsar Alexander I in the gardens of the Villa Volkonsky, Rome

Painting of the 3rd Earl of Egremont receiving the allied sovereigns in the marble hall at Petworth House on 24 June 1814, by Thomas Phillips. Princess Volkonsky is on the far left seen from behind

Princess Maria (Madeleine) Vlasova, Zinaida's sister, by H. Reisner

complicated the issue at Vienna. Austria's chief aim was to prevent Prussia from swallowing the whole of Saxony and, thus strengthened, threatening Austria's dominance in German-speaking Europe. Metternich himself was more concerned about Russia's annexation of Poland. He thoroughly distrusted the Tsar and agreed with Castlereagh that a strong Prussian-Austrian central bloc was greatly in the interests of European stability.

> In the first place, so to conduct the arrangements to be framed for congress, as to make the establishment of a just equilibrium in Europe the first object of my attention, and to consider the assertion of minor points of interest subordinate to this great end.

By this he meant an independent Poland and a strong Prussia allied to Austria, which would constitute a bloc between Russia and France.

The British government, on the other hand, with no territorial ambitions in Europe, cared little about Poland. Britain's mastery of the seas and the security of the Low Countries ensured her own safety and that of her trade routes. The Cabinet had little interest in foreign affairs, its main concern being to avoid irritating Russia; Castlereagh's policy was constantly attacked as too bold. The one issue which British public opinion was keen to see settled in Vienna was the abolition of the slave trade. Castlereagh behaved with extraordinary independence. Sharing Metternich's distrust of the Tsar, though there was no personal antipathy between them as in the case of Alexander and Metternich, he was determined that the Tsar should be checked. 'You must make up your mind to watch him and resist him as another Bonaparte. Acquiescence will not keep him back, nor will opposition accelerate his march,' he wrote to Liverpool.[20]

Talleyrand's main interest was to re-establish France as one of the great powers. He spent the first three months in Vienna ensuring that France would be included in the negotiations. To do this he had to make it clear that France wanted nothing outside her own frontiers, that she had abandoned any thoughts of conquest: in short, that she was now set on moderation. France's chief interests boiled down to four points: 1. that Austria should not make one of her princes King of Sardinia, 2. that Naples should be restored to her former Bourbon ruler, 3. that Russia should not annex the whole of Poland, and 4. that Prussia should not acquire the whole of Saxony. Talleyrand was as opposed as Castlereagh to any country gaining too much dominance in Europe. In this respect the last two points were of particular importance.

Talleyrand's first exchange with the Tsar on the subject of Poland had infuriated Alexander. With his army in Poland, how dared the representative of the nation he had just defeated question his intentions or his right to 'keep what I occupy'? 'Your Majesty will wish to keep only what is legitimately his,' Talleyrand had answered silkily. Surrounded by three powerful neighbours, Poland had been subjected to three partitions during the eighteenth century. As the Congress began in September Poland was again occupied by a vast Russian army.

By the end of November 1814, the statesmen of the Quadruple Alliance were in deadlock. News came that Prince Repnin, the eldest of the Volkonsky brothers, and in command of the Russian occupying forces in Saxony, had handed over the administration of the kingdom to Prussia. From Warsaw came the news that the Poles were being urged to unite and fight for their independence. On hearing this, Austria immediately moved troops up to the Galician border and France began a partial mobilisation. Talleyrand, meanwhile, was rounding up the minor German states and urging them to make a collective protest against the annexation of Saxony by Prussia. Prussia's angry response was that any denial of her claim to Saxony was tantamount to a declaration of war. The situation was serious enough for Castlereagh to write to Liverpool warning of 'actual or impending war', and to recommend that, as Britain could hardly avoid involvement, she should be prepared to act as 'armed mediators' together with France. War was now more than a possibility. Mistrusting the Tsar most of all, Metternich and Castlereagh believed that the time had come to bring France back into the fold. The British Cabinet meanwhile answered Castlereagh's despatch with an unequivocal instruction.

It is unnecessary for me to point out to you the impossibility of His Royal Highness consenting to involve this country in hostilities

at this time for any objects which have hitherto been under discussion at Vienna,

Lord Bathurst replied on behalf of the Cabinet on 27 November.[21]

On New Year's Day 1815, Castlereagh got word that a peace treaty
between Britain and the United States, ending the American war, had
been signed at Ghent. This welcome news would give him a freer
hand. Three days later, a secret treaty was signed between England,
France and Austria, which stipulated that the three powers would act
together and that each would defend the other in the event of attack.
The fact that it was common knowledge that the British government
had no intention of going to war weakened Castlereagh's hand, but it
did concentrate the minds of the Tsar and the Prussians. France was
now back at the negotiating table. A jubilant Talleyrand reported to
his master, Louis XVIII: 'So great and fortunate a change can only be
attributed to the protection of Providence which has been so plainly
visible in the restoration of Your Majesty.' Having given God his due,
Talleyrand was unable to resist mentioning the real author of the change:

After God, the main causes of this change have been:
– My letters to M. de Metternich and Lord Castlereagh and the
effect produced by them.
– The suggestions that I made to Lord Castlereagh, concerning an
agreement with France, which I reported in my last letter.
– The pains that I took to calm his suspicions by showing complete
disinterestedness on the part of France.
– The peace with America.[22]

While Europe's statesmen spent their days struggling with the task
of redrawing the map of Europe, the evenings and nights were wholly
given over to pleasure and frivolity. Salons, ballrooms and bedrooms
were in any case excellent places for getting information or sowing
disinformation. Only a small proportion of the people who had
flocked to Vienna actually had anything to do. The endless social
round kept them occupied. Balls, dinners, redoubts, theatre, opera
and concerts, private and public, *tableaux vivants*, balloon ascents, drives

in the Prater (Vienna's magnificent park), picnics, and – as it grew colder – sleigh rides and skating parties for which snow was brought in from the surrounding areas, were only some of the entertainments designed to keep the Congress amused.[23] Outside the city, at the Imperial estates, huge hunts were organised where the assembled guests watched the sovereigns slaughter thousands of animals: boar, hares, deer and foxes, which had been specially rounded up by the Imperial gamekeepers and driven towards the royal guns.

On 18 October, the anniversary of the battle of Leipzig was celebrated with an immense victory parade of the Austrian army in the Prater. After a religious service, three orchestras led the thousands of assembled voices in a hymn to peace, accompanied by the pealing bells of all the churches in Vienna, 'a sublime and poetic scene beyond all description', wrote La Garde Chambonas, a young man-about-town, ecstatically.[24]

That evening Metternich and his long-suffering wife hosted one of the most memorable parties of the Congress. Their 'Peace festival', in the presence of the sovereigns and their suites, took place at Metternich's new summer palace on the Renweg. Eighteen hundred guests climbed the steep flights of steps, 'as tall as a house', carpeted in red, canopied with Turkish tents and lit with torches, into a reception room. From there they were conducted out into the gardens to fanfares of trumpets and drums, to watch the ascent of a balloon which released firework displays of their coats of arms into the night sky. The guests were then left to wander around the gardens and admire the various *tableaux vivants*, music groups, acrobats and entertainers who were performing in strategically placed pavilions and arbours. They were then conducted, in order of precedence, into an amphitheatre facing the main lawn on which three pavilions had been erected, the central one to 'Peace' and the other two to the 'Arts' and 'Industry'. After a theatrical performance, they all watched a parade of chariots, after which supper was served at round tables while representations in fireworks turned Discord into Concord. After supper the Metternichs led their guests to a specially constructed ballroom which had been decorated in blue and silver, colours symbolising peace, to dance till dawn. The ladies wore ballgowns in the same colours, with olive wreaths in their hair.[25]

The Renweg villa was the scene of another famous party, a costume ball given by Metternich on 8 November, at which all the ladies wore national costume. In the sophisticated atmosphere of Vienna, the dowdy and strait-laced Lady Castlereagh decided to wear her husband's Order of the Garter in her badly coiffed hair. At the end of the month she was seen wearing the same Garter in her hair again at the Carousel. This extraordinary event, held at the Hofburg's Spanish Riding School, for which people were prepared to pay a huge black-market price for tickets, was a re-enactment of a medieval tournament, modelled on the famous carousels of the time of Louis XIV. Twenty-four 'knights', mounted on black horses and chosen from among the best riders of the young Viennese aristocracy, entered the arena to fanfares of trumpets, riding around the vast hall first at a trot then at a canter and finally at a gallop. In the spectator boxes sat twenty-four *'belles d'amour'*, identifiable only by the different colours of velvet and satin they were wearing. At the climax of the scene each horseman reigned in dramatically before the damsel of his choice, who cast off her veil to greet her knight. After the jousting and supper, to the accompaniment of minstrels, the ball opened with a quadrille danced by the *belles d'amour* and their knights. Zinaida, in the last stages of pregnancy, was not one of the *belles* and unlikely to have attended the Carousel although it was one of the most spectacular events of the season.

The Tsar, who was ill, also missed the pageant. He must have been very disappointed as chivalry and all its trappings was what he liked particularly. His mood at the time, as a result of the stalemate in negotiations, was in any case so black that only his closest confidants dared to approach him. Sergei Volkonsky recalled the following evening when all the Volkonskys were at the Russian embassy for a magnificent dinner for 360 guests hosted by the Emperor and Empress of Russia. The house was lit with so many candles that the heat caused them to melt, dripping wax. The Prince de Ligne couldn't resist punning: *'Nous avons à Vienne une pluie de Sire'* – 'It is raining wax in Vienna.'[26] (The Prince was joking about the huge numbers of kings and princes present, all addressed as *Sire*, and punning on the same sound of the French word for wax – *cire*.)

Alexander was now spending many hours with the Empress's lady-in-waiting, Roxanne Sturdza, a follower of Jung-Stilling, a famous mystic who preached a higher form of ecumenical Christianity and professed occult knowledge of the imminent end of the world. He encouraged Alexander to think of himself as the elect of God, who would save Christendom. Alexander sent him special grants and joined with Jung-Stilling and Roxanne Sturdza in a spiritual marriage. Mystic marriages were common among Pietist sects at the time. Two people sharing religious convictions could by this process unite for the purposes of prayer and meditation, regardless of a formal earthly marriage to someone else. A fourth person in this spiritual ménage was Baroness de Krüdener who was soon to gain a serious influence over the Tsar. Alexander was still able to reconcile the bible reading and his spiritual marriage with a punishing social life, which he gave every evidence of enjoying to the full. 'The Emperor of Russia dances almost continually, he is a magnet for women,' wrote Gentz, Metternich's secretary.[27]

On 29 November in the presence of the Tsar and the King of Prussia, Razumovsky arranged a gala concert of Beethoven's music, in the vast Redoutensaal of the Hofburg, at which the by then completely deaf composer conducted his Seventh Symphony, followed by a piece he had just written to celebrate Wellington's victory at Vittoria.[28]

'Le congrès danse, mais n'avance pas,' remarked the old Prince de Ligne.[29] On 3 December, Zinaida's twenty-sixth birthday, the much-loved Prince died. The whole of Europe mourned the death of the famous octogenarian. A lifelong inability to resist a pretty woman had driven the old man out into the freezing night for a romantic rendezvous, as a result of which he had caught a fatal chill. Witty to the end, he remarked to the friends gathered around his death-bed that at least he would be able to offer another fine show to the visitors of the Congress – a funeral of a Field Marshal of both the Russian and Austrian Empires. His death must have been a great blow to Zinaida, but it was overshadowed by a closer personal tragedy. Soon after her old friend's funeral, Zinaida gave birth to her second son but, weak from the outset, he died after a few days in which his mother must have hovered between hope and despair. He had been hastily christened Grigory, his grandfather's name. The loss of her child filled

Zinaida with misery and a sense of failure. She blamed herself for not resting enough, for lacing herself too tightly during those months of social whirl in Paris, London and Vienna. Her baby might have been stronger if she had taken better care of herself. Zinaida saw this as punishment for her sins. Her bitter sense of loss and guilt is evident in a poem she wrote soon after, when she was thinking of leaving Vienna to go to Italy. In it she likens herself to a swallow:

Alas! like me the poor swallow/ makes ready to leave these parts where the cruel arrow/ pierced her poor babe with its sting./ She pauses, thinking in her bitter grief/that she has failed in a mother's duty / by depriving him of her presence.

But she can hear the voices of her sweet companions/calling her in chorus to fly over the mountains./ Let us leave, they cry, let us live for the day! / I see them stream towards the celestial plains./Let us flee too, let us flee from pain,/ let us fly towards spring.[30]

In spite of her grief, Zinaida recovered more quickly from this birth than she had from her first. Though deeply mourning the loss of her baby, she does not seem to have suffered from a recurrence of the post-natal depression which had cast her down for almost a year after the birth of her son Alexander. The second stanza of her poem bears witness to a youthful optimism and a desire for happiness.

December had been a cruel month for Zinaida, with the death of a dear friend and the loss of her baby. The Congress however continued to dance. 'The Emperor of Russia dances while Rome is burning,' wrote Edward Cooke disapprovingly. But it was not Rome that was burning. In the early hours of New Year's Day 1815, traditionally the start of the carnival, Vienna awoke to the smell of burning from a huge fire. A few hours later the whole of the Razumovsky Palace, with its priceless collections of art and furniture, had burnt down. Throughout the day the ambassador received his friends, including the Emperors Alexander and Francis, with stoical calm among his charred treasures.

Heavy snow fell in January. To entertain her visitors the Empress of Austria planned a day of festivities at Schönbrunn, the Emperor

Francis's baroque palace just outside Vienna. Thirty sleighs lined with fur, driven by horses bedecked with ribbons and escorted by twenty-four pages in medieval dress and a detachment of the Imperial Guard, set off from the centre of Vienna. In the front sleigh the Emperor of Austria escorted the Empress of Russia, dressed in white ermine, a green silk hat topped with ostrich feathers and magnificent diamonds. Bringing up the rear, a huge sleigh carried an orchestra in Turkish costume which, in spite of wind and weather, played heroically all the way.[31]

By February the haggling over Saxony and Poland was nearly over, and a final agreement was being reached on the 11th. Castlereagh had made some progress over the abolition of the slave trade. All that remained was to brief Wellington who was taking over from him, as Castlereagh himself had hoped he would. Castlereagh left Vienna on the 15th to return home, where Liverpool's government, under attack over the Corn Laws, was clamouring for his presence on the front benches. Wellington had arrived in Vienna before Castlereagh's departure, with the celebrated Italian soprano, Madame Giuseppina Grassini, in tow. Once again the Congress hostesses outrivalled each other in their efforts to entertain the great hero. Once more, Baron Hager's agents sent in daily reports on the goings-on in the various palaces. The rest of the month passed uneventfully. There were many issues still to be decided, not least, what to do with Napoleon who was still on Elba.

Tired of Vienna and of the relentless social life, Zinaida suddenly decided to go to Italy. As always towards the end of the northern winter she longed for the sun. Cardinal Consalvi, still in Vienna where he remained until June, had urged her to come to Rome after the Congress but she was unwilling to wait that long. It was well known that the Cardinal was keen to continue to convert as many influential Russians as possible to the Catholic faith. The Princess would be a prestigious convert and was ripe for conversion. The Cardinal was a friend of the Russian ambassador to the Papal States, A. Italinsky, and corresponded with him on this subject.[32] Consalvi was also interested in attracting rich foreigners, as was noted by his contemporary, Cardinal Massimo D'Azeglio, who wrote of the policy 'of attracting foreigners, or rather their money'.[33] There is no doubt too that, in

spite of these more practical reasons, the Cardinal had grown fond
of Zinaida and wished to help her find her place in the world. Zinaida
was very anxious to visit Rome. She would be able to study music
more seriously away from the ceaseless social round, and she wanted
to learn more about the Church. She began to make the necessary
preparations for a visit with her sister-in-law Sophia, whose husband
Prince Peter Volkonsky would remain in Vienna with the Tsar while
Nikita escorted the ladies into Italy. The two Princesses had decided
to stay in Italy at least until the end of the Congress, whenever that
might be. In early March, however, their plans had to be postponed
abruptly, as news arrived in Vienna which had the impact of a
bombshell.

On 7 March 1815, a despatch reached Metternich which galvanised
not just the Congress but the whole of Europe. Napoleon had escaped
from Elba! Metternich recorded the event:

> A conference between the plenipotentiaries of the five Powers took
> place in my house on the night of March 6th and lasted till three
> o'oclock in the morning. Since the Cabinets had met in Vienna, I
> had given my servant orders that if a courier arrived at night he
> was not to awake me. In spite of this order, the servant brought
> me, at six o'clock in the morning a despatch, sent by courier, and
> marked *urgent*. When I saw on the envelope the words 'From the
> Consul-General at Genoa', having been only two hours in bed, I
> laid the despatch unopened on the nearest table, and turned round
> again to sleep. Once disturbed, however, sleep would not come
> again. About half past seven I resolved to open the despatch. It
> contained the information in six lines: The English Commissary,
> Campbell, has just appeared in the harbour, to inquire whether
> Napoleon has been seen in Genoa, as he has disappeared from
> the island of Elba; this question being answered in the negative,
> the English ship has again put to sea.

Dressing hurriedly, Metternich was with the Emperor Francis
before eight o'clock. Having read the despatch, the Emperor sent

Metternich to Alexander and to the King of Prussia, with the message that he was ready to order his army to march back to France. The important thing now was to secure peace. Metternich went straight to the Tsar, as commanded:

> At a quarter past eight I was with the Emperor Alexander, who dismissed me with the same words as the Emperor Francis had used. At half past eight I received a similar declaration from the mouth of King Frederic William III. At nine o'clock I was back at my house, where I had directed Field Marshal Prince Schwarzenburg to meet me. At ten o'clock the ministers of the four Powers came at my request. At the same hour adjutants were already on their way, in all directions, to order the armies who were returning home to halt. Thus war was decided on in less than an hour.[34]

The coalition, which had all but dissolved during the first three months of the Congress, was now united in the face of the common enemy. The Tsar had not hesitated: 'We are both Christians; our holy law commands us to pardon offences. Let us embrace and let all be forgotten,' he had said to Metternich. The next day a declaration of eight powers was signed, effectively proclaiming Napoleon an outlaw: 'Napoleon Buonaparte has placed himself outside the pale of civil and social relations, and rendered himself subject to public vengeance.'

The chief protagonist of all the excitement was to record the event in a few laconic words:

> I left the island of Elba on the 26th February 1815 at 9 o'clock in the evening. I boarded the brig *Inconstant*, which flew the white flag studded with bees throughout the journey. On the 1st March at 5 o'clock in the afternoon, I landed on the beach of the Golfe Juan near Cannes. – At length on 20th March at 8 o'clock in the evening, on my son's birthday, I entered Paris.[35]

'The Congress is dissolved,' Napoleon is said to have announced on landing in France as men flocked to his standard once again. At Grenoble, Colonel Charles de La Bédoyère, together with his seventh regiment, went over to him. Worse, Marshal Ney, who had promised to bring back Napoleon in a cage, now rejoined his former master. The King fled from Paris to seek asylum in Belgium.

From the Tuileries, into which he had moved on arrival in Paris, Napoleon now sent conciliatory messages in all directions. He also sent the Tsar some files which had been left behind in the hurry of evacuation, proving the secret alliance between France, Britain and Austria signed on 3 January. The Tsar, on reading this confirmation of his suspicions, paced about the room, his ears red with rage, as one of his advisers, the Corfiote Count Capo d'Istria, recorded. He decided, however, that what mattered now was a united front against Napoleon.[36]

There was no doubt in Wellington's mind as to how he could best serve his country. 'I am going into the Low Countries to take command of the armies,' was his brief message to Lord Burghersh on 22 March. Easter Sunday fell on 25 March that year. The following Tuesday, the Duchess of Sagan gave a large party to bid farewell to the Duke. On the 29th, Lord Clancarty wrote to announce that the Duke had left Vienna and that he was taking over. Wellington was in Brussels on 4 April. 'We wait with impatience for intelligence from all quarters,' Castlereagh had written to him on 26 March.

The great question is, can the Bourbons get Frenchmen to fight *for them* against Frenchmen? – If we are to undertake the job, we must leave nothing to chance. It must be done upon the largest scale. You must inundate France with force in all directions.[37]

The 'job' was undertaken, as preparations for the Waterloo campaign began. Britain promised £5,000,000, and Russia, Prussia and Austria at least 150,000 men each.

In Vienna, 'a thousand candles seemed to have been extinguished in a single moment,' wrote La Garde Chambonas. As Easter approached, Zinaida decided to postpone her plans no longer. In Vienna she had enjoyed the company of the most interesting men of her time and suffered great pain at the death of her child. She was still only twenty-six, in the full flower of her youth, but in Vienna, with all the opportunities for every form of sensual gratification, we hear only of her lovely singing voice and her friendships with Consalvi, Razumovsky and Ligne, all men old enough to be her father. Her desire to go to Italy after Easter was characteristic of the sudden bolts of her early life. 'Let us flee, flee from pain,' she had written in her poem. The swallow would now fly south, to Rome.

The Belgian campaign was now under way. In Brussels, Wellington waited with almost 100,000 English, Dutch, Hanoverian and Belgian troops, while Blücher had arrived in Namur with 120,000 Prussians. The Austrian and Russian armies were on the move, but unlikely to arrive before an engagement with the enemy, which must be soon. In Vienna Alexander waited in the bleakest of moods.

The prospect of more war, the enervating and exhausting months in Vienna, guilt at his own self-indulgence, all served to tip the unbalanced Tsar into despair. He missed his spiritual conversations with Roxanne Sturdza who had left Vienna with the Empress. Through her he had been in constant touch with Madame de Krüdener who, only recently, had given proof of her extraordinary gift of prophecy in a letter to Mademoiselle de Sturdza, written in her inimitable style, in which she had announced Napoleon's imminent return:

We are going to see guilty France, who according to the decrees of the Eternal was to be spared by the Cross that had subdued her, we are going to see her chastised. Christians should not punish, and the man that was chosen and blessed by the Eternal, the man we are privileged to love as our Sovereign, could not bring other than peace. The storm is approaching; those lilies which the Eternal has preserved, that emblem of pure and fragile flower that broke an iron sceptre, because the Eternal wished it, those lilies which should have summoned men to the love of God, to repentance, have appeared only to vanish again. The lesson has been given, and men more hardened than ever dream only of tumult.[38]

Alexander pondered this message as he left Vienna at the end of May to join the Emperor Francis at the headquarters of the eastern armies. His daily readings of occult works had overheated his imagination and made him increasingly superstitious. The war was now in Wellington's hands; an engagement with Napoleon was imminent while his own troops hadn't even crossed the Rhine. As he waited in the little town of Heilbronn for his forces to arrive, he felt that he, who had only recently been hailed as the liberator of Europe, had lost his role. Late on the night of 4 June as the Tsar sat alone thinking of Madame de Krüdener and wishing for guidance, Prince Peter Volkonsky knocked on the door. He was sorry to disturb the Tsar at such a late hour but there was a woman outside who insisted on speaking to him. It was Madame de Krüdener! That she should be there when he most needed her! 'Such an immediate response to my desire could not be mere chance,' the Tsar later wrote to Mademoiselle Sturdza. They were closeted together for several hours, and the mystic begged Alexander to repent of his sins and be worthy of his mission, 'speaking strong words of consolation' which calmed his soul.[39]

Julie de Krüdener was then fifty. Of Latvian origin, she had had a somewhat racy youth which she recorded in an autobiographical novel, *Valerie*. She had hoped to become a famous woman of letters like Madame de Staël. When that failed she had turned to the Pietist movement which was attracting a wide variety of people at the time. The Baroness, always keen to be at the centre of events, turned to evangelism, passing herself off as an intermediary between the spiritual and material worlds. Like all successful charlatans she exploited the Tsar's weaknesses with a combination of intense personal attention, which he craved, and a professed mystic faith, perhaps partly sincere, in the greatness of Russia and her sovereign.

'If you knew, Sire, how He loves you,' she wrote, 'you would not resist him in anything. Before the ages, God prepared a path for each one of us.' She added more specifically, 'You who are so great yet such a child, I tell you without the slightest doubt that you will not be able to advance without me as long as God wills that it should be I; this has so often been my experience as a spiritual guide.' In the exalted language he loved, she told him that when he had been 'regenerated in the stream of life' he would lead Europe and Christendom to redemption. From then on she never left his side. He utterly depended on their daily readings and talks, during which she reinforced the idea that he was indeed the elect of God. He in turn was to keep her and her impoverished family in funds. She even referred to him as her 'celestial banker'.

The Congress was now winding up its work as successive treaties established the new Europe. Northern Europe had been largely settled in February, with Prussia and Austria each regaining a part of their lost Polish territories, while Russia took the rest of Poland. Saxony retained more than half her land, Prussia taking the rest, together with a substantial slice of the Rhineland. By early June, Genoa and its territory had been given to the Kingdom of Sardinia, while Austria took a substantial share of Lombardy and the Veneto. A new German confederation came into being. A declaration condemning the slave trade, the best which could be achieved on that issue, was included in the final act of the Congress, which was signed on 9 June 1815.

6

Travels: Rome, Paris and 'the Mud of Odessa'

'What a pity that so much talent should have been wasted on a
lady of high birth.'

Zinaida left Vienna a month after Napoleon's flight from Elba,
immediately after Easter 1815, with her sister-in-law Sophia. Nikita
accompanied them. Since earliest childhood she had loved crossing
the Alps and that moment of first looking into Italy. 'What bliss to
be streaming towards Italy,' she wrote many years later.

We are coming down towards Italy. The further you come down
the more nature loses her harshness; rivers flow more freely, more
easily towards Italy – and mountain plants grow into and merge
with the fragrant vegetation of the south – around me the graces
of nature and melodious voices – I am in Italy![1]

They went first to Florence, where they spent a week, from where
Sophia wrote to their friend in Paris, Louise de Cochelet:

The bearer of this letter is a ladies' maid whom my sister [Zinaida]
engaged in Paris. In view of events she was afraid of not being
able to get back to her own country and prefers to go back from
here. My dear friend, if you could possibly recommend her when

you have the opportunity, we would be so grateful. Recent events have forced us to return to Germany. We leave lovely Italy without having seen Naples. We were also to have spent a week in the city of the Caesars; but since my brother [Nikita] is a military man we thought it more prudent to leave at once.

We have been here for a week, and are about to leave for Pisa. We take a boat from Livorno to Genoa after which, having spent three or four days there, we go back the same way via Verona and on to Venice. The latest news from there, as well as from my husband is good.

Sophia also asks Louise for news of her brother Sergei, who was to have met them and escorted Sophia, while Zinaida and her husband stayed on a little longer:

Where is my darling brother? My husband writes that he was to go to London. I hope that he has given up the idea of coming to fetch me here. I shall go back with the couple [Zinaida and Nikita]. I can't imagine that we will be able to stay much longer.

A hasty postscript from Zinaida adds her pleas to Sophia's for Louise's protection for her maid, whom she was sending back to Paris. Napoleon's escape from Elba had worried the girl, who was afraid that she might never get home. Characteristically, Zinaida not only sent her back to France but, concerned for her future, also gave her excellent references and made sure she would have the protection of her influential friend.

My dear Louise, we are literally about to leave; I can only add a few lines to send you my warmest good wishes. I am very sad that my journey to Paris will have to be postponed to the Greek Calends [indefinitely], my main regret is that I shall miss you. I beg you recommend the bearer of this letter. Circumstances force her to leave me. I am most satisfied with her and beg your protection for her. *Au revoir*, but when? My husband and Sachon [her son Alexander, then four] kiss your hands. Zénaïde[2]

Napoleon's dramatic return had thrown everything open once more; nobody knew quite what would happen next. The Volkonskys had planned to travel as far south as Naples and then stay in Rome for a week, but now Princess Sophia decided to rejoin her husband who was in Germany with the Tsar. As an officer, Nikita too had to hurry back to headquarters in Heidelberg. Zinaida, however, had no intention of returning so soon. She had decided to go on to Rome until the summer when, all being well, she would see her friends and family in Paris. This journey was a watershed in Zinaida's life. The uncertain young woman was gone. Henceforth she would live her life on her own terms.

Rome in the spring and early summer was balm to her soul. She did some serious sightseeing, deepening her knowledge of the city that would one day be her home. The beauty of the city was like a benediction to her trained and sensitive eye. The warmth of the climate and of the people restored her happiness.

As always, she was drawn towards artistic circles, particularly musical ones. She was determined to train her voice and may well have taken singing lessons. It must have been in her musical circles that she met the young painter with a beautiful tenor voice, Michelangelo Barbieri.[3] Alone in one of the most romantic cities in the world, Zinaida was greatly drawn to him. He was not of her world, but they sang together and he was young, handsome and attentive. Zinaida was once again beginning to enjoy life and the love affair that began in Rome meant enough for her to take Barbieri back to Russia with her later as her secretary and as Italian tutor to her son. In Moscow the relationship certainly caused gossip.[4] Zinaida would once again flee, but after Vienna she began to take charge of her life, living much less conventionally than her friends and family, and especially the Tsar, would like.

During this three-month stay in Italy, Zinaida also met a brilliant young composer whose music enchanted her. Only three years younger than the Princess, Gioacchino Rossini was born in Pesaro in 1792, the son of the town trumpeter and a baker's daughter who had become a singer. Taught to sing and play from an early age in order to help with the family finances, Rossini studied at the Liceo Musicale in Bologna, where he won a prize for a cantata in 1808. In

1813, with 'his youthful genius bursting into flower' as Stendhal put it, he had had great success with his two operas, *Tancredi* and *L'Italiana in Algeri*, both first performed in Venice.[5] *L'Italiana* might have been written for Zinaida. She loved the role of Isabella, which was perfect for her rich young contralto voice. Zinaida was always more artist than princess in her friendships. Her rank might preclude her own participation in anything but private performances, but, natural and warm-hearted, she never allowed it to exclude genuine friendships with people she liked. Her attitude was entirely patrician, on the other hand, when it came to ignoring the world's opinion and following her own wishes.

Soon after news of the victory at Waterloo at the end of June, in spite of the pleasures of Rome, Zinaida set off for Paris with her two children. She had completely recovered her spirits and leaving her beloved Rome was no hardship this time since Michelangelo Barbieri went with her. She had always adored Paris which was, once again, the hub of European affairs. Napoleon, who had cast his strong shadow over her life as he had over all Europe, was finally gone. But he had swept away the old world. It was a time of new beginnings, of optimism and progress, which her friend Rossini expressed so excitingly in his music, and it was a new Zinaida who now rejoined the Tsar's suite in Paris.

Zinaida found Paris seething with excitement. Word of Wellington's decisive victory over Napoleon had reached the Imperial Allies' head-quarters in Heidelberg on 21 June. It had already reached England as Wellington's famous 'Waterloo despatch' to Lord Bathurst, the Minister of War, was published in *The Times*. He had lost 35,000 men. Now he paid tribute to those who most deserved it: 'It gives me the greatest satisfaction to assure your lordship that the army never, upon any occasion, conducted itself better.' It had been, in Wellington's own words to Creevey on the day after the battle, 'a damned nice thing, – the nearest run thing you ever saw in your life'.[6]

While the Allies argued about Napoleon's fate and the second restoration of the Bourbons in France, Wellington made his own position absolutely clear in a letter to Sir Charles Stewart:

Blücher writes, to kill him; but I have told him that I shall remonstrate, and shall insist on his being disposed of by common accord. I have likewise said that, as a private friend, I advised him to have nothing to do with so foul a transaction – that he and I acted too distinguished parts in these transactions to become executioners – and that I was determined that, if the sovereigns wished to put him to death, they should appoint an executioner, who should not be me.[7]

The period which came to be known as the Hundred Days was nearly over. The second week of July saw the return of Louis XVIII as well as the arrival of the Tsar in Paris. On 15 July, a hundred days after his return to France, Napoleon embarked on a British ship, the HMS *Bellerophon*, hoping that he might be permitted to live in England. For two weeks he languished as a prisoner on board this ship at Portsmouth, where he became a spectacle for large crowds who rowed out daily to see him. On 9 August he boarded HMS *Northumberland* for the tiny, mid-Atlantic island of St Helena to which the Allies had decided to exile him. Two months to the day after the final act of the Congress of Vienna, Napoleon was gone from Europe for ever. He remained on St Helena, writing his memoirs and reliving his past glories, until his death on 15 May 1821.

Louis XVIII, enormously fat and gouty, was back again on the throne of France. The two men responsible for putting him there, Talleyrand and Fouché, attended an audience of the King, the former leaning on the arm of the latter. Chateaubriand, who witnessed the scene, could barely contain his disgust, leaving a memorable description:

Suddenly a door opened; in came Vice, leaning on the arm of Crime. It was M. de Talleyrand, supported by M. Fouché; the infernal vision passed slowly before my eyes, entered the King's chamber and disappeared. Fouché had come to swear allegiance to his lord; on his knees the loyal regicide placed the hands which had caused the beheading of Louis XVI, into those of the martyred king's brother, while the apostate bishop stood surety for the oath.[8]

All the protagonists of the Congress now reassembled in Paris. The Castlereaghs, who had arrived in early July, were installed in Wellington's new embassy on the Faubourg St Honoré. The elegant Hôtel de Charost, standing between courtyard and garden, which had belonged to Napoleon's sister Pauline Borghese, had been bought for Wellington in August 1814.[9]

The Tsar entered Paris for the second time on 10 July. On this occasion he stayed at the Elysée with his spiritual adviser, Madame de Krüdener, installed in a house nearby. Zinaida and Sophia once again rejoined their husbands in the Tsar's entourage. They found Alexander in an uncertain mood, torn between depression, anger and exaltation. Madame de Krüdener was delighted to be in Paris with the Tsar, delighted too with her spacious apartments which were covered in grey toile, adding an other-worldly atmosphere to her seances when she would speak for as long as an hour and a half on religious matters, her face taking on a trance-like expression.[10] At first people flocked to her salon out of curiosity and as a way of seeing the Tsar. Queen Hortense of Holland, now Duchess of St Leu, the Duc de Richelieu, former governor of Odessa but now back in France, Benjamin Constant the liberal thinker and chief theorist of the left, his former lover Madame de Staël, his present one Madame Récamier and her future lover Chateaubriand were among those who visited, although most soon drifted away. Many of them were part of Zinaida's Paris circle of friends, but although she was increasingly drawn to religion herself, Zinaida kept away from Madame de Krüdener's salon. Perhaps this was because she had moved even closer to the Catholic Church, but it may also have had something to do with an antipathy towards Madame de Krüdener and her ascendancy over the Tsar. Happier away from court circles, she was glad to keep as much distance as she could between herself and the Tsar's inner circle.

Chateaubriand quickly saw through the bogus mystic. 'While I have my dreams, I hate unreason, abominate mistiness and despise charlatanism,' he wrote. 'I was soon bored, the more I tried to pray, the more I felt the emptiness of my soul. I could think of nothing to say to God while the devil was tempting me to laugh.' Castlereagh dismissed her as 'an old fanatic, who has a considerable reputation among the few high-flyers in religion that are to be found in Paris.'[11]

The 'old fanatic's' influence on the Tsar, however, could not be so lightly dismissed. She made him fast and pray for hours on end. Madame de Boigne recalled with amusement how on one occasion Madame de Krüdener had boasted that it was she who had persuaded the Tsar to renounce Maria Narishkina, his mistress of sixteen years. It had taken immense courage for him to sacrifice a liaison of sixteen years to duty, she said. Casting her eyes to heaven, one of the company present that day, Elzéar de Sabran, replied, 'Alas! sometimes it is easier to renounce a liaison of sixteen years than one of sixteen days!' Even Madame de Krüdener had been unable to resist joining in the general merriment at this sally, before returning to more serious matters.[12]

As part of the Tsar's entourage, Zinaida would have been at the spectacular review of his armies organised on the Plain of Vertus, near Montmirail, on 10 September 1815. From the top of a small hill the Tsar, his guests and their suites looked down at the plain on which 150,000 men, 520 pieces of artillery and the carriages of every European nation made an unforgettable picture. Below them uniforms of every colour wove a moving tapestry as the Emperor Alexander and his party waited for his royal guests. As the entourage of the Emperor of Austria appeared, Alexander, accompanied by his Chief of Staff, Zinaida's brother-in-law Prince Peter Volkonsky, his aides-de-camp and his generals, rode half-way down the hill to meet the sovereigns. Afterwards, at a signal from the Tsar, a cannon roared, to be answered by other cannon in the three lines in which the army was drawn up. The troops then formed a huge square, the cavalry and artillery taking up their positions at full gallop, and at such speed that the Duke of Wellington remarked admiringly that they had the precision of a machine. Lady Shelley, watching with the Duke 'from atop her dear chestnut mare', thought that the 30,000 light cavalry, cuirassiers and uhlans with their many-coloured flags looked like the celestial hosts as they approached from afar. 'The Russian artillery is so beautiful that I cannot find words to describe it – the horses in perfect shape and well groomed. It was a splendid sight to see them on the march,' she wrote.[13]

Alexander returned from Vertus in an ecstatic mood. The day had been the finest of his life; he had heard interior voices, he told Madame de Krüdener and her friend, the preacher Empaytaz, who had come with her from Heilbronn. His 'heart was filled with love' for his enemies.[14] He had also read Madame de Krüdener's booklet, *Le Camp de Vertus*, which, nothing if not diligent, she had published immediately after the event.[15] Giving full reign to her feelings, she had confirmed that 'all breathing people implored, from the seven altars, the blood of the man-God, a new union of nations based on the Gospel.' In this feverish mood the Tsar drafted a proposal for a new style of diplomacy, presenting it first to the Emperor Francis. Alexander's text proposed that the three Allied sovereigns would sign a Holy Alliance, based on the precepts of the Gospels. They would be 'delegated by Providence to govern the three branches of a single family, namely, Austria, Prussia and Russia; thus confessing that the Christian nation of which they and their people form a part has really no other sovereign than Him to whom all supreme power belongs.' Other nations too were invited to join his Holy Alliance.

Alexander's original text was, in fact, both liberal and internationalist, based on respect for the rights of people and on ideas of international brotherhood and morality. Metternich thought it 'an empty echoing monument' but, consummate politician that he was, and aware of how he could make use of it in the future, he set about redrafting it. Thus the document which Alexander had hoped would change the style of diplomacy was turned by Metternich into one which confined any attempts at international fraternity to the sovereigns personally. The pact of the Holy Alliance, as amended by Metternich, was signed by the Emperors Alexander and Francis as well as Frederick William of Prussia on 26 September 1815.

Castlereagh also thought it 'a piece of sublime mysticism and nonsense', to which he and Wellington had found it difficult to listen 'with becoming gravity', adding, 'The fact is the Emperor's mind is not completely sound.'[16] To save the Tsar's face, a constitutional reason had to be found which would make it impossible for the Prince Regent to sign the Holy Alliance. A solemn personal letter from him apparently satisfied Alexander, who was in any case keen to conclude the whole business and leave Paris.

The Quadruple Alliance between Britain, Austria, Prussia and Russia, and the treaty with France, took much longer, largely because Castlereagh and Wellington had to fight hard against Prussian demands for Alsace Lorraine and Lille, which would have undermined the newly returned King Louis XVIII's authority, and might well have led to another war. The second Treaty of Paris was finally signed on 29 November. After much bargaining, France was able to retain her 1790 borders, although she was forced to pay war reparations and accept the occupation of her territory by 150,000 men for the time being. An important article of this treaty stipulated that the signatories would meet at regular intervals to discuss matters of common interest, establishing the so-called 'congress system'.

One of the most burning subjects of conversation in the salons was the article in the treaty which promised to return to their respective countries the works of art which had been looted by Napoleon. It caused great anguish to most of Zinaida's circle.[17]

Zinaida was thoroughly enjoying Paris, delighted to be among so many friends. Her young brother-in-law Sergei, who had been in Paris when Napoleon returned from Elba, was still there. When Sergei was on his way to Paris from the Congress of Vienna, his sister Sophia and his friend Prince Eugène, who was the Queen's brother, had recommended him to Queen Hortense. Sophia had written to Louise then: 'My darling brother leaves here in a fortnight. I recommend him to your friend's [the Queen] kindness and to yours; you will like him. What an excellent young man he is! Zinaida sends all her love. Love my Serge, I think him perfect.'[18]

Sergei later wrote warmly of the Queen and of Louise de Cochelet, as 'people who stood out not only because of their importance under the Empire, but also because they were able to retain that social importance, by virtue of their intelligence, and a brilliant education, as well as their hospitality and kindness.' The liberal Sergei had been less happy that 'My acquaintance with Countess Laval [Zinaida's step-aunt] brought me unwittingly and I would even say unwillingly, into contact with the St Germain set, that is the main legitimist circle,' but through her he was also invited to the salons of the Duchess of Courland and Madame de Staël, as was Zinaida herself.[19]

The liberal faction was led by Benjamin Constant and Madame de Staël, who had once again returned to Paris after Napoleon's final exile to St Helena. Indefatigable as ever, she lobbied the Tsar and Wellington for a liberal parliament and for an end to the military occupation of France which caused her particular anguish. The Prussians had behaved savagely after Waterloo, raping and pillaging as they went. In Paris, the Prussian commander Blücher had even intended to blow up the bridges of Austerlitz and Iéna and, when Talleyrand protested, he had expressed the hope 'that Monsieur de Talleyrand would be on it when it blew up'. Wellington posted a British sentry on the bridges pending the intervention of the Allied sovereigns who had at that time just arrived in Paris.[20] Writing to Lady Burghersh, then in Florence where her husband had been appointed minister, Madame de Staël spoke highly of Wellington: 'The Duke has made himself very much liked. He is behaving as a generous conqueror, but still it is sad to be conquered.' Although she irritated him occasionally, Wellington's admiration for her was no less great than hers for him. Sergei Volkonsky was another admirer:

She was the possessor of a fine mind and a wide range of interests, she had the gift of conversation perhaps even greater than the talents of her pen; she was not good-looking, but her eyes were full of fire, expressing both the loftiness of her thoughts and the sacred flame burning in her heart.[21]

Madame de Staël had less than two years left. She died in her beloved Paris on 14 July 1817 and was buried at Coppet.

While the fate of France was being decided and the country was under occupation, parties, balls and all kinds of entertainments went on as usual. Zinaida threw herself into musical and artistic life, singing regularly at private recitals. Keen to introduce her friend Rossini's music in France, she helped to stage his opera *L'Italiana in Algeri*, herself singing the role of Isabella. Albeit in a private performance, Zinaida brought Rossini to French audiences for the first time. The Tsar frowned on her amusements but she took little notice, re-establishing contact with her old teacher, the French composer Boieldieu, from whom she took singing lessons again. In her mid-twenties, the slim and blue-eyed Zinaida was determined not to be merely decorative. She was too artistically gifted to take her talents lightly, but at the same time she was well aware of the limitations which her social position imposed on them.

She was not alone in this. Mademoiselle Mars, a famous actress of the time, whom French society flocked to see at the Comédie Française where her interpretations of Molière women were particularly admired, so admired Zinaida's acting and singing, which she was able to enjoy at the private performances which Zinaida delighted in, that she was heard to exclaim: 'What a pity that so much talent is wasted on a lady of high birth!'[22] She was not, however, received by society. 'I never realised what sentimental and genteel comedy could be until I came to Paris and saw Mademoiselle Mars. – However, actresses are much less received in society than with us,' wrote Lady Shelley.[23] Zinaida, to whom she was a much-admired fellow artist and friend, had no such inhibitions. Sending her a bouquet of viburnum and roses for the opening of *Le Secret du Ménage*, she included a poem, 'A Mademoiselle Mars', in which she celebrates the 'Muse who hides her real name under such a warlike one'.[24]

In spite of Zinaida's many friends in royalist circles, that summer she took an active and passionate interest in the fate of a young officer who had been condemned to death for joining Napoleon during the Hundred Days, considerably annoying the Tsar in the process.

Charles Huchet, Comte de La Bédoyère, was a young and handsome officer from an old aristocratic family, who, after the Restoration, had been persuaded against his better judgement into the service of the King by his wife's royalist relations. He was a colonel quartered at Grenoble when Napoleon escaped from Elba. Forgetting his new loyalties, he had assembled his regiment and, against the orders of General Marchand and the Prefect, left at once to welcome Napoleon, returning to Grenoble with the Emperor in triumph. From his mount, he had shouted to a friend as he left, 'Farewell, Madame. In a week's time I shall either have been shot or I shall be a Marshal of France!'[25] He did not quite achieve that rank, but subsequently, as a general, fought bravely with Napoleon at Waterloo. After Waterloo he had made an impassioned speech in the Chamber of Peers, demanding that Napoleon's son be recognised as his father's successor. The Allied Powers, annoyed by the treachery of the whole French army, decided to make an example of him together with General La Valette and Marshal Ney, whom Napoleon had called 'the bravest of the brave'. La Valette escaped on the eve of his execution with the assistance of some British officers. Ney, who refused at his trial to allow his defence counsel to plead that he had been born in Saarelouis, which was outside French territory, with the words, '*Je suis français et je saurai mourir français*' ('I am a Frenchman and I will know how to die as a Frenchman'), was executed on 7 December.[26]

Sergei greatly admired La Bédoyère, and attracted criticism by intervening on his behalf with those of his royalist acquaintances who he thought might have some influence at court. The Tsar, though fond of 'Monsieur Serge', was not amused. He was even angrier when he received the original copies of the letters which Zinaida and Sophia had sent out to their friends on behalf of La Bédoyère. Sophia's husband Prince Peter Volkonsky, as Chief of Staff, was delegated to reprimand Sergei severely, expressing, as he later wrote, 'the Tsar's displeasure that I had not only involved myself in unwarranted activities but had also dragged my sisters into them, and to inform me that I should stop interfering in the affairs of France and turn to those of Russia.'[27] Little did Alexander realise how literally the future Decembrist would take his advice, and with what tragic consequences.

Knowing that he could count on her help, Sergei asked Zinaida to intervene with the Duchesse d'Angoulême, the King's niece, whom she knew through her aunt Laval. Although the Duchess was herself an Ultra,[28] the Volkonskys had hoped that the well-known royalist sympathies of La Bédoyère's wife's family would help his cause. Zinaida herself had friends on both sides. Horrified by the sorrow of La Bédoyère's young wife, Georgine, she threw herself into their cause with all her heart, petitioning anyone who might help and even going to the Tsar personally. Georgine de La Bédoyère meanwhile tried to enlist Alexander's support through Madame de Krüdener, whose influence on the Tsar was then at its height.

Moved by Zinaida's pleas but unwilling to interfere in France's internal affairs, Alexander went to consult Madame de Krüdener. Perhaps her 'Voice', which she was hearing more and more often at this period, would provide an answer? He found her in a dreadful state, agitated and in tears. She had spent the whole day in her oratory wrestling with her 'Voice', without – alas! – obtaining permission from it to present her petition to the Tsar. This could only mean that Alexander should refrain from taking any action at all. The sentence was all the more serious, she knew, because La Bédoyère's soul was not in a state of grace.[29]

La Bédoyère was duly executed on 19 August, going bravely to his death. At his trial for treason the young man interrupted his defending counsel with the words:

> No, I am not a traitor. I may have been mistaken in what might bring the greatest happiness to my country. Now as I await the inevitable sentence of death, I only ask that my still-young children should not carry the burden of their father being called a traitor to his country and theirs.

'All our efforts were to no avail, but in all conscience my sisters and I had done our duty,' Sergei Volkonsky wrote later.[30]

After the execution, Madame de Krüdener persuaded the Tsar that he had a great duty to fulfil. Alexander must now intervene with God on behalf of the young man's soul. She kept the Tsar kneeling on cold marble for eight solid hours, freeing him only at two o'clock in the morning. At eight, he was woken with a note from her telling him that her 'Voice' had announced that his prayers had been heard. She then wrote to the desperate young widow to inform her that, after spending only a few hours in purgatory, her husband was now in Heaven, thanks to the Tsar's personal intervention. She was sure that this news would help to alleviate her sorrow. Far from being comforted by this news, Madame de La Bédoyère poured out the story to her friends with rage now added to sorrow.[31]

The Tsar, who had never forgiven Talleyrand for his secret treaty with Britain and Austria, had the satisfaction of seeing him removed from power before he left Paris in October 1815. The elections in August had swept the extreme royalist Ultras to power. Talleyrand's government would now have to deal with this reactionary assembly, the famous Chambre Introuvable, whose deputies were much more extremist than the King. Madame de Boigne, whose sympathies were Orleanist, described them as 'mad, unbalanced, ignorant, hot-headed and reactionary, dominated by the interests of their caste.'[32] The Tsar's influence – he was now Talleyrand's implacable enemy – did the rest. Louis accepted Talleyrand's resignation and appointed the Duc de Richelieu in his place. 'He is certainly the man in France who knows most about the Crimea,' was Talleyrand's cutting remark as he bowed out.

Richelieu, of whom Wellington had said that his word was equal to a treaty, was the great-nephew of the famous Cardinal. Betrothed at the age of fifteen to the twelve-year-old Rosalie de Rochechouart, he discovered on his return from the Grand Tour that his future wife was a hunchback. He married her nevertheless. Like many brilliant young men of his time, he was drawn to the Russia of Catherine the Great, where he fought against the Turks under Suvorov and was decorated for his bravery. He returned briefly to France, but his dislike of Napoleon and his friendship with Alexander took him back to Russia, where his exceptional administrative abilities were put to use. He became a very efficient governor of the Crimea and was responsible for the growth and development of Odessa, from a village sunk in mud in 1803, when he went there, to one of the main cities of the Empire. He returned to France in 1814. Brave, cool-headed, generous, friendly and approachable in manner, the Duc was universally loved and respected in Odessa. In Europe he was generally considered one of the most enlightened, capable, disinterested and honourable men of his time.[33]

Zinaida was, of course, aware that Alexander was very displeased with her for her part in the La Bédoyère affair. She had been glad to be able to talk to him at a reception at the Duchess of Courland's before he left Paris. He had been kind enough to her then and not reproved her, but he seemed gloomy and disapproving. She knew that he took little pleasure in social amusements these days, but he seemed more severe than usual. Perhaps the execution of La Bédoyère had upset him more than he realised? Or had her efforts to win La Bédoyère a pardon seriously annoyed Alexander? He may even have felt a little left out. She had sensed the coldness between them. It did not stop her from writing to him to ask if he were still cross 'and wished to scold her'. Nor did his displeasure inhibit her from soliciting his help as she invariably did – this time about her luggage, which had been sent ahead to Russia. She was never afraid of him, always sure, somehow, that she could depend on his affection.

Alexander left Paris two days after signing the Pact of the Holy Alliance. He was exhausted and, in his new serious and severe mood, deeply disenchanted with Paris and the French. From Brussels, he wrote to his sister Catherine: 'Here I am away from that accursed Paris!' where he could find no softening of his cares, except in the 'sublime consolations that flow from the Supreme Being'.[34] Madame de Krüdener, however, did not go with him. She was beginning to bore him. On his return to Russia, still in a black mood, he refused all celebrations, publishing instead a manifesto about the Holy Alliance so illiberal in tone and content and so bitter about the French that it drew a protest from his old tutor, La Harpe.

Zinaida remained in Paris, where six months after the Tsar's departure she received a reply to her letter. Alexander wrote from St Petersburg. His tone was much friendlier. She was mistaken to suppose that he was angry with her about the La Bédoyère affair:

If it was perhaps wrong of you to become involved, I certainly never doubted your motives, and I am well aware of the sensitivity of that angelic heart, so much a part of you. – Also the way in which I spoke to you at the Duchess of Courland's should have dismissed any idea that I wished to scold you, as you put it, in your letter.

If I was cross with you, it was not over La Bédoyère, but, and I admit it openly, for your predilection for Paris with all its empty amusements [he continued, more in sorrow than in anger]. A soul as elevated, as noble as yours seemed to me little suited to such frivolity.

One day she would understand, he continues, that loving her as he does, he could not look on, but with regret, at the way she was wasting her time in occupations which were so unworthy of her interest. He ends with reassurances that he has given orders with regard to her belongings, and looks forward to her speedy return.[35]

Zinaida might well have reflected ruefully that it was not so long ago that the Tsar was engaged in all manner of frivolities himself. She knew that he could not be objecting to her friends, most of whom were also his. She realised that what had probably annoyed him particularly was the very thing that mattered most to her – her artistic interests. Perhaps most of all, the Tsar was disconcerted by a new and independent Zinaida. The adoring young girl who had enchanted him in St Petersburg, the radiant lover, the unhappy young wife was gone. In her place was a young woman aware of her strengths, rejoicing in her talents, self-sufficient and free. Zinaida took note of the Tsar's request that she return home to Russia – in those days tantamount to a command. She ignored it for almost a year.

Zinaida returned to Russia in the spring of 1817 after another brief visit to Rome. Michelangelo Barbieri accompanied her as her secretary. He had been part of her household for a year and must have been part of the reason for her happiness. As well as being lovers, they shared a passion for music, often singing together. He was also a gifted painter and designer as well as a constant reminder of her beloved Italy. After a brief vist to St Petersburg, where she gave a lunch for Sophia – 'Yesterday – a surprise outside the town on the St Petersburg road, where Princess Zinaida was giving a lunch for Princess Sophia,' wrote Alexander Turgenev to his brother[36] – she went to Reval (now Tallinn in Estonia) for the rest of the summer.

Little had changed in St Petersburg during her absence. Lavish receptions and balls succeeded one another as before. Now there was a new craze for the ballet where the ballerina Istomina was all the rage. Her magic feet were to be immortalised by Alexander Pushkin. The young poet had only recently left school and was now busy sowing his wild oats. He and Zinaida would meet some years later. For the moment, together with the romantic poet Zhukovsky and Prince Viazemsky, he had joined a literary society, Arzamas, whose members hotly defended the new wave in literature against the likes of Admiral Shishkov, who had so disapproved of Zinaida's views when they were all travelling in the Tsar's suite during the German campaign. Shishkov had founded the Society of Lovers of the Russian Word which sought to expunge all foreign words from the language and base the written word on Church Slavonic.

In October, together with all of Petersburg society, Zinaida went to Moscow for the founding ceremonies of the new Cathedral of Christ the Saviour, due to take place on the 12th, which was to commemorate the victory of the Russian people over Napoleon. The presence in Moscow of the entire court and the Diplomatic Corps threw the great aristocratic houses into a fever of entertaining. Muscovites had long felt patronised by St Petersburg. But it was the old capital that had saved Europe! Now, as new buildings rose everywhere, obliterating the memory of the terrible fire, the Moscow aristocracy felt a new sense of pride. With the whole court assembled, princes and merchants vied in the splendour of their entertainments. The Tsar had appointed the architect Vitberg to design the cathedral, taking a great personal interest and supervising the design himself. On 8 October, he wrote to Zinaida asking if he could come to see her that evening if she were free. He would have come sooner but his engagements prevented him from doing so. It is just a short note making an arrangement to meet, but it shows a new and more equal phase in their relationship – one of warm and lasting friendship.[37]

Zinaida took up residence in her father's house on the Tverskaya. She had always preferred Moscow to the cold northern capital. Nikita had gone to London on the Tsar's business, one contemporary joking that it was Zinaida who managed to send him so far away.[38] This was not altogether fair. Throughout the early, more unhappy phase of her marriage Zinaida had always assiduously pleaded on behalf of her husband with the Tsar. But there may have been some truth in the accusation since Barbieri remained with her. His presence set the tongues wagging. Zinaida remained in Moscow throughout the winter. She may have intended to stay indefinitely, but by March, tired of the northern winter and perhaps also of the interest and gossip occasioned by the presence of Barbieri – the '*monsieur de compagnie*' as he was called – she suddenly left for Odessa, on the Black Sea. One of the Empress Elizabeth's ladies-in-waiting, Princess Volkova, writing to her friend Princess Lanskaya in St Petersburg, gives her 'an excerpt from the scandal sheets': 'Princess Zinaida Alexandrovna

Volkonsky, having compromised herself, has gone to Odessa with Signor Barbieri. Everyone, even the Tsar himself, advised her not to go. Fine people you send us here!'[39] Behind this small piece of gossip lay a great deal more. Zinaida was too beautiful, too unconventional and too well known to have escaped from a great deal of such unwelcome attention. Perhaps Alexander's visit to her had included a little lecture on behaving more circumspectly? Barbieri's presence in her life may also have been in his mind when, in his letter to her when she was in Paris, he talked of frivolities unworthy of her. As she had no intention of altering her way of life, she may well have felt a great need to get away from her circle in Moscow.

Odessa with its sea, its mild climate and southern vegetation was known as the Russian Italy. Under the governorship of the Duc de Richelieu, this charming port had expanded rapidly, becoming a centre of both commerce and culture, and attracting a number of interesting foreigners. There was a splendid new Italian opera, with first-class singers and musicians. Zinaida had had enough of Moscow and its gossips. She was always happier in a warm climate, but there was a much more important reason for her move to Odessa; she had heard in St Petersburg of the Jesuit Abbé Nicolle and wanted to consult him about her son's education.

The abbot, who had been a prominent educationist in France, came to St Petersburg in 1793, where he opened a small and select school which did so well that he greatly enlarged it. He moved first to Moscow, and then, in 1811, to the south because of his health, settling in Odessa where he set up teaching programmes for two schools for the nobility. In May 1817, almost a year before Zinaida travelled to Odessa, the famous Lycée Richelieu, organised according to the abbot's educational theories, had opened in the city. Zinaida had decided to take charge of her son's education herself. She had greatly benefited from her father's teaching and wanted to do the same for her beloved son. She asked the abbot to draw up an educational programme for Alexander, then eight years old. The programme, which was to cover twelve years beginning in September 1819, dealt not only with academic subjects but also with physical, religious and moral education, including methods of encouragement, punishment, and supervision. The abbot recommended that the pupil should always be under the tutelage of parents or tutors. Vladimir Pavey, only a little younger than Alexander, shared in this programme.[40]

In Odessa, far from hiding discreetly with her lover, Zinaida was surrounded by family. Her sister-in-law Princess Sophia, from whom she had been almost inseparable since her marriage, came south with her children. They were soon joined by Sergei Volkonsky, who had come down from Kiev to visit his favourite sister and sister-in-law while inspecting some land which he had acquired two years before. Nikita's elder brother, Prince Repnin, on an inspection tour of the region, and his wife were also in Odessa, as were more distant relations, the Muravievs. Finally the Tsar, who was constantly touring his empire at that time, perhaps attracted by Zinaida's presence there and the amusing company she always gathered around her, paid his first visit to Odessa in 1818.

Zinaida took a house in the centre of the picturesque old quarter of the town, its garden full of lemon trees and umbrella pines, which at once became the centre of social life. 'St Priest and I are just off to Princess Zinaida's. She has settled here and we are all at her feet. I hear that she sings wonderfully and is quite delightful,' wrote one young poet, Batyushkov.[41]

Life in Odessa, as recalled in the memoirs of Sergei Volkonsky, could not have been more agreeable. The atmosphere was unstuffy and cosmopolitan, with French, Italian, Polish and Greek residents mixing with local families and aristocratic Russians. Comte Andrault de Langeron, now governor of the Crimea, commander of the Don Cossacks and resident in Odessa, was an old friend of Sergei's and delighted to welcome them. Zinaida's friends were mainly young and entertained each other at dinners, picnics, fancy-dress parties, and musical and theatrical soirées.[42]

She named many of them in seven couplets which she wrote in 1819 and illustrated with charming watercolours. Her 'Verses on the Mud of Odessa' (to the tune of 'A Morning in Paris' a song popular at the time) not only recall the mud which enveloped the city streets in the spring, but celebrate her friends and acquaintances. The Count (Langeron), the Danish consul, Raynaud the French commercial counsellor, Guibal another Frenchman, Cobley the English commander of the garrison, the priest Boisvin who taught at the Lycée Richelieu, the Austrian consul Thom (or his son; they were known as Thom I and Thom II, a play on the word for volume in both French and Russian), Barbieri and a French engineer named Poitiers all appear in the charming and light-hearted verses, which bear witness to the diversity of Zinaida's circle. There is no doubt that she enjoyed her time in Odessa, creating a lively and unconventional atmosphere in her salon, which became known for its brilliant conversation, its music and its sheer fun. Card games, which she loathed, were banished here as they would be from all her houses.[43]

While Zinaida was in Odessa, in September 1818 the Tsar had attended the first of a series of congresses at Aix la Chapelle (Aachen), where, largely thanks to Richelieu's influence, the Allies finally agreed to withdraw their troops from France and reduce the indemnity imposed by the Treaty of Paris. In effect France could now take her place among the great nations. Alexander returned to Russia to the devastating news of the death of his beloved sister, Catherine, Queen of Württemberg since 1816. The court was plunged into mourning, as he withdrew into stony and silent grief.

St Petersburg was already under the twin influences of a religious ferment and the growing and malign ascendancy of Alexander's new military leader, Count Arakhcheev. Although generally considered the evil genius of the last part of Alexander's reign, Arakhcheev was, rather, his loyal and brutal watchdog, faithfully and unquestioningly carrying out the commands of the increasingly paranoid Tsar.

Europe in general was to witness a strong religious revival in the aftermath of the Napoleonic wars, a reaction to the rationalism of the Enlightenment and the upheavals of the Revolution. In Russia, every kind of religious sect flourished. Martinism and Illuminism jostled with Freemasonry and the more extreme forms of occult mysticism, such as the flagellant Dukhobors, the even more extreme self-castrating Skoptsy, and a sect founded by Caterina Tatarinova, the German widow of a Russian colonel, who dressed in white at her religious meetings, whirled like a dervish and when exhausted would speak of visions and prophecies. The Tsar's primary concern now was to encourage spiritual regeneration. He saw himself more and more as the defender of the Christian faith against a growing atheist liberalism which threatened the principle of monarchy as well as the Christian order.

Alexander's love of all things military, inherited from his father Paul, coupled with great inner turmoil, was becoming manifest in a growing passion for order. One of his ideas, enthusiastically espoused by Arakhcheev, was to form military colonies all over Russia. During the next few years a simple process was devised which would combine military service with farming, enabling peasant soldiers to live a normal family life and greatly reducing the cost of the army. A regiment would be moved into an area in which all the male inhabitants would automatically be absorbed into the army, constituting that regiment's reserves. They were then housed in special and identical units, made to work in the fields together, and drilled mercilessly. More horrifically, they were deprived of all liberty, obliged to marry – there were to be no widows or old maids, who were also forced to marry – often by the choice of the military authorities, and required to produce a child a year. By 1821, about a third of the army was established in these military colonies which, not surprisingly, were deeply hated. Arakhcheev himself became the subject of universal loathing, except to the Tsar who appreciated his uncomplicated and total loyalty. Alexander had moved an extraordinarily long way from the young idealist of the days of his Secret Committee.

In spite of the new repressive atmosphere, Russia was embarking on a period of unequalled cultural development, which came to be known as her golden age of literature (usually considered to fall between 1820 and 1880.) The eighteenth century had been a period of learning and rapid absorption of Western, mainly French, culture. In the early nineteenth century, the intellectual scene began to shift away from the Enlightenment and the French *philosophes*, towards Romanticism and the German idealistic philosophers, particularly Schelling and later Hegel. These opposed rationalism, substituting a more mystical and religious view of the world. The tensions between these competing philosophies in Russia produced a uniquely creative climate for the growth and development of a new culture which, while it incorporated Western ideas, developed new literary forms. Based on Russian folklore and popular speech, they helped to fashion a modern Russian language which, in the hands of writer's of genius, was to produce a great literature as Russian as it was universal.

Zinaida left Odessa for St Petersburg early in 1819, staying with the Repnins at their estates near Poltava on the way.[44] She had grown tired of Odessa and of social pleasures and was now determined to pursue more seriously the literary activities on which she had embarked. Nikita was still abroad, sent to buy thoroughbred horses for the Tsar; they would be apart for eighteen months.[45] Here she remained closeted until the summer, when her *Quatres Nouvelles* were published. Written in elegant French and dedicated to Sophia, these four stories, *Les Maris Mandingues* (Africa), *Une Tribu du Brésil* (America), *L'Enfant du Kachemyr* (Asia), and the partly autobiographical *Laure*, have the exotic settings which were then becoming fashionable. *Laure*, representing Europe, is set in France, in Montpellier. The novel's eponymous heroine marries young, is caught up in the social round, but soon tires of her empty life. She sets off on her travels, a little à la Corinne, and dedicates herself to art in which she finds new strength. The birth of her child gives new meaning to her life. The story is based on Zinaida's feelings about her own life hitherto, as she makes clear in the dedication to Sophia:

> In the European novel, I have attempted to show the customs of our society, which have wounded us both so painfully, and especially to show how reprehensibly superficial are its judgements of others.

The other three titles are Rousseauesque tales, celebrating noble savages in different continents. Her stories were moderately well received.[46] Soon afterwards she left again for Europe, stopping on the way in Warsaw, which the Tsar was visiting at the time. She had evidently decided to return to Rome even before she left Odessa, because she had already sent her maid Avdotia Naumova ahead with some of her heavy baggage and had obtained a passport for her from Langeron in Odessa.[47]

In Warsaw, a letter from Sosthène de La Rochefoucauld, evidently in reply to one she had written, was awaiting her. Aware that Zinaida continued to enjoy the Tsar's friendship and confidence, he hoped that she might be in a position to influence him or at least report to him La Rochefoucauld's opinions on the affairs of France. 'The Emperor Alexander loved her wit, her woes, her qualities, as pure as they were lovable. His feelings towards her were of friendship and trust which give the letters which follow some importance,' La Rochefoucauld writes in a footnote to his letters, published eighteen years later. This footnote confirms that Zinaida's relationship with Alexander was very solidly based, and had survived beyond the chivalrous and romantic feelings expressed in the Tsar's letters during their love affair.

In France, Richelieu, who had tried to govern as a moderate royalist, resigned in December 1818, the Chambre Introuvable having proved ungovernable. The political regime in France, at that time still more monarchical than parliamentary, meant that the choice of ministers rested with the King. The King's favourite Decazes, like Richelieu a moderate monarchist but looking to the left rather than to the Ultras for support, now went to the country. The result was an electoral victory for the left.

La Rochefoucauld was himself a royalist to the core; his father-in-law the Duc de Montmorency was one of the Ultras' chief spokesmen in the Upper Chamber. In his letter to Zinaida, written in September 1819, he makes clear his disapproval of Richelieu and of his influence over the Tsar: 'The departure of foreign troops of which you write had become essential.' He agrees with Zinaida's point that, of course, a certain amount of instability was inevitable after the departure of these troops, but his predictions about Richelieu, who should have known who his real friends were, had only too unhappily come true. Richelieu, he writes, had lost control and was now completely finished. Zinaida was not to think that he (La Rochefoucauld) was calling for foreign interference or troops to sort out France's problems. He was too good a Frenchman for that, indeed it had been foreign influence which had done France the greatest harm, in his opinion.

I don't know what kind of liberal madness went through all the sovereigns' heads [he continues pointedly]. It is they themselves who seem to be in thrall to all the chimeras of false freedom, whereas revolutions in other countries, as well as the trials of our unhappy France, have taught us only too well how pernicious these ideas were. Equality before the law, government to the King, and administration to the country, that is the only true foundation of liberty, the only system which, in our country at least, might give people some peace.

In his long letter La Rochefoucauld reminds Zinaida that the cause of France is that of all Europe:

> The demon of revolt is everywhere. It is war to the death declared on all the sovereigns, passionately sustained by the spirit of revolution which is in league against everything legitimate. They fight principles because they do not believe in duty; they deny God because they will not obey. But I believe that we are living through memorable times, because it is God Himself who is under attack, and it is He who will avenge Himself. The triumph of the lie has lasted thirty years. How much longer can it last? . . . This is what I believe, my dear Princess, since I believe in Providence.

Finally, after defending the heir to the throne (the future Charles X) to whom La Rochefoucauld is particularly close, he gets to the point. The Emperor Alexander, who has always done much good to France, is now, in seeming to support a 'diplomatic influence', doing France much harm and doesn't realise that this might lead to undesirable results.[48] Although, as is obvious from her future actions, Zinaida was a liberal and La Rochefoucauld clearly the opposite, she remained a loyal friend.

Zinaida enjoyed her stay in Warsaw and remained in the Polish capital for several months. One of her oldest and closest friends, Prince Peter Andreevich Viazemsky, then living in Warsaw, was a distinguished littérateur, and future editor of one of the better literary journals, the *Moscow Telegraph*. Through him Zinaida frequented all the fashionable salons. As always she shone at the musical soirées and her voice was much praised. Viazemsky, who had often heard Zinaida singing since their childhood, was so much struck with it that he compared it to the then famous Borgongio.[49] In February 1820, unable to bear the severe Polish winter, she left for Italy.

7

Rome, Verona and Paris

'Madame Volkonsky is quite remarkable ... she sings contralto
like an angel.'

STENDHAL

Zinaida arrived in Milan in February 1820, after her long stay in
Warsaw. As always, she was swept up in the social round. Her talents,
especially her voice, were well known and she had many friends in
musical circles. Her friend Rossini, after his triumphs in Rome where
The Barber of Seville had opened in 1816, was then living in Milan. One
of his greatest friends was Henri Beyle, better known as Stendhal,
the *nom de plume* he adopted in 1814 when, after the fall of Napoleon,
he returned to Italy where he spent about seven years.

Stendhal had taken part in most of Napoleon's campaigns from
1800, including the Russian campaign. A liberal and a freethinker, as
well as a Bonapartist, he represented the opposite political extreme
in France from that of Zinaida's Ultra friend, Sosthène de La Rochefoucauld. The great clash between royalists and liberals would come
to a head ten years later in the revolution of 1830, which swept away
the Bourbons and which Stendhal described in his masterpiece *Le
Rouge et le Noir*.

Stendhal liked Zinaida immediately, easily discerning the unconventional and imaginative artist behind the society lady. A lover of music
and also of women, he was lavish in his praise of her musical talent
and her voice. Strangely, whilst almost all of her contemporaries
invariably described the thirty-year-old Zinaida as beautiful, he obvi-

ously did not agree. In a letter to his friend the Baron de Mareste, dated 3 March, Stendhal describes his social round. It was the season of Carnival.

> I spend my evenings with Rossini and Monti; all things considered I prefer extraordinary people to ordinary ones. I leave you to now dine with Rossini.
>
> There have been some masked balls, four of them charming; all of society present; among them a Russian princess. Madame Volkonsky is quite a remarkable woman, utterly unaffected, who sings contralto like an angel. She is bringing up a son [by herself] whom she adores; she writes passable French and has recently published novels. She is thirty-two, ugly, but with a pleasant kind of ugliness, and she composes lovely music. She is charming and mad beneath the mask.[1]

With his finely tuned eye and ear, Stendhal captures Zinaida in a paragraph – her considerable musical talent and wonderful voice, her writing, her love for her son, her ability to communicate with people directly with a complete absence of affectation, and the charm and 'madness' beneath the mask. What did he mean by mad? Probably that she was unconventional, a bohemian rather than an aristocrat by nature, but perhaps he also saw the streak of instability and emotional fragility, like a metallic thread in the warm texture of her personality, always present, sometimes overheated, but an indispensible conductor of the artistic sensibility which was at the centre of her.

Zinaida was now educating her son at home. She had tried to follow the educational programme drawn up for Alexander by the Abbé Nicolle, but, as her kinswoman and biographer N. A. Belozerskaya wrote severely in 1897, thirty-five years after Zinaida's death,

> her own wayward nature to which any systematic approach was foreign meant that she soon abandoned it, teaching her son as she had been taught by her father, with the difference, that her son, Prince Alexander Volkonsky, spoke and wrote Russian perfectly and, since childhood, had known and loved Russia.

Zinaida and her father had belonged to generations for whom Russian was a foreign language. Responding to changing times, she was determined not to repeat the same mistakes with her son.[2]

Zinaida set off for Naples on 3 March 1820, as we know from Stendhal's letter, longing for the south. She had been unable to visit that city during her last sojourn in Italy, when Napoleon's escape from Elba had forced her to cut her journey short. This time, she stayed in Naples for two months, arriving in Rome in May accompanied by Barbieri.

Throughout this time her husband Nikita was in London where King George III had recently died. The Prince Regent was now King George IV and London teemed with important visitors coming to pay their respects. It was also buzzing with rumours about the impending return of the King's estranged wife Caroline, who had been racketing around Italy for several years, creating endless problems for the Vatican's Secretary of State Cardinal Consalvi, who was unsure as to quite how to treat her. At the end of April, to the Cardinal's relief, Caroline left Rome, but, to her husband's horror, was preparing to return to England.

'The Queen – that is the great question of the moment – what is wanted is to un-queen her, but how is it to be done?' wondered the sharp-tongued Countess Lieven, in a letter to her brother, as she happily contemplated the scandal ahead. 'Our friend Nikita is here,' she adds – 'a magnificent "Highness"; it must be said that the English don't think him any the cleverer on that account.'[3] Nikita clearly had an inflated sense of his own importance, or perhaps of his office when on the Tsar's business.

The revolutionary conquests of Napoleon after 1796 had destroyed the existing system of states in Italy. Many Italians had looked on his invasion as a deliverance from rigid government unchanged for centuries. Neither the use of men for his armies, nor the imposition of swingeing taxes on his Italian possessions to finance endless campaigns, nor even the wide-scale looting of Italian art treasures, succeeded in turning them against him. They continued to support him, as the main catalyst of much-needed social and economic change.

The settlement of 1815 at the Congress of Vienna returned much of Italy, already held by right of conquest, to Austria. The Napoleonic kingdom of Italy was parcelled out into various states, turning Italy once again into Metternich's 'geographical expression'. Lombardy and the Veneto were restored to their former status of provinces of the Habsburg Empire. Tuscany and Modena were ruled by an Austrian archduke apiece. The House of Savoy, reinstated in Piedmont and Sardinia, also annexed the once-independent republic of Genoa. Elsewhere, princelings and dukes were back on their thrones. The Pope returned as temporal ruler of the Papal States which stretched right across central Italy from Ferrara in the north-east to Rome. To the south, with the exception of the tiny papal enclaves of Benevento and Pontecorvo, the Spanish Bourbons were restored in the Kingdom of the Two Sicilies, while a Habsburg princess married to the King of Naples further reinforced Austrian influence.

Pope Pius VII, who had negotiated the concordat with Napoleon in 1801 through his friend and Secretary of State, Cardinal Consalvi, and had so unwillingly presided over the Emperor's coronation in 1804, was a cultured and open-minded man. He had tried hard to reconcile the Revolution with the Church, retaining some of the reforms of Napoleon's administration, adopting his civil code, and even giving asylum to members of his family. Napoleon's mother Letizia, his brothers Joseph Bonaparte and Lucien, and sister Eliza all lived in or near Rome. Most of these reforms were reversed by Pope Leo XII after the death of Pius VII in August 1823. The restored *ancien régime* was, on the whole, as authoritarian, rigid and repressive as ever. Once again police spies were everywhere. Feudal and clerical privileges were restored, censorship was reimposed, state and tariff barriers re-established. But the citizens of the Italian states had changed. A new middle class was beginning to emerge as a result of the Napoleonic administration, which had been determined to open careers to talent. The winds of the French Revolution, though quieter, continued to blow over the Italian peninsula, as indeed, over the rest of Europe.

When Zinaida arrived in Rome in May 1820, it was for an indefinite stay. She plunged happily into artistic life, immediately becoming the centre of a circle of Russian artists who were all studying in the city. Young art students mixed happily with the distinguished Italian and foreign artists who flocked to her salon, among them the sculptors Canova and Thorvaldsen, and the painters Camuccini and Vernet. The Princess also entertained members of the Roman aristocracy and an endless stream of her foreign friends visiting or living in Rome. In addition to her own considerable talents, which she was now developing and using, she always had the ability to make others happy and to bring out the best in them. Her generosity, unaffected warmth and charm made people feel at ease, while her quick mind and sound education made her conversation a delight. Among the young Russian artists in Rome were the painters Bruni, Bruilov and Schedrin and the sculptor S. Galberg, who, thoroughly smitten, in a letter home described the Princess as 'the most charming, most intelligent, most kind of women, an author, musician and actress, a woman with the most enchanting eyes, in short the very same famous Zinaida Volkonsky of St Petersburg', adding that 'she has brought the painter Bruni with her, who lives in her house.'[4]

At first, Zinaida simply invited the Russian art students to her musical soirées. Little by little, Galberg recounts, the soirées turned into opera productions while the art students, from making up the audience, found themselves pressed on to the stage. No one escaped Zinaida's eager eye. She didn't require much from them by way of acting: they were mostly spear carriers, asked to stand on the stage and above all not make any noise. In spite of endless rehearsals the students made unconvincing soldiers, throwing Prince Volkonsky and Count Osterman-Tolstoy into fits of laughter at their attempts to march on stage. A young Russian painter, Schepkin, newly arrived from Naples, also found their efforts amusing – until his next visit when he too was dressed up as a soldier and made to march and fight on stage. 'During this battle scene, he hit Toni [another artist] so enthusiastically on the head, that he knocked him out. Now it was our turn to laugh!'[5]

Prince Nikita, who had been absent from his wife's life for some time and, after a separation of a year and a half, hadn't known exactly where she was in Italy, had found her in Rome. The Princess and her husband seem to have settled down amicably together. What kind of man was he? The English traveller Mary Berry, who had met Nikita in London and again in Geneva, in the summer, visited the Volkonskys in Rome, in January 1821, describing Nikita as 'a man whose character is something like his voice – rough, untuned and half polished.' However, she continues, 'They seem on the best footing possible, and he boasts to everyone of the talents, cleverness and charms of his wife.'[6] Although one of Zinaida's nephews had written that Nikita Volkonsky did not love his wife,[7] perhaps now things had changed, or absence had made a difference. Perhaps the ten-year-old Alexander, who, although his education was entirely undertaken by his doting mother, was much loved by his father too, had brought them together, or maybe it was the benign atmosphere of Rome where Zinaida was always so happy. A tendency to occasional bouts of depression never left her, but she seems to have come to terms with her undistinguished, lazy, but good-natured husband, while her son fulfilled her need for a close and uncomplicated love. Writing about their relationship much later, their great-nephew Prince Sergei Volkonsky revealed that Nikita was always spoken of in the family as '*l'entiché*' (the infatuated) because of his devotion to his wife, while she was known as the enchantress.[8] The truth is that Zinaida was by far the stronger and more interesting of the two. Once she had overcome the disappointments of the early years of her marriage, she was perfectly happy to live with her husband around. He relied on her entirely and seems not to have interfered with her way of life, while she helped his career and managed their finances, but otherwise left him to his own devices.

Miss Berry was much taken with the charm and talent of her young hostess. At a Twelfth Night party at the Volkonskys (6 January 1821), for about thirty people, Zinaida had recited 'Le Songe d'Athalie'. 'It was not possible to recite Racine better, nor with more expression than she did: she also gave us the "Declaration de Phèdre", quite equal to the other,' enthused Miss Berry. After commenting on the poor supporting cast, she reports that Zinaida showed

not the least degree of shyness about the exhibition of her talent, nor of affected modesty or of *amour propre* about the praises she received and the admiration she excited, but seeming quite as much at ease and quite as much amused herself as any of the company. For music she is an enthusiast; an excellent musician, singing with much and varied expression. She takes entirely the charge of the education of her son, a boy of eight to whom she dedicates much time. She speaks well on most subjects, with good sense, frankness and an absence of all affectation; but with the sort of self-satisfied pride and *délibéré* which mark the character and manners of the Russians of this day, and which has thrown quite into the background the sulky silent pride of the English.[9]

Like Stendhal, Miss Berry was impressed by Zinaida's absolute lack of affectation or grandness. She was clearly delighted with her, and the feelings must have been mutual, for she was invited again three nights later. This time the Princess was staging and singing in the title role in Rossini's *Tancredi*:

Very well acted; costumes perfect; and she herself had quite the air of a noble cavalier. The accessories wonderfully well arranged, and altogether it made a very pretty little spectacle, and a very agreeable evening.

The costumes and accessories so much admired by Miss Berry had been designed and made by Barbieri. He was a very talented stage designer, responsible for the sets and costumes of all Zinaida's opera productions, including her costume and the sets for an opera of her own composition, *Giovanna d'Arco*.[10]

Soon after her arrival in Rome, Zinaida had joined the Accademia Filarmonica where she continued to study music and composition. Now she was composing an opera. The Italian libretto which she also wrote herself was adapted from Schiller, with Galberg helping her to translate from the German. The three-act opera, entitled *Giovanna d'Arco, Dramma per Musica ridotto da Schiller*, was published in 1821. Zinaida wrote a charming preface in Italian in which she apologises to those 'born under the lovely skies of the most beautiful country in the world' for her inadequate command of Italian, and for music whose meters were meant for other languages.[11] She had intended this work to be performed only in her tiny theatre. Now that it was being published she begs indulgence for her 'poor Joan', since destiny has decreed that she should be known to a wider audience. Zinaida sang the title role of Joan of Arc in her household theatre in Rome, and was later painted by Bruni in her costume.

One of the first people with whom the Princess made contact in Rome was her old friend Cardinal Consalvi. As Secretary of State of the Vatican and the Papal States, he would have greeted any distinguished visitor to Rome. Consalvi numbered many prominent women among his friends. Madame de Boigne thought him as good as he was intelligent[12] while the Duchess of Devonshire, though a Protestant, remained devoted to him for more than twenty years. In a letter to Lord Byron in August 1821 from Spa, she promises to use any influence she may have in Rome, where she had lived for many years. Apparently in response to Byron's strong doubts about the restored order in Rome, she reassures him:

> Believe me also that there is a character of justice, goodness, and benevolence in the present Government of Rome. – Of Consalvi it is truly said, '*il a établi une nouvelle politique formée sur la vérité et la franchise. L'estime de toute l'Europe le paye ses fatigues.*'

(He has established a new form of politics based on truth and openness, and is respected by all Europe for it.)[13] In a telling postscript, she adds, 'I give up the Austrian Government to all you choose to say of them.'

Stendhal, who did not know the Cardinal and was bitterly opposed to the Church, nevertheless respected him. Writing about the staging of Rossini's masterpiece *The Barber of Seville* in Rome in 1816, and Consalvi's involvement in the censorship of parts of it, he remarks:

> Could one possibly believe that a statesman like Cardinal Consalvi, a man who knows how to rule – his master above all, and the state not too badly – and who once had the wit to be an intimate friend of Cimarosa, would waste three hours, scanning the words of a miserable libretto of an *opera buffa*?[14]

In Zinaida the Cardinal was welcoming not only a friend, but also someone with significant political and social connections, particularly with the Tsar. The Vatican was still preoccupied with the question of Roman Catholicism in Russia, both in terms of the Church's independence and authority in the appointment of Catholic clergy there, and in the treatment of the Jesuits who had just been banished from Russia. One of the Cardinal's main aims was the conversion of Russian Orthodoxy to Roman Catholicism – indeed, in the previous two decades, a number of prominent Russians had been converted and he was anxious that nothing should impede the process. Consalvi may also have had a secondary aim – to bring about the conversion of Zinaida herself and to persuade her to leave her money to the Church. While their relationship had its practical side, it was undoubtedly based on great personal affinity and developed into a warm and loving friendship. The Cardinal, then in his late sixties, became something of a father figure to Zinaida, taking an interest in her various activities and in the welfare of her son. Zinaida turned to him, just as she always did to the Tsar, for everything from help with clearing her heavy luggage through customs to finding jobs for, or otherwise helping, her many friends and dependants. Busy as he was with affairs of state, the all-powerful Cardinal was always delighted to be of service to her:

> If you think I could possibly forget ... anything that comes from you, then I tell you you do not know yourself and you do not know me either. My devotion to your incomparable person will be your gage that I will not forget M. Oloué. It is I who should thank you for accepting the little or almost nothing that I do for you,

he wrote on 22 October 1821.

He was a frequent guest at her house. A letter from the music-loving Cardinal (19 January 1822) accepts Zinaida's invitation to come and hear 'the incomparable Curioni', a famous and very handsome singer from the San Carlo in Naples, then singing in Rome.[15] He hopes to get away in time from a reception given by Count Apponyi, the Austrian ambassador, whose wife Thérèse was also a friend of Zinaida's.

*   *   *

The 1820s were marked by uprisings and revolts all over Europe. In the years immediately following the Napoleonic wars there was famine, the result of several bad harvests and economic depression. Thousands of unemployed ex-soldiers caused great hardship everywhere. The five great powers, Austria, Britain, France, Prussia and Russia, were wary of social revolution. The Congress system which they had set in place to police Europe soon began to crack, however, under the strain of the differences which appeared between them. In Britain, both Castlereagh and Canning after him had supported a policy of non-intervention in the internal affairs of the Continent. In France opinion would swing from rigid absolutism to more moderate views while the three signatories of the Holy Alliance, Austria, Prussia and Russia, were determined to stamp out liberalism and uphold legitimacy everywhere.

At the Congress of Troppau, in October 1820, they reaffirmed their right to overthrow all revolutionary governments which they considered a danger to other states. Castlereagh was alone in protesting vehemently against any such action. In February 1821, the Tsar went to Laibach (Lubliana) to attend another of the regular congresses which had been set up in 1815. Revolutionary secret societies, chief among them the Carbonari, were springing up all over Europe. This, together with a recent mutiny of the Tsar's own Semyonovsky regiment while he was attending the previous congress at Troppau, had greatly upset Alexander. Torn between the impossibility of reconciling liberal and absolutist principles, and mistrusting his own advisers, the Tsar once again turned to Metternich for guidance. Metternich was only too happy to provide it, later writing: 'He regards Capo d'Istria as a chief among the Carbonari. He distrusts his army, his ministers, his nobles, his people. A man cannot lead in such a state of mind.'[16]

Alexander wrote to Zinaida from Laibach. After his usual reassurances as to how much he thinks of her, he wrote wistfully:

As you say we are quite close and yet I dare not hope that I shall have the chance of seeing you – if it was only up to me I would move the Conference of Laibach to Rome, but there are so many things in this world that one cannot arrange as one would wish![17]

Zinaida had been pressing him to come to Rome, doubtless at the request of Cardinal Consalvi who attached great importance to such a visit. Alexander had accepted the Pope's invitation at first, but later he thought better of it. It was thought at the time that the Empress Dowager, alarmed by the Tsar's mystical turn of mind and fearing the influence of the Catholic Church, had dissuaded him.

The Carboneria was a secret society. Some of its followers wanted constitutional government, others merely wanted more freedom, or some changes. A generalised protest movement at first, it became more focused on nationalism later. There were cells of Carbonari all over Italy, but it was especially strong in the Neapolitan army. A revolt in July 1820 had forced the Spanish Bourbon King Ferdinand to adopt a constitution and the Neapolitans made similar demands. The King of Naples, however, responded by calling on Austrian assistance to suppress the insurgents. This provoked strong fears of a revolutionary counter-attack in Rome, although the indefatigable Miss Berry, writing in her journal on 7 February 1821, seemed unworried:

> In the night an estafette (courier) arrived here, announcing to the Austrians that their army had passed the Po, and were on their march to Naples in three columns – so there is no more hope for the poor Neapolitans!

A papal proclamation was pasted on the walls of Rome announcing the Pope's neutrality, and requiring his subjects not to treat the Austrians as an enemy. Miss Berry, her sympathies clearly with the Neapolitan revolutionaries and her imagination running riot, speculates on what the Neapolitans might do. If the regular army can't make it to Rome perhaps irregular troops together with some of the bandit gangs which then infested the countryside might come and ransack the treasury, kidnapping some of the richest bankers and nobles to be ransomed later? Or the banditi might unite and, having released the galley slaves in the Castel Sant'Angelo, 'pillage the town for several hours, retiring to the mountains with their newly acquired allies (who would certainly have all declared themselves to a man *Carbonari*, before any regular defence could be made,' she writes breathlessly.[18]

It was the season of the Carnival. The Romans, torn between their traditional celebrations and the imminent arrival of Austrian troops, prepared for both with their customary gusto. The Austrian Embassy had just moved to the recently refurbished Palazzo Venezia and the Emperor of Austria's great ball and supper were held there on 12 February as planned in spite of the general feeling against him. Even the English, though indignant at Austria's conduct, couldn't, it seems, resist the party. On the day after the ball, however, Zinaida got a hurried note from Consalvi, telling her that the Vatican had just received a warning from the governor of Albano some twenty kilometres south of Rome, that the revolutionary Neapolitan forces were approaching Rome via Velletri, and urging her to leave at once. The Pope, he added, was himself leaving Rome.[19] Zinaida stayed in Rome, however, and was unconcerned enough to give another of her musical parties on the 27th, singing in Cimarosa's opera, *Gli Orazi e i Curiazi*.[20] 'She herself taking the part of the Curiace wonderfully well in singing, expression and grace. Madame Renaudin as Sabine, good for the music but not for the acting,' reported Zinaida's faithful admirer, Miss Berry.

Thereafter, throughout the ten days of the Carnival, the population of Rome and the foreign community divided their time between gawping at the Austrian troops near the Ponte Molle and enjoying the Carnival processions along the Corso. On the morning after Zinaida's performance as the Curiace, Miss Berry was again on hand to describe the arrival of the Austrian troops, having managed to secure a good vantage point:

> Several open carriages by the Corso (for we were *en plein Carneval*), filled with grotesque masks, had prolonged their drive hither to the great amusement of the Austrian cavalry, as they passed by![21]

During that same revolutionary spring of 1821, the Tsar was faced with another nationalist uprising nearer to home, when one of his own aides-de-camp, Alexander Ipsilanti, crossed into Turkish-held Romania at the head of a small band of Greek soldiers and called for Greek independence. Revolt soon spread all over the Peloponnese and Attica. Alexander, usually only too happy to send his troops to stifle revolt, was suddenly faced with the problem of whether to support his fellow Orthodox Christians against the legitimate Ottoman government. Public opinion in Russia was strongly pro-Greek. Capo d'Istria, Alexander's able and liberal Foreign Minister, himself a Greek, did his best to persuade the dithering Tsar to defend his fellow Christians. Metternich, who did not wish to see part of the Ottoman Empire under Russian control, managed to dissuade the Tsar from intervening. Castlereagh, concerned about the effects on the balance of power if the Tsar's armies were allowed to overrun the crumbling Ottoman Empire, had sided with Metternich. British sympathies were overwhelmingly in favour of the Greeks, however. Young liberals educated in the classics flocked to the cause of the Philhellenes, who had caught the imagination of a romantic new generation, greatly helped by figures like Lord Byron.[22]

In England, too, there had been growing radical activity as a result of economic hardships caused by the war. The 'Peterloo' massacre in Manchester in 1819 (so called in ironic reference to the great victory of the previous year), when a regiment of hussars called out to assist the local yeomanry had charged a large crowd asembled in St Peter's Field killing eleven people, was part of a series of industrial and rural riots. Castlereagh was under pressure from the mob in London following these disturbances, and deeply unpopular after the trial and subsequent unexpected death of Queen Caroline. His mental balance, by then precarious, began to slip. 'Everyone wanted the honour of cutting his throat,' wrote Countess Lieven to her lover, Metternich.[23] On 12 August 1822, worn out and deeply grieved by the attacks against him, he cut it himself with a penknife. He was succeeded as Foreign Secretary by George Canning, in spite of the King's reluctance, while Wellington was despatched to represent Britain at Verona where another Congress was to be held in the following month.

The Congress of Verona, which had been summoned principally to deal with the question of Greece, found itself having to deal first with the Spanish civil war. The affairs of Spain and France concerned Metternich rather more than the Eastern Question, and it was now Metternich who led the Congress. Britain was categorically against intervention in Spain, in France the Ultras were at first divided but the war party won, while Russia and Austria were determined to support the divine right of rulers everywhere.

In October 1822 Zinaida left Rome for Verona, summoned by the Tsar. It was a happy reunion with Alexander, their relationship now in the calmer waters of friendship. The Tsar was accompanied as always by his Chief of Staff Prince Peter Volkonsky and his wife Sophia. His Foreign Minister Nesselrode and his ambassadors to London and Paris, Lieven and Pozzo di Borgo, were also present. Alexander took up residence at the magnificent Canossa castle. Waiting for him in Verona were the Emperor Francis with Prince Metternich and his secretary Friedrich Gentz, as well as the Austrian ambassadors to St Petersburg, London and Berlin. King Friedrich William of Prussia, Napoleon's widow Marie Louise now Duchess of Parma, the Grand Duke of Tuscany, the Duke of Modena, and the Kings of Naples and Sardinia were some of the crowned heads present. Representing France was the Ultra Prime Minister, the Duc de Montmorency, accompanied by his ambassadors to the other great powers, among them Chateaubriand, then French ambassador to London, who came with the beautiful Madame Récamier. For Britain there was the Duke of Wellington accompanied by the Marquess of Londonderry, Castlereagh's brother (formerly Sir Charles Stewart), who was ambassador to Vienna and who came with his wife. In spite of his new religious zeal, the Tsar had not quite lost the habit of flirting with pretty women, especially at congresses, and Lady Londonderry soon caught his eye, to the fury of Countess de Lieven:

> Mme de Lieven does not at all like the Emperor coming so much to see me, especially as he never sees her. I have had some good scenes with her. The other day I received a note from the Emperor during dinner, and her curiosity was so excited that after repeatedly asking who it was from, she put out her thin red paw to snap at it, but Metternich, who was sitting between us, interposed and said '*Ce serait une indiscretion impardonable pour une jeunne femme de produire ses billets.*' She was not to be pacified, and as I took care she should not see the note she turned sulky.[24]

The work of the Congress was accompanied by the usual social whirl. This time it was Zinaida who outshone all the ladies present. 'I've had news of you from M. de Montmorency, dear and lovely princess,' wrote Sosthène de La Rochefoucauld from Paris. 'You find yourself on a very great stage, but your success is as certain as on smaller ones. You are the toast of Verona!' The rest of La Rochefoucauld's long letter, all about the affairs of France, was once more written with the hope that Zinaida would act as an intermediary with the Tsar, and was generally an apologia for the Ultras.

'Heading the government,' he writes, referring to the Comte de Villèle,

> is one whose intimate friend I've been for seven years, who is certainly the most distinguished of men, bringing to politics the only sure foundation which the world can count on. His moral and religious opinions are a happy guarantee of his feelings. As for me you know the feelings of deep veneration which I have for this Sovereign [Alexander]; it is extreme and his character inspires such confidence in me that I am convinced, that in perfect agreement with the King of France, it will be for those two princes to regenerate Europe, and to put politics on a new basis.

Finally he comes to the King's new favourite, Madame du Cayla, coyly referred to only by her initial, to whom he is devoted, and who has been grossly slandered. Zinaida, he is sure, would find her a sister in spirit. The Comtesse du Cayla, a beautiful and witty young woman who had captured the affections of Louis XVIII, was also a close friend of Villèle, leader of the Ultras and now President of the Council, who advised her on what to say to the King. Villèle did not like Chateaubriand who was close to the Tsar during the Congress of Verona. La Rochefoucauld probably hoped to counter Chateaubriand's more moderate influence on Alexander.[25]

Zinaida enjoyed Verona enormously. Happy in her beloved Italy, and ever more confident of her talents, the Princess was probably also delighted to be among so many Russian friends. Her friend and sister-in-law Sophia was there and had brought her daughter Alina, who was a great favourite of Zinaida's. There was also her cousin

Prince Tatishchev, the newly appointed Russian ambassador to Vienna. Everywhere in demand, she sang opera and recited French tragedy. Knowing that the otherwise unmusical Alexander liked Paisiello's operas, she privately staged his favourite, *La Bella Molinara*, as a surprise. Alexander, who, as Chateaubriand noticed, now often looked unhappy, was delighted. Zinaida always cheered him up. Madame de Lieven, her nose out of joint and not on good terms with the Tsar's entourage as a result of her affair with Metternich, wrote to her brother that while she was much enjoying Verona, 'the feminine element is weak, there is not a single woman [of distinction?]here – and those who are gathered here are thorough barbarians, so that I am the sole representative of my species.' An extraordinary remark in view of the presence in Verona of both Princesses Volkonsky, and Madame Récamier. 'Every evening the Congress assembles *chez moi.*' Metternich and Wellington are constant guests, Madame de Lieven asserts. In fact she sees everyone but her fellow Russians who, because she has been ten years in England, think of her as an Englishwoman and, because she sees Metternich so often, think of her as an Austrian.[26] The fact was that no one, least of all the Tsar, trusted Madame de Lieven.

The British had had strong reservations about the way in which the uprising in Naples had been crushed. Canning's orders to Wellington were to prevent any intervention in Spain. Another issue which was passionately felt in Britain was the slave trade. Since the Congress of Vienna, thanks to Castlereagh's and Wellington's determination, but above all to constant and heroic pressure from William Wilberforce, most of the leading maritime powers had been persuaded to abolish the slave trade, without (except for Britain) doing very much about the enforcement of the prohibition on their own nationals. The trade had, in fact, increased. Canning urged Wellington to press this subject at Verona. At loggerheads on this and every other question with the others throughout the Congress, Wellington left abruptly on 30 November, 'displeased with us all', as Metternich observed.[27]

The Congress of Verona, which ended in December 1822, was the last of the post-1815 congresses. It was not a success. The great powers parted barely able to paper over the differences between them. Canning, who wanted to scupper the congress system anyway, was well pleased with this outcome: 'Things are getting back to a wholesome state again. Every Nation for itself and God for us all,' he wrote to his ambassador. He refused to attend a congress in St Petersburg in January 1825, to discuss the Greek question. Madame de Lieven, who thought him a dangerous radical, rightly understood it as 'a complete revolution in the political system of Europe; it means the breaking up of the Alliance. In a word, it means that Mr Canning gets his own way.'[28]

Alexander returned to Russia from the last journey he would make to Western Europe in a mood of bitter disappointment. Verona had been a failure. Chateaubriand, who had had long talks with him there, remarked on the Tsar's depression and on the great change in his political position. The liberal young Tsar of 1814 had become a complete reactionary.[29]

Before he left, Zinaida had once again taken the opportunity to petition Alexander on behalf of friends and family and even of a cook, a Crimean Tartar who had been unjustly punished and sent to Siberian exile. She intervened on behalf of her friend Prince Viazemsky, whose lifelong liberal views had clashed with those of the Tsar.[30] There were problems relating to the Beloselsky property of Krestovsky Ostrov. It was the wrong moment to importune Alexander who at forty-five was not as resilient as he used to be. He was tired, cross, and disappointed with the results of the Congress, and in a mood of gloom and depression. Once again he spent hours praying. A terse note to her headed 'Brixen, 13/25 December 1822' betrays his irritation with her:

> You have sent me so many papers in your last letter that it is only fair that I should do the same. As to your papers, Madame, allow me to speak of them another time, since I haven't a spare minute at present. Please be sure of my sincere attachment to you. My respects to Princess Sophia and Alina.[31]

At the beginning of 1823 Zinaida's sister Maria (Madeleine) Vlasov and her husband came to Rome, where, unexpectedly, Vlasov died.

Nikita wrote to Barbieri in Rome, from St Petersburg to which he had returned with the Tsar after the end of the Congress of Verona, as a serving member of the Tsar's household.

> I cannot sufficiently express my gratitude to you, my dear Barbieri, for all your help and efforts concerning the funeral. It has been a tragedy for us all and a terrible one for Madeleine. It was a particular blessing from Providence that Zinaida was near her sister at the time of this fearful catastrophe. I read two of your letters to Maman Volkonsky [his mother]. She is terribly worried about Madeleine and about her financial situation. She is writing to Zinaida about this. Tell me please, Monsieur Barbieri, what has happened to the sum of 94 thousand roubles which Labensky sent recently through the commercial bank to the late lamented? He left no power of attorney. What a misfortune about the money. Please keep me posted about all developments. You know that Zinaida's health may suffer as a result. We all know that nobody could be more clear and precise than you. I count on you not to leave me without news.

In his postscript the Prince adds:

> I embrace Alexander. Tell me what effect has his uncle's death had on him? Today is the 12th anniversary of my marriage, and he was born in the same year. At 13 he is no longer a child. The Turgenevs send you their greetings.[32]

Madeleine, who had no children, must have returned to Russia soon after her husband's funeral. There is no mention of her in any of the letters written to Zinaida during the next eighteen months. Madeleine, who was left in difficult financial straits, probably went to live with her sister soon after Zinaida settled in Moscow, never to leave her again. Zinaida spent her remaining months in Rome working quietly on her romantic novel based on a history of the Slavs. Her book, the *Tableau Slave du Cinquième Siècle*, was published in Paris the following year.

Throughout her three-year stay in Rome, Zinaida remained very close to Cardinal Consalvi. Consalvi hoped that she would settle in Rome for good. Passionately fond of gardens, he presented her with some huge garden urns, almost as if he hoped that such large objects would help to anchor her.[33] Consalvi loved entertaining Zinaida and his other close women friends, the Duchess of Devonshire and Countess Albany, at his several beautiful houses around Rome. While he was a Prince of the Church, with exceptional political and diplomatic skills, it was his wisdom, kindness and genuine concern for their spiritual welfare and their happiness that made him so much loved by the people who knew him. Zinaida, although her life seemed full and gay on the surface, was dogged by depression and a sense of futility as was apparent only a few years later from letters written to her by the Archimandrite Pavsky, which show her to have been overcome by a sense of guilt and fear of death. She was much concerned about punishment for her sins. At this time Zinaida was still hoping to give greater depth and meaning to her life through the arts, but her spiritual odyssey would eventually lead her to the Catholic Church. Consalvi's letters to Zinaida show much warmth and affection, something she desperately needed and sought. Although Consalvi lived on a grand scale, he was unconcerned with riches for himself, wrote his friend and biographer Crétineau-Joly. His only personal expenses were the flowers and plants in his garden at Ponte Rotto, which was his great passion.[34]

In the summer of 1823 Zinaida suddenly decided to leave Rome for Paris. Her pretext was that Sophia had been unwell and needed her there. Still not sure of the direction her life might take, Zinaida's emotional instability, referred to indirectly as her 'illnesses' by her husband and friends, made her incurably restless. The Cardinal wrote her a sad and touching letter on the day of her departure, sending his love to 'little Alexander', wishing her a happy journey and a swift return and assuring her that she could count on him for anything which he might be able to do for her in Rome during her absence.[35]

Zinaida was welcomed to Paris with delight by her many friends. The change provided some sort of temporary respite and a week or so after her arrival she was reading 'a novel of her writing' to Miss Berry and several English friends, 'but the MS was so confused that she could not even continue it herself'. The novel in question must have been *Tableau Slave du Cinquième Siècle*, which she based on several foreign sources of the history of the Slavs, together with Karamzin's account. In the preface, Zinaida explains that she wanted to write about the customs and habits of the Slav tribes who lived along the banks of the Dnieper in the fifth century. Written in French, it is the romantic tale of an already civilised Slav chieftain, Ladovid, a member of a tribe renowned for the valour of its men, who falls in love with Miltiada, a girl from the still-savage forest tribe. He first sees her naked but for her long blonde tresses, as is the custom of the forest tribes, at the annual tribal gathering to celebrate the festival of the river god. Saving her from death at the hands of another female savage, Ladovid marries her and takes her home to his mother and sister who dress and civilise her. Miltiada is miserable among the plainsmen, and homesick for the freedom of her native forests. One day she escapes on Ladovid's faithful horse Lety. Ladovid finds her and brings her home. Touched by his love and kindness she settles down, bearing him two sons and a daughter. Finally Miltiada has a dream about her children's future, particularly her eldest son, Kiyé, who will one day found the city of Kiev.[36]

The novel, published anonymously in Paris in 1824, received wide critical acclaim. 'If Madame is not French she deserves to be; France counts her among her daughters, while the beautiful work with which she has enriched French literature must be her gage of citizenship,' wrote A. Martainville, critic of the legitimist *Drapeau Blanc*.[37] The critic Colnet of the *Gazette de France* preferred the work to 'any number of modern novels, which die as soon as they are born', praising it for its purity of language and its historical accuracy.[38] Yet another praised the unknown author, a worthy rival of French-born writers, for the delicacy and freshness of her pure harmonious style.[39]

When Zinaida arrived in Paris in early July, she renewed her acquaintance with the queen of the classical theatre – the Théâtre Français – Mademoiselle Mars. Although well into her forties, Mademoiselle Mars had recently appeared in *Tartuffe* and in *Valerie*, 'in a manner to make one cry and to quite enchant all who have taste enough and mind to appreciate her inimitable talent' wrote Miss Berry enthusiastically. After also seeing her in *Le Misanthrope* and *Les Fausses Confidences* Miss Berry thought her more perfect than ever and was delighted to be given the opportunity to meet her heroine on Monday 18 July, at a small party in her honour given by Zinaida, at which there was a group of French, English and Russian friends.

> In society she is as natural and as intelligent as upon the stage, talking with much cleverness and very willingly about her art, about Talma, and about a new piece in which she is to appear with him.[40] In short she is in the drawing-room what she is on the stage – the same charming tone of voice, the same finesse, the same simplicity. I was very glad to have seen her. Her dress is very simple, her hair without ornament – a plain muslin gown, with gold beads round her neck. We left her at Princess Zeneide's near midnight.[41]

Zinaida quickly created a salon in Paris, where one of her regular visitors was Rossini, who became the director of the Théâtre Italien in the following year. Thoroughly enjoying her artistic pursuits, she decided to spend the winter in Paris, after which it would be difficult to ignore the Tsar's insistence that she return to Russia. Her husband was once again travelling, but Barbieri had accompanied her. He was an accepted member of the family, and Nikita no less than Zinaida herself completely relied on him. Zinaida, meanwhile, continued to write, working on a prose-poem, based on her studies of Russian and Scandinavian archaeology. The poem, *Olga*, though never completed, was published posthumously by Zinaida's son. Based on the life of the eponymous heroine Princess Olga, its lyrical descriptions of nature bear witness to a real talent.[42]

In August, Zinaida received a miserable letter from Cardinal Consalvi, in reply to hers announcing her plans to stay in Paris for the winter: 'I had not expected the thunderbolt (such was your letter from Paris to me) which announced your intention of spending the winter there and then going directly to Vienna and St Petersburg in the spring, without even being able to assure me that the following winter would bring you to Rome.' They ought to reconsider their plans, the mild climate of Rome would do them both good, he begs. He is not sure that he will live long enough to see her again. Old and ill himself, the Cardinal was now shaken by the failing health of the Pope, his close friend for almost a quarter of a century. His letter also mentions the destruction by fire of the Cathedral of St Paul which had greatly saddened him. 'You were adored here, everyone misses you,' he adds. He implores her to take care of her health and not to tire herself out with 'all that her incomparable heart embraces'. The Cardinal ends with an emotional appeal to her that she turn to him for any help she might need in Rome, which would be the only compensation for her absence. 'I kiss your hand with all my heart, and beg you to believe that no one is more devoted to you for life than myself.'[43]

In October the Cardinal wrote his last existing letter to the Princess. Thanking her for two letters which reached him at the same time, he promises to look after a young man she has recommended to him, the son of friends from Odessa who was now studying in Rome. Consalvi was very touched by her loving condolences on the death of Pope Pius VII – in August 1823 – 'in which I recognise your heart, and all the nobility and excellence of your fine character.' The tenderness with which she had written to him had made him weep. Consalvi had watched over his dying friend for three days and nights. After that there had been an exhausting month during which the Conclave took place which had ended with the election of Pope Leo XII, with whom Consalvi did not get on. He is so grateful to be considered a friend, he writes; 'I am one and will be for ever. Dispose of me as something wholly yours.' When she returns, if he is still alive, she will find him as devoted as ever, he ends.[44]

Consalvi died on 10 January 1824. Zinaida kept her promise to him to return to Rome, never to leave again. That when she did so, five years later, it was as a convert to the Catholic faith undoubtedly had much to do with the Cardinal, whose death she felt keenly. Unwilling for the moment to return to Russia, especially in the winter, Zinaida stayed in Paris until June 1824, spending the rest of the summer not far from the city, at Château Brou. After a decade of wandering around Europe, she was reluctant to settle in Russia, but could no longer continue to ignore the Tsar's wishes.

PART II

Moscow

8

The End of an Era

'It seemed like the enchanted castle of a musical fairy.'

PRINCE VIAZEMSKY ABOUT ZINAIDA'S MOSCOW HOUSE

Zinaida returned to St Petersburg in late July 1824. Nikita was in Moscow but, unlike the Tsar, was unaware of her arrival and unsure of her whereabouts.[1] Two letters awaited her. The first was from Sosthène de La Rochefoucauld, lamenting her departure:

One can only love you in a manner worthy of you, of your spirit, your soul, your heart, so how can one love you half-heartedly? Accursed piece of paper, and yet one must bless it for enabling me to express the most tender friendship to you, at a month's distance![2]

The second letter, delivered by Prince Peter Volkonsky personally, was from the Tsar. Full of apologies for his silence, he had been unable to reply to her letters because he had been away travelling for almost three months on an inspection tour of the army. He had also been dangerously ill in the early part of that year after being struck down by a horse. After repeated reassurances to Zinaida that her fears that he may have something against her were totally unjustified, and that she could always count on his affection, he comes to the question she raised in her letters. 'As to your requests on behalf of your husband, what you envisaged was not feasible and was contrary to usage here. We will talk about it when we meet.' Alexander was referring to the matter of her husband's appointment to a position

[171]

at court. Nikita had not yet received a civilian post, although he had been given various commissions. The Tsar had never much liked him but Zinaida's persistence on his behalf finally bore fruit and he was soon appointed a general of the Tsar's suite.[3]

Zinaida may have been wrong in thinking that there was an estrangement between them, but it was undeniable that Alexander's mood in the past two years had been particularly sombre. Zinaida was concerned for him, understanding only too well the debilitating effects of depression. Though he was still the all-powerful Tsar, in many ways their situations were reversed. In the early days of their friendship soon after her marriage, it was Zinaida who was struggling through depression and unhappiness while Alexander, young and at his zenith, was about to become the 'saviour of Europe'. Now, a decade later, Zinaida was a successful and confident woman in her mid-thirties, while Alexander, in his late forties, broken by disappointments and undermined by his all-pervading sense of guilt, seemed an old man. No sooner had she arrived in St Petersburg than she wrote him several encouraging letters. Knowing that his doctors had recommended a fruit diet after his illness, she sent him some, together with a copy of her *Tableau Slave*. Touched by her care, Alexander replied at once. In a short, undated note he asks if he might come and visit her after dinner. His longer letter expresses all of his former affectionate warmth, and a genuine sense of pleasure, so absent from his life at this time:

> I am at your feet, Princess, for the very kind note which I have just received. The joy of seeing you again is too great for any other feelings and I beg permission to present myself to you this evening. I am so much looking forward to it. – It is with the greatest gratitude that I received the lovely fruit which you sent me in your infinite goodness. – with respectful attachment.[4]

Zinaida's letter, full of praise and encouragement, was balm to his soul though Alexander believed her to be treating him far too kindly. He was confined to his palace, seeing almost no one, and she was an old friend with whom he shared so many memories. Above all, he trusted her. Her devoted friendship was one of the few things which the inreasingly paranoiac and lonely Tsar could still count on, and which gave him pleasure in what was to be the last year of his life.

Zinaida's return to Russia, now as a mature and confident woman whose friendship with the Tsar was closer than ever, brought another letter from La Rochefoucauld announcing both private and public griefs – the death of his own third child, and that of King Louis XVIII. After long descriptions of the King's last moments and his customary special pleading for the noble bearing of Madame du Cayla, he described the entrance of Charles X in Paris amid, as he saw it, great popular enthusiasm. 'For the moment the first acts of his reign leave nothing to be desired and everything to be hoped,' wrote La Rochefoucauld, who had just been made the King's aide-de-camp in charge of the arts.[5] The truth, however, was that Charles X's reception had been distinctly lukewarm. His reign, which lasted five years, was characterised by uncompromising reactionary stupidity, ensuring the final fall of the Bourbons in 1830.

That autumn in St Petersburg, the Tsar had to face fresh woes when, on 7 November, the Neva, swollen by south-westerly gales, broke its banks. More than 500 people lost their lives as the furious river tore through the city, bringing down bridges, destroying houses, and flooding cellars. The catastrophe deeply affected the Tsar, intensifying his feelings of guilt: the devastation of his beloved city must be another punishment for his sins. Pushkin later immortalised the flood in his poem *The Bronze Horseman*, using it as an allegory of the crushing power of the state over the individual. In it, his humble hero Evgeny, whom the flood deprives of his beloved and his future, sees the cause of all his misfortune in a hallucinatory come-to-life bronze statue of Peter the Great, who, regardless of the human cost, had arrogantly built the city on a marsh prone to flooding.

Moscow, to which Zinaida moved later that month, had now become the centre of intellectual and artistic life. Far from the court and the repressive influence of Arakhcheev, it enjoyed greater intellectual freedom. Zinaida had always preferred the old capital. Once again she moved into the magnificent neo-classical Beloselsky Palace surrounded by gardens, on the corner of the Tverskaya. The palace boasted a beautiful private theatre designed and decorated by Barbieri, with the motto 'Ridendo Dicere Verum' inscribed above the stage which was flanked on either side by busts of Molière and Cimarosa.[6] Here the Princess began to entertain at her famous Monday soirées. Before long her salon had attracted all that was best in Moscow. 'Writers and painters turned to the Princess as to a Maecenas. She made everybody feel at ease. – She had the gift of bringing everyone together. Everything about this outstanding woman breathed grace and poetry,' wrote her admiring friend A. N. Muraviev.[7]

Zinaida's return to Moscow and the success of her salon, which became the hub of an extraordinary gathering of talent, coincided with a new philosophy in Russian intellectual life, and new perceptions of the role of the artist in society. The near-veneration of the artist in Russia, which persisted throughout century, followed logically from romantic philosophy, particularly that of Schelling, who had believed philosophy to be closer to art than to science. The artist became at once priest and prophet, the keeper of the sacred flame, and, most importantly in Russia, the discoverer of a national identity. While art was not yet required to carry a strong social message, it was already being seen as a force which could transform society. As censorship gripped the country in the last years of Alexander's reign, to be intensified in that of his successor – his brother Nicholas – literature became the only medium for the free expression of philosophical or political opinion. Those few in Russia who had a key to this magic kingdom created the 'intelligentsia'. In the years following the Decembrist revolt of 1825, which profoundly shocked Zinaida's generation, a generation brought up on the values of the Enlightenment and with a belief in progress, educated Russians had been forced to realise that they were different. The state remained oppressive, indeed became more so, while their Western education had actually widened the gulf between them and the great mass of the people. The questions of what it meant to be Russian and of the nature of Russian culture and identity assumed immense importance.

The first of the literary journals, the so-called 'thick journals' (*tolstiye journali*), which were to play such an important role in the development of that culture, was founded by Prince Vladimir Odoevsky and the poet Küchelbecker, two close friends of Zinaida's who became the mainstay of her salon. Entitled *Mnemosyne*, it was intended to help create a truly Russian poetry. Throughout the 1820s poetry was considered the purest and greatest of the arts. For the next half-century, the 'thick journals' gave an unprecedented moral authority to literary critics, of whom the radical firebrand Vissarion Belinsky was the greatest and most influential. Belinsky believed that literature was not merely an agreeable intellectual pastime but the best medium for the dissemination of ideas which would change society. Far from being a mere utilitarian propagandist, however, he believed that beauty of form was an essential component of art. As Russia sank into the repression of Nicholas's reign, the journals became the main forum for political, philosophical and social discussion.

Moscow University was still a centre of intellectual life. Two successive curators, Prince Golytsin and Count Stroganov, both Zinaida's friends and kinsmen, had attracted many interesting professors, around whom formed small discussion groups, known as *krushki*, or circles. Professors Pavlov and Daviydov were noted followers of Schelling. Another of these circles, called the Obshestvo Liubomudria or the Society of Lovers of Wisdom, centred on Prince Odoevsky in whose house they met on Saturday nights. Among its members were the philosopher Ivan Kireevsky, the poet Dimitri Venevitinov and his brother Alexander, Professors Shevyrev and Pogodin, Melgunov, and Sobolevsky and Chaadaev. All of them became regulars at Zinaida's salon.

In 1824, Griboyedov's masterpiece *Gore ot Uma*, usually translated in English as *Woe from Wit*, was circulating in Moscow in samizdat form. A brilliant satire of Moscow high society, it was staged only in 1831, and then heavily cut. The embittered aristocratic hero, Chatsky, many of whose satirical asides at once entered everyday speech, was the personification of the deep disappointment and frustration felt by his generation at the end of Alexander's reign. Young men of vision and energy with a Western liberal education and a wish to change society saw service to an increasingly repressive state as pointless and shaming. 'I'd love to serve, but am sickened by servility,' says Chatsky, the prototype of the 'superfluous man', the recurring hero of Russian literature, alienated, cynical, inactive and doomed.

Zinaida's house became a natural magnet for several of these circles.

The Princess, influential, rich and beautiful, was now known for her literary talents as well as her lovely voice. Her *Tableau Slave*, translated into Russian, had been published in several Moscow journals, together with the highly flattering opinions of French literary critics. Her salon swiftly assumed a central role in the intellectual life of Moscow: the meeting place not only of her more talented aristocratic friends, but of university professors, artists of all kinds, state officials and journalists. Her love of all the arts, and her wish to learn more about her own country, attracted the most gifted and interesting of Moscow's intelligensia to her circle. She treated everyone with the same simple friendliness, with the same sympathetic interest in their troubles, and a readiness to believe the best of everyone.

At the end of March 1825, Zinaida paid a short visit to St Petersburg. She always avoided the gloomy Volkonsky residence on the Moika, presided over by her stiff-necked old mother-in-law, and stayed instead at her family house, the Beloselsky Palace, just missing the arrival of her new sister-in-law. Sergei Volkonsky had recently married the twenty-year-old Maria Raevsky in Kiev. The daughter of General Nicolai Nicolaevich Raevsky, hero of the battle of Borodino, Maria was a slender, dark-eyed young beauty almost twenty years younger than her husband. Lonely and unhappy in the northern capital after a childhood spent in the sunny Ukraine, Maria had gladly accompanied her husband on his military posting to the headquarters of the Second Army in Tulchin, in southern Russia. In May the young couple were in Uman, where Sergei was to take command of the ninth division.

Maria later described those days, when she was newly pregnant and unwell as a result of a chest infection:

> I was sent off with my mother and my English governess, to Odessa for some sea bathing. Sergei couldn't accompany us as he had to remain with his division. I had hardly known him before our wedding, and as I remained in Odessa all summer, we had only really spent three months of the first year of our marriage together.[8]

Although Sergei loved her and she greatly admired him – 'the most worthy and honourable of men' – he was busy with his regiment and fatally busy as a member of a secret organisation. When Maria and Zinaida met in Moscow, it was to be under tragic circumstances.

On 2 April, Easter Day, while Zinaida was in St Petersburg, a letter arrived from the Tsar from Tsarskoe Selo:

> To treat me with such kindness, when you could have well thought me ungrateful and insensitive, is a measure of the boundless indulgence you have always shown me; and yet I am neither. The huge burden which weighs on me and takes up all my strength, may make me seem so. But let me tell you first that my joy at knowing you to be so near, of seeing you in a few hours, is extreme. I shall be at your door between four and five, in the greatest impatience to be able to express to you in person, how touched I am by the friendly way you treat me in spite of my sins. Having so little time to myself, I waited to reply until I had managed to arrange what you asked. It has taken time because there were several problems in the way.[9] Farewell then and please accept the assurance of the sincere and respectful attachment which I bear you for ever.[10]

And indeed, only sincere attachment could have brought the Tsar out to visit Zinaida on Easter Day, the most important day in the Orthodox calendar, and only two days before he was to set off on a journey to Poland on 4 April. It was his last letter to her and this would be their final meeting.

While in St Petersburg, Zinaida also renewed her friendship with the poet Kozlov, who was by then completely blind and paralysed. Passionately fond of music, he was a friend of the composers Glinka and Dargomyzhsky. In spite of his physical disabilities, his spirited and warm personality kept his circle of musical and literary friends at his bedside. Among them were Krylov, Griboyedov, Viazemsky, Alexander Turgenev and Baratinsky. Kozlov, who kept an intermittent diary, was completely entranced by Zinaida. Blind since 1821, he immortalised her looks in a poem written in 1825, so he must have met her on one of her previous visits to St Petersburg, either before she went abroad in the Tsar's suite in 1813 or during her subsequent visit in 1817. Of their first meeting he writes in his poem:

I only remember that I saw/the singer's form beyond compare/Oh I remember with what fire/ her blue eyes shone/ and the golden curls weaving around her young head,/ her ethereal figure – I remember the sound of her voice/as one remembers a cherished feeling / and whatever is dear on earth /when she sings, becomes more precious.

An entry in his diary for 14 April 1825 records a visit to Zinaida when he presented her with a copy of his long poem *The Monk*:

I went to the residence of Princess Beloselsky to see Princess Zinaida Volkonsky. The charming Zinaida treated me with such touching tenderness. I read a poem which I had dedicated to her. She enchanted me with an aria from *Paresi* and the song 'Isolina Veluti'. She sings marvellously: she has everything – voice, youth, soul – and she sang for me! I recited my 'Venetian Night' to her from memory. She spoke with such grace, this musical Zinaida, truly a romantic Peri! I came back home, with my heart full of her. She has sworn me the most tender friendship for ever.[11]

The Princess did not stay long in St Petersburg, returning to Moscow as soon as she could. She had toyed with the idea of another journey to Europe, perhaps to Spain now that the war was over, but too much was happening in Russia that was of real interest to her. Sophia and Alina had gone to Paris in June. That Zinaida did not go with them was a sign of great change in her. A letter from La Rochefoucauld, dated 1 June, confirms their arrival, and laments Zinaida's absence. It would have been wonderful to travel to Spain together, he tells Zinaida:

Like you, I was opposed to this war, so long as I thought it avoidable. But the situation had deteriorated. The honour of France, the upholding of the principles of civilisation, the country's safety, and Europe's interest had all made it impossible to hesitate.

The remainder of La Rochefoucauld's letter is concerned with his usual theme: the unimpeachable virtue of Madame du Cayla, and the

rightness and goodness of the King and his ministers. He was determined to present the case of the Ultras at every opportunity.[12]

Soon after her arrival in Russia, Zinaida had embarked on an
earnest study of the Russian language which she was anxious to
resume. Surrounded by literary figures at a time when a true Russian
literature was just emerging, she had been stung by criticism following
the publication of her *Tableau Slave* in Russia. Some declared that she
was really a French writer. Her friend Prince Viazemsky, however,
writing to Alexander Turgenev about her first publication, thought
that her novella *Laure* was full of sensitive observations and beautifully
expressed. Shevyrev also praised her writing, but expressed the wish
that she had learned Russian in her childhood. Zinaida was determined
to learn her native language properly and was also engaged in the
study of early Russian history. This was necessary for her prose-poem,
Olga, about the saint and princess from whom the Beloselskys claimed
descent. She was studying under the Swiss historian Baron André
Mérian and the Russian orientalist Gulianov. Zinaida had also
developed an interest in Russian popular culture, collecting songs,
proverbs, legends and superstitions on which she made many notes.

In 1825, Zinaida's *Letters from Italy* were published in the Petersburg
journal, *Northern Flowers*, in her own Russian translation. The journal's
editor, Delvig, was criticised by the literary critic of the *Son of the Fatherland* for publishing the work of someone who was obviously not a Russian writer, but rather a French one. Zinaida must have been hurt and
discouraged by this as well as by the disapproval openly expressed by
some members of Moscow society who wondered why a woman in her
position could not be satisfied with being simply a social ornament. Her
friend the diplomat Prince Kozlovsky tried to comfort her:

Do not be distracted from your path by the mockery of these cold,
ignorant souls. Society has its points, but not when it comes to serious
matters. One can only pity them. Please keep alive for your friends
that source which refreshes and renews whatever it touches.[13]

Despite criticism of her Russian, Zinaida's history of the Slavs
was well received and she was praised by several academics for her
knowledge and research into the period. In October she was elected

an honorary member of the Society of History and Russian Antiquities, the first woman to be so honoured. Her letter of acceptance on 10 November was addressed to the president and written in Russian. Expressing her thanks for the signal honour, she asks him to 'assure the honourable members of my sincere readiness to justify in any way possible, their kind opinion of me'.[14]

The Princess certainly improved her command of the Russian language sufficiently to be able to write more easily, but for all her efforts her real language clearly remained French, as it did for most of her generation and class. As the Slavophile writer Ivan Kireevsky wrote a few years later:

> Not to speak French is still impossible; such is the education of our society. But at least whoever has begun to write now writes in Russian, and probably it is no longer possible to think of examples of Russian talent taken away from Russia by French literature. There is no need to add that I am thinking here of a writer who has given a poetic account of the life of our ancient Slavs, but to French literature. Can you tell me, to whom has nature given more means to influence the success of the fine arts in Russia? Born with a poetic spirit, open to all that is beautiful, gifted with the rarest talents, educated in the most refined enlightenment, surrounded from earliest childhood with the most shining examples of art, – she herself seemed one of the happiest and most delicate creations of fate. What others dreamed of from afar, what they guessed at from hearsay, to her was alive and accessible. All the rarities of European culture, all the marvels of enlightened countries: great painting, famous writers, historical figures, today's great men, – all this flowed quickly and brightly before her eyes, all this could only leave precious traces on her young imagination; – she could have shared it all with her countrymen, been a wonderful bridge between them and the most noteworthy achievements of a century of enlightenment – but this was not to be.[15]

When Alexander returned to Russia from Poland in June 1825, he found the Empress in very poor health. The doctors recommended that she should winter in a warmer climate. Italy and France were rejected by the Empress herself who wished to be nearer home. Finally, it was decided that the Imperial couple should spend the winter in Taganrog, on the Sea of Azov. In November, however, disturbing rumours began to circulate in Moscow about the Tsar's health. Charlotte Disbrowe, the wife of the British minister in St Petersburg, was writing a letter describing a ball where she had chaperoned Alina Volkonsky:

My charge looked extremely well though she would wear her old black ballgown. She had pink marabouts in her hair, and her mother's emeralds and diamonds on.

Suddenly, on 27 November, news came of the Tsar's death.

Little did I think to add such a postscript. The Emperor is dead. Only six days ill; of typhus fever. The poor Empress Elizabeth had the melancholy consolation of being with him the whole time and of performing the last duties of a wife. She has known little of the happiness of one, poor thing, but he had returned to her latterly, and they were united at the last. – The poor old Empress [Dowager] learnt it this morning, and dropped as if shot on reading the news. They thought she was gone also, for as she is laced from head to foot, she turned quite black directly. The Grand Duke Constantine succeeds.[16]

Taking her daughter Alina for company, Sophia immediately set off for Taganrog to be with the Empress and to accompany her on her return journey to St Petersburg. As a general of the Imperial suite, Nikita too hurried down to Taganrog to accompany the Tsar's body back to St Petersburg via Moscow, where his remains were to lie in state for three days. Zinaida remained in Moscow with her son. In her anguish at the death of a man she had loved deeply, she collected eyewitness accounts of Alexander's last days. She also wrote her first poem in Russian, 'To Alexander I', which she set to music in a cantata.[17] In her notes of Alexander's last days, later published by her son, Zinaida gives an account of the Tsar's premonition of his death. General Diebitsch, who had accompanied the Tsar as he left

St Petersburg, told Zinaida that as they were crossing the Nevsky bridge Alexander, who normally would enthuse about the beauty of the city, this time looked back at the capital attentively, wordlessly and with an expression of deep sadness and regret. On his way to Taganrog, while he was in the south, Alexander had agreed to go on an inspection tour of the Crimea. Zinaida continues:

A few days before His Majesty's departure for the Crimea, the Emperor was working in his study. The weather was wonderful. Suddenly clouds covered the sky and it became so dark that he was obliged to call for candles; then suddenly, the weather changed again, the sun came out and Anisimov returned without candles. 'I notice you haven't brought candles,' said the Emperor. 'I expect it's because you were afraid that if you appeared with lighted candles in brilliant sunshine, people would think there was a dead person in the room. The very same thought had crossed my mind.'[18]

On his return to Taganrog from the inspection tour of the Crimea, with which the Emperor had been very pleased, he said to Anisimov as he came into the room: 'Do you remember that you didn't want to give me any candles, and I guessed the reason? You know, I think it is highly likely that it will all come to pass.'

It was in that very room that the Emperor breathed his last on 19 November 1825 at 10.50 a.m.[19]

In February, Zinaida poured out her anguish in a letter to her friend and teacher, the Baron Mérian. She had never really been able to see Alexander clearly. Even at the end of his life when there was scarcely a trace left of the idealistic young Tsar she had first known, the image of the chivalrous knight was the one she always carried with her, an image which was reinforced by what came later. Though increasingly reactionary at the end of his reign, Alexander had, as Herzen remarked, the enormous advantage of being sandwiched between his mad father and his uncompromisingly repressive brother. To Zinaida, however, he would always remain her beloved friend. Now she wrote to Mérian:

I have already spoken to you of my pain and of that of all Russia. Europe shares it and therefore understands. It is a colossal misfortune, but above all nothing can console me and others for the loss of our angel of protection, our angel of consolation, who guarded our peace, our happiness, our future.

I shall tell you in detail about his illness and of what happened. These cruel memories console me in my agony. It is still as if his beloved remains have left Moscow this very day. I can still see the black sheets hanging from the windows and balconies of every house and I ask myself: for whom is all this?

My heart bleeds. Could it really be the body of the Emperor Alexander who has just passed through these streets? How is this possible? These very same streets where only a few years ago he inspired such joy and enthusiasm, where people would stop his horses to look at him, where the same people tore his handkerchief to pieces so that each might keep a shred. Can this really be him!

My courage failed me as the heartbreaking procession passed beneath my windows. I did fulfil my duty at Kolomenskoe, some seven versts from here, where they had stopped for the night before entering Moscow. It was there that I prostrated myself beside the coffin and prayed for him. There were no crowds, almost no movement in the church where the Emperor had been placed. Only a few peasants, a few local women who, like myself, had come to kiss the sorrowful bier, around which stood those of his aides-de-camp who were on duty that night. The priest was chanting prayers; his voice the only sound. How can I describe what I felt? My heart failed me. How can I describe what I felt when, in the darkness, I glimpsed the funeral carriage that had brought him here from Taganrog standing by the church door. I who used to be so happy when I caught sight of his travelling coach bringing him back into our midst, when I would say to myself: I shall see him soon; I shall hear him speak with that grace which was his alone.

Zinaida describes the 'heartbreaking and tragic' way in which the Empress Dowager heard the news while attending a Te Deum in her chapel. She went there every day to pray for her son's recovery. That day, she had just received better news. Suddenly, Grand Duke

Nicholas entered and said to the priest, 'Present the cross to my mother.' 'The Empress Maria understood at once, took the cross and holding it to her bosom, fainted.'

In her long letter, Zinaida spares no detail. Prince Peter Volkonsky supervised all the ceremonial duties, a task which he performed 'with the zeal of a most tender friend' in spite of the huge difficulties of finding all that was needed in the midst of the steppes, in a town with no resources. But, Zinaida goes on, everything was perfect and worthy of the dignity of the man. The funeral cortège left for Moscow. 'From town to town it passed amid funeral chanting or a religious silence. Sometimes the Russian people, especially the women, would express their pain in words inspired by the sadness of the moment.' Zinaida continues her account:

The Tsar's coachman Ilya, who had never left his side and who had been a familiar figure to everyone in Paris in 1814, himself drove the funeral carriage from Taganrog. Hearing the peasants along their route say that it couldn't be the Tsar, that the Tsar wasn't dead, he replied:

'My friends, how can you doubt it, would I be here if it wasn't him?' and when they recognised him they all said;

'It is Ilya, we can believe him.'

When they reached Moscow, the Court Chamberlain explained the procedures of the solemn procession through the city to Count Orlov-Denisov. 'But where is Ilya?' asked the general. He would never allow anyone else to drive the funeral carriage. The Court Chamberlain explained that the occasion demanded that the coachman be properly dressed in ceremonial clothes, and without a beard. Gently, the Tsar's aide-de-camp tried to break the news to Ilya:

'As you have a beard,' he said, 'they say that you may not drive the carriage in Moscow.'

'Well then, I'll shave my beard off,' replied Ilya with no hesitation.

You know how important the beard is to a man of the people in Russia. Ilya kept his beard. He is a man of about sixty. Never was anyone seen to weep so much. They had wanted to paint his portrait for me then, but it was impossible to catch his features, altered as they had become by the truest and most simple pain. Nothing could be more touching than that man, driving his master for the last time.

A small crown of laurel and everlasting flowers was found on the coffin and everyone believed that these were from Zinaida, but she denies it in her letter to the Baron Mérian:

It was thought that they were from me; no, I was too upset. I wrote some Russian verses, the first in my mother tongue; and I am setting them to music. I needed to express the feelings flooding my heart.

The Empress Elizabeth had been touched by them, and his mother too, Zinaida writes, but she had not done it for them. 'My soul was comforted when I had paid him this tribute, it was what I needed to do.'[20]

The last years of Alexander's reign had been overshadowed by growing disappointment among young liberals about the failure to abolish serfdom and to establish basic freedoms in Russia. Indeed, Russia was moving decisively in the opposite direction. Young men, changed by their experience of the Napoleonic war and with contact with Western life, wanted political and social change in their own country. They also argued for reforms adapted to suit Russia rather than the imposition of other countries' ideas. Patriotism and nationalism were high on the agenda when the Union of Salvation was set up in 1816, later to be replaced by the Union of Welfare (Soyuz Blagodenstvia), better known as the Green Book, from the colour of the cover of its statutes. The Green Book incorporated the declared aims of the Union of Welfare. These were to co-operate with the government in promoting greater civic responsibility, philanthropic activities, justice, education, and morality. The other, secret half concerned political change. In 1821 the Union of Welfare, aware that the authorities were about to close in, pretended to disband. Dividing in two, the Union emerged as the first revolutionary group in Russia, later known as the

Decembrists after their failed uprising in December 1825, immediately following Alexander's death.

The Decembrist movement, made up mostly of aristocratic young officers of the Imperial army, had two branches. The Northern Society in St Petersburg, led by Nikita Muraviev, was essentially reformist, in favour of a fairly conservative constitutional monarchy. Prince Trubetskoy, Nicolai Turgenev, and Princes Obolensky, Odoevsky and Bestushev were among the members of this group. Among the civilian minority who joined it were the idealistic poet Conrad Ryleev who, in a perpetual mood of breast-baring, romantic self-sacrifice, urged more radical measures. The Southern Society, based at Tulchin, the headquarters of the Second Army, was revolutionary. This much more radical, indeed republican group was led by the intellectual political firebrand, Colonel Pavel Pestel, who, as well as believing in the abolition of the monarchy and in free enterprise, was also a passionate nationalist zealot who believed in colonising the borderlands, and then enforcing Russification. Assimilation would be compulsory; Jews, being more difficult to assimilate, should, he believed, be deported to form their own state in Asia Minor. Poles were to be treated as a special case – allowed to become an independent republic but obliged to swear perpetual alliance with Russia. Pestel was joined by the highly idealistic Sergei Muraviev-Apostol. Sergei Volkonsky, who also joined this radical group, first met Pestel in 1819 in Tulchin when he stopped there on his way to visit his sister-in-law Zinaida, in Odessa. He recorded the meeting:

> There were many young thinkers there [in Tulchin], among them Adjutant Pavel Ivanovich Pestel, a man of exceptional intelligence and education, in whose heart burned the noblest feelings of patriotism.[21]

Another of Zinaida's friends closely connected with the Decembrists was the Polish poet Adam Mickiewicz, who had been imprisoned by the Russian authorities in 1823 for belonging to a student brotherhood, The Philomathians, and banished to Russia. He arrived in St Petersburg in 1824 where he met Ryleev through his friend Pushkin. Ryleev, in turn, gave him letters of introduction to Pestel and Muraviev when

Mickiewicz was banished to the Crimea in October 1824. Describing a meeting in Ryleev's house in St Petersburg, Mickiewicz recalled a romantic scene: Odoevsky, Bestushev and the other officers, their tunic buttons undone, some sporting high Byronic cravats, sprawled on sofas and deep windowsills in the thick blue haze of cigar smoke, drinking toasts of 'Death to the Tsar', proposed by their young host, Ryleev, 'his jet black eyes alive with an inner flame'.[22]

Mickiewicz was loved by all his Russian friends and trusted absolutely by the Decembrist conspirators. An outstanding gift for poetry was combined with a no less remarkable facility for improvisation, which aroused the admiration of all who knew him. Mickiewicz and Zinaida shared a passion for music. It was often music that would inspire the poet to improvise. Like Zinaida, he had an extraordinary capacity for friendship. Pushkin, Polevoi and all his friends noticed how there was no bitterness in him towards his Russian oppressors. Although fierce in his opposition to the Tsar's government, and in his love for his native land, he was a genuine idealist, believing in a time when nations would unite as one family, laying aside mutual hatred. Zinaida loved and admired the romantic young Pole no less than did the brilliant group of poets and writers whose friend he remained. Later she wrote a pen-portrait of him in which she noted his sad air even among friends.

> His spirit is free and pure. His virtue beyond reproach. Noble in action, generous in sacrifice, everything that is true, everything that is beautiful, warms and exalts him. His sadness is due to exile and the fate of his tragic country. He carries the thought of home with him always, the source of all warmth and light.
>
> For him it is the column of light which led God's chosen people through the desert, the fire from the motherland, which Greek colonisers took with them to foreign lands.[23]

In his turn Mickiewicz wrote: 'I had the privilege of knowing and enjoying the friendship of the purest and the noblest of Russian youth,'[24] whom later he commemorated in his poem 'To My Russian Friends'.

Whether the Decembrists were romantics or revolutionaries, young idealists or hardened Jacobins, they did have one thing in common:

the determination to do away with the autocracy. Matters came to a head after Alexander's death. The logical successor to Alexander had been his next brother Grand Duke Constantine, who, however, had renounced his rights in 1820 when he had married a Polish commoner. In 1822, Alexander had drawn up a secret manifesto to the effect that he would be succeeded by the next brother, Nicholas, with the agreement of both brothers. In spite of this agreement, when Alexander died, for some reason Nicholas himself swore allegiance to Constantine who, not at all keen to be Tsar and wishing to continue to lead a quiet life in Poland, was naturally horrified. He rushed to Moscow to confirm that Nicholas should be Tsar. Nicholas, who had prepared himself to rule Russia, nonetheless swore allegiance again to Constantine. He was determined not to appear a usurper. The two brothers then swore allegiance to each other in competition, passing the crown between them like a hot potato. Ignorant of Alexander's secret manifesto, the army too had naturally sworn allegiance to Constantine after Alexander's death. On 14 December (old style), after the position had finally been clarified, the guards regiments assembled in St Petersburg to swear allegiance to Nicholas.

Taking advantage of the general confusion, the Northern Society decided that this was the moment to stage its rebellion. Pestel had been arrested the day before. On the pretext that Constantine had been usurped, the officers incited mutiny in the ranks, alleging that it was about the succession. Three thousand men had gathered in Senate Square that cold winter morning calling for Constantine as the legitimate king. Soon the mutineers were surrounded by a larger body of troops loyal to Nicholas. Unwilling to inaugurate his reign by a wholesale massacre of his subjects, Nicholas attempted to convince the rebels to give up peacefully. Meanwhile in the rebel camp all was confusion, resulting in a complete failure to act. Their leader, Prince Sergei Trubetskoy, had changed his mind, slipping away to swear allegiance to Nicholas, the man he was supposed to depose, after which he hid in the Austrian Embassy. Talks between the two sides went on throughout the day. When General Milarodovich, the popular, much-decorated hero of 1812 and Governor General of St Petersburg, rode out across the square to try and convince the mutineers to return to barracks, he faced Prince Obolensky, who had taken command of the rebels. As he turned his horse, he was shot in the back and killed by the highly strung idealist, Peter Khakovsky, who had long aspired to the role of self-immolating regicide. Despite this act, there were several more futile attempts at talks, but as dusk fell the artillery was sent in. By the end of that cold winter day, some seventy rebels lay dead on the icy square.

'It was dreadful to hear the firing. – Some say the mutineers have retreated across the river and dispersed,' wrote Charlotte Disbrowe, the wife of the British minister. Two days later she records that the soldiers had received a general pardon, 'but of course a similar clemency could not be extended to those who incited them to revolt and a great many officers are arrested . . . The traces of the sad event on Monday were horrid: pools of blood on the snow, and spattered up against the houses.[25]

The rebellion was joined by the Southern Society but that too was quickly suppressed. Maria Volkonsky, wife of Sergei, who was a member of the Southern Society, later recalled those days:

> He [Sergei] came to fetch me towards the end of autumn, and took me to Uman, where his division was stationed, himself leaving for Tulchin, the headquarters of the Second Army. He came back a week later in the middle of the night; waking me and saying, 'Get up at once.' I woke up trembling with fear. I was heavily pregnant and the suddenness and noise had frightened me. He began to stoke the fire and started to burn some papers. I helped him as best I could, asking what had happened. 'Pestel has been arrested,' he replied. 'Why?' – no reply. All this secrecy upset me. I could see that he was unhappy and preoccupied. Finally he told me that he had promised my father that he would take me to him in the country for my confinement; and so we left. He handed me over to my mother and left at once. He was arrested as soon as he had returned and sent off to Petersburg.[26]

All the officers were rounded up and imprisoned in the days following the failed coup. 'Did we free Europe in order to be put in chains ourselves? Did we grant France a constitution so that we dare not talk about it, and buy pre-eminence among nations with our own blood, in order to be humiliated at home?' wrote one of the Decembrists, Prince Bestushev, to the Tsar Nicholas from his prison cell.[27]

Sergei Volkonsky was tried by Nicholas I personally on 14 January 1826, and urged to give the names of his co-conspirators which he refused to do. His wife, meanwhile, had given birth to their son on 2 January. That night at a grand ball given by Prince Kochubey, the Tsar danced with the relatives of those who had plotted against him. Although the conspiracy had been a failure, and it seemed that nothing had changed, Russia would never be the same again. The first blow against the autocracy had been struck.

The events following the Decembrist revolt touched Zinaida directly. Not only her brother-in-law, almost the same age as herself and with whom she had shared so many happy times over the past fifteen years, but also many of her close friends were implicated. Sergei Trubetskoy was married to Zinaida's cousin, Katasha Laval; Muraviev was a distant relation and friend.

The prisoners remained in the Peter and Paul Fortress through the winter. In April, Maria Volkonsky, still weak after a very difficult birth, was able to visit her husband there. Sergei's mother, a courtier to the marrow of her bones, had at first refused to see him, declaring that it would kill her, and leaving with the Empress Dowager for Moscow where preparations were under way for Nicholas's coronation.

Suddenly news came of the death of the Empress Elizabeth in Belev, in the province of Tula. She had been returning to St Petersburg from Taganrog, but exhaustion had forced her to stop at Belev. Princess Sophia Volkonsky accompanied the body of the Empress back to St Petersburg. In May all the Volkonsky women were in Moscow, where Maria was received by the Empress Dowager who made polite small talk but uttered not a word about her husband.

On 13 July 1826, all the Decembrists were sentenced – Pavel Pestel, Sergei Muraviev, Conrad Ryleev, Mikhail Bestushev-Rumin and Peter Khakhovsky to death, and the others to life imprisonment and exile. Lined up on the battlements of the fortress at dawn, they stood facing the five gallows. Fires had been lit in which the uniforms and decorations of the condemned were to be burnt. Sergei, his wife recorded, quickly took off his military uniform, throwing it in the fire, as he did not wish it to be ripped off him. Their swords were then broken over their heads, so clumsily that some of them were wounded. The five men condemned to death were then hanged, but the execution was bungled. Three of them fell into the pit still alive and had to be hanged again. Refusing help, Muraviev remarked that in Russia they couldn't even hang a man properly, while Ryleev went to his death with the words, 'I am happy to die twice for the fatherland.' Afterwards, their bodies were placed in two large boxes.[28]

Those not condemned to death, however, were now dead in the eyes of the law, losing not only their property but their names, and even their married status which was annulled so that wives could marry again if they so wished. Children were excluded from the punishment, and wives were given permission to follow their husbands into exile if they chose, though any children born in exile were to be deprived of their titles of nobility. Sergei Volkonsky's punishment was harsh: 'My husband was deprived of his titles, his wealth and his civil rights, sentenced to twenty years of hard labour and life exile. On 26 July he was sent to Siberia together with the Princes Trubetskoy, Obolensky, Davidov, Artamon Muraviev and the brothers Borisov and Jacubovich,' wrote Maria Volkonsky.[29]

Herzen, then a schoolboy, saw Nicholas riding into Moscow on the day after the execution of the Decembrists (14 July 1826). He recalled the Tsar's impressive good looks, but noticed something more:

He was handsome but with a cold beauty. Never did a face show a person's character so mercilessly as his. – It showed an iron will but a weak mind, more cruel than sensitive. But the most striking thing were the eyes, with no vestige of warmth or mercy; they were wintry eyes.[30]

In Moscow, Zinaida and all her circle had been horrified by the execution of the five Decembrists although relieved that Sergei's life at least had been spared. There had been no death sentences for more than a generation. In a horribly tense atmosphere, everybody waited to see what would happen next. Zinaida's friend Prince Odoevsky, afraid that they might be taken for political agitators, closed down the circle of the Lovers of Wisdom, calling his friends together one last time when they ceremoniously burnt the circle's rule book. Their fears were justified, as can be seen from police files of the following year in which it is stated: 'All those involved in Jacobinism are from Moscow. Titov, Kiriievsky, Sobolevsky all work for the *Telegraph*. Their patrons are Prince Viazemsky and the former Professor Daviydov, the most important Jacobin.[31]

Prince Peter Andreevich Viazemsky, Zinaida's close childhood friend, was undoubtedly one of the few who openly supported the Decembrists:

> For me Russia has been defiled, and bloodied: I can't bear it here,
> I feel stifled. I cannot, I do not wish to live peacefully in this place,
> the scene of the execution! How many were sacrificed and what
> an iron hand has fallen on them.[32]

A convinced liberal, he had been in trouble with the authorities as early as 1821 when, while serving in Warsaw, he had disagreed with the government and was believed to sympathise with the Polish opposition. At that time Zinaida had interceded for him with Alexander. Now she fearlessly did so again with Nicholas. She was not close to the new Tsar but her connections at court were still good. She was not altogether powerless. Moreover, the Princess never failed her friends.

The new Emperor was even more determined to preserve the autocracy than Alexander had been in his last years, and quite untroubled by any liberal inclinations. A military man to the core, Nicholas was obsessed with order. Deeply unpopular in the army, where from the earliest age he had been a harsh martinet, he too had inherited his father's passion for drill, uniforms and precise arrangements. Marriage to a Prussian princess and the close ties he established with her country reinforced his natural inclinations. From the beginning Nicholas's reign was marked by the three principles which were to be officially expressed in 1833 by the Minister of Education Sergei Uvarov, in a doctrine known as 'Official Nationality': orthodoxy, autocracy and nationality. To enforce this doctrine he set up a new bureaucracy, which included a secret police. For many Russians, the infamous but incompetent Third Department, dressed in their sky blue uniforms, became the very symbol of Nicholas's reign.

A poem dedicated to the Decembrists by the Romantic poet, Tuut-chev, ended with the words, 'An iron winter has set in, removing all traces of the blood with which you hoped to melt the polar ice.' While politically Nicholas's long reign was characterised by stagnation, incompetence and repression, under the ice there was a ferment of thought, questioning and idealism which gave birth to the Russian intelligentsia and to the outstanding artistic and literary achievements of the next quarter-century.

9

A Salon in Moscow

'Queen of the Muses And of beauty'

ALEXANDER PUSHKIN IN A POEM TO ZINAIDA VOLKONSKY

Young Alina Volkonsky, in Moscow for the coronation of Nicholas I in August 1826, hurried to visit her favourite aunt as soon as she arrived. Alina wrote enthusiastically to her mother Sophia, who would be arriving later with the royal family, about Zinaida's newly decorated apartments in the Beloselsky Palace:

> Yesterday morning I saw the apartments which Aunt Zinaida has arranged for herself upstairs in the Beloselsky house. Her dining-room is of a mustard-green colour, with Caucasian divans rather like the one in Taganrog [the house where the Tsar Alexander had died], the walls covered with landscapes and watercolours. The main drawing-room is mauve, the paintings framed in dull gold, the furniture in dark green velvet. The billiard room is covered in old damask. Her study is hung with Gothic paintings, with small busts of our tsars placed on consoles attached to the walls, with matching furniture. The floor of the mauve salon is painted in a wonderful imitation of black and white mosaic. I can't tell you how lovely it all looks and what wonderful taste![1]

The mosaic floor, so much admired by Alina, had been painted by Michelangelo Barbieri. P. I. Bartenev, describing Zinaida's house much later, in 1901, was full of admiration for his work. 'The Italian painter Barbieri painted the reception rooms magnificently in Princess Volkonsky's house on the corner of the Tversky and Kozitsky Street. The painted ceilings have survived to this day.' S. B. Beselovsky wrote that Barbieri had also decorated the walls with paintings at the Volkonsky country estate of Sukhanovo.[2]

Whether or not Barbieri was still Zinaida's lover, he was her main-stay, and had become a trusted member of Zinaida's family circle; a friend who took a full part in her artistic and social life. He was well liked by many of her friends. Count Buturlin, who had met him in Italy, wrote: 'Barbieri, who is a Roman, sang with her on stage, managed the affairs of the house, and was also tutor to her son. He is a talented man and very pleasant company.'[3] He had in fact become indispensable to the whole family. The previous summer, when he and Zinaida were staying at Vorontsovo, her mother-in-law's estate just outside Moscow, the old Princess wrote to Barbieri from Tsarskoe Selo:

> I take the liberty, knowing that I can count on your kindness, to ask you through my daughter-in-law, Zinaida, to do me a great favour and deal with the complaints of my peasants from the village of Vorontsovo. Make them tell you what the problem is but please, make sure that neither they nor my factor, Filip Koshelev, know that I have asked you to do this. If you could do this and send me a letter with their complaints as well as your own views on the matter, I will be greatly in your debt, and beg you to believe, Monsieur Barbieri, that I will be most grateful and that I remain yours very truly and respectfully.[4]

Other friends of the period also mention Barbieri, as a matter of course. Thus Bulgakov writing to his brother about the death of a friend and distant relative of Pushkin's, recalls that 'In the evening there was music at Princess Zinaida's. Barbieri came from there and announced the sad news. Turgenev and Viazemsky left at once.'[5]

Zinaida's Moscow drawing-room, so much admired by her niece, was immortalised by the Polish poet Mickiewicz, in his poem 'Pokoj Grecki' ('The Greek Room'). He also left a lively description of its decor and atmosphere in his memoirs:

It was a huge room in neo-classical style, painted white, with Greek columns and Greek statuary. At one end of it was a library full of works by Voltaire, Rousseau, Chateaubriand, André Chénier, Bernardin de Saint-Pierre, Madame de Staël and by many others, recent and classical, both French and English writers. The books were arranged in Empire-style, glass cases. Alfred de Vigny and Musset occupied prominent positions in the bookcase nearest the window – as did Byron. There were some splendid pieces of furniture by renowned French cabinet makers, and many comfortable armchairs, in which elderly visitors and assorted aged relations dozed – reminiscent of the days of Catherine the Great and Potemkin. The other end of the great salon was dominated by a piano, which seemed to be in constant use; it was the rallying point of the room. Flowering orange trees, chrysanthemums and hothouse plants in huge tubs filled the air with a most pleasing aroma. Waiters in white gloves, blue and gold livery and red slippers moved silently among the guests with trays laden with food, champagne and every kind of drink. It was a most luxurious atmosphere. From the fertile soil of central Russia and the labour of thousands of slaves flowed the money for the Moscow salons. Nevertheless it was a joy to go there, for the Princess collected all the literary lights of her day, and her charm and hospitality made these gatherings unique. She made only two demands on her guests: a modicum of talent, and punctuality at meals.[6]

Mickiewicz could not help but notice the contradictions between liberal views and the ownership of thousands of serfs. The Decembrists had wished to abolish slavery in Russia, as Alexander had once wished to do in the early days of his reign. Doubtless Zinaida was against serfdom. Her house was a centre of liberal and enlightened thought. As she was active on behalf of all her causes, it must have seemed to her almost impossible to do more, especially in the wake of the Decembrist plot and her family's involvement in it. She was usually careless of her own interests and safety when any of her friends were under attack, and fearless in their defence. Mickiewicz himself owed it to Zinaida's intercessions that he was able to obtain a passport and leave Russia. Zinaida, however, was an aristocratic liberal, not a revolutionary. As Herzen observed of those years: 'The aristocratic independence, the cavalier boldness of Alexander's time vanished after 1826.[7] They were always very much present in Zinaida. She was, at this stage in her life, still a child of the *ancien régime*, part of a romantic generation which worshipped art, adored nature but on the whole avoided the cruder realities of life. The Decembrist coup, while revolutionary in aspiration, had shown complete lack of organisation or understanding of the need for popular support. Although in the last years of her life Zinaida would devote herself entirely to the poor of Rome, while she was in Russia she seems to have accepted serfdom as an inevitable part of the natural order, at least for the time being, and had to be content, perhaps, simply to treat her own people well.

The coronation of Nicholas I, postponed because of the death of the Empress Elizabeth, eventually took place with great pomp and splendour in Moscow on 22 August 1826. It was as if the horror of the Decembrist trial and the execution of five of the revolutionaries on 13 July was to be obliterated in a show of excess. All of Moscow had turned out. Huge tiers of benches were erected outside the cathedral, so that to Charlotte Disbrowe 'even the sky seemed crowded, for some of the scaffolding was raised to the steeples.'[8] In the packed cathedral, there was only enough room for the first two classes of the nobility; the rest had to remain outside.

Prince Peter Volkonsky was created Ministre des Appanages and Ministre du Cabinet, while Zinaida's mother-in-law, still Mistress of the Robes to the Empress Dowager, received the order and star of St Catherine in diamonds in spite of the disgrace and exile of her youngest son Sergei. Count Lieven was created Prince, to the delight of Princess Lieven and the dismay of her many enemies.

A splendid court ball attended by 5000 people was held on 1 September. The banqueting hall, hung in crimson velvet emblazoned with the arms of the provinces, provided a magnificent backdrop for the ladies in court dress and the men in full dress uniform. The vast hall was lit by a huge bronze chandelier holding 2500 candles, their light reflected in the sparkle of diamonds. Guests dined at tables set with heavily embossed silver gilt, an orange tree in the centre of each. Afterwards, only polonaises were danced. The exceptionally tall and handsome young Tsar towered over his guests.[9] Foreign embassies and Moscow grandees vied in the splendour of their entertainments. A ball at the French Embassy for 800 guests, for which a special supper room had been built and painted with flowers, was attended by the Imperial couple, dressed in white as a compliment to France. The Empress Alexandra's dress, trimmed with marabout and studded down the whole front and all round the bodice with diamonds, drew all eyes. Not to be outdone, the British ambassador, the Duke of Devonshire, gave a ball two days later, duly reported by Charlotte Disbrowe:

> The only ornaments were pink roses without leaves, an immense circle of wax lights supported on a wreath of roses was suspended by very fine wires, so that it appeared to be held by magic. Our King's and the Imperial ciphers were traced in roses on the walls. The supper was laid out in the Orangerie, on two long tables, the Imperial table was placed across in a raised alcove at the end of the gallery, the hangings were in crimson and blue silk. This time the Imperial couple were dressed in red for England![10]

Hard as they might try, foreign missions could not match the Russians in magnificence. At Prince Youssoupov's, the entrance to the house had been transformed into a garden. A performance of opera was followed by a ball, after which supper appeared as if by magic, in the now transformed theatre, where the ceiling was covered with silver netting and lit by two silver chandeliers, each holding 200 candles.[11] The celebrations were wound up by a huge *fête populaire* held on 16 September at which there were 200,000 guests. Charlotte Disbrowe was amazed that:

> The guests had full liberty to carry away whatever they could lay hold of. The table cloths were torn to pieces, the tables broken up, the provisions appropriated, the wine was swallowed in a twinkling, and no sooner were the contents disposed of than they began to demolish the very buildings.[12]

Although she had been deeply shaken by the fate of the Decembrists, Zinaida had been obliged to join in the festivities to celebrate the coronation. Her own house, as recalled by a young hussar, was the scene of several concerts, at which her guests enjoyed performances by Italian singers.

When the coronation festivities were over Zinaida's house remained open to those of her friends who were not already on their way to Siberia, many of whom remained under shadow of suspicion, closely watched by the Tsar's spies. A report dated August 1826 to Count Benckendorff, head of the Third Section of the Imperial Chancery (the secret police), stated that among the ladies the two least sympathetic, always ready to tear the government to pieces, were Princess Zinaida Volkonsky and the wife of General Konovitsyn (whose two sons and son-in-law were among the rebel officers). 'Their private circles are hotbeds of malcontents, and no one curses the government and its servants more thoroughly than these two.'[13] Zinaida's house was indeed full of liberal sympathisers. Her circle included the poets and writers Viazemsky, Baratinsky, Venevitinov, Odoevsky, Küchelbecker and Vieligorsky as well as Zhukovsky, Mickiewicz and Pushkin. She entertained the philosophers and thinkers Khomiyakov and Kireevsky, who were to become prominent Slavophiles in the great debate about Russian identity in the next decade. An older member of her circle was Chaadaev, who was to initiate that debate with his bitter *Philosophical Letter* (published in *Teleskop* in 1836), in which he argued that Russia belonged to neither East nor West and had contributed nothing to culture. Delvig, Pushkin's greatest friend and publisher of the journal *Northern Flowers*, Polevoi, the editor of the *Moscow Telegraph*, and several of the professors from Moscow University, among them Shevyrev and Pogodin, remained frequent guests. When, after the Decembrist coup, some of her friends were forced to wind up their philosophical circles, their discussions continued under Zinaida's roof.

Herzen paid a special tribute to the women of Russia at that bitter time:

The tone of society had changed visibly. No one, except for the women, dared to show sympathy, to utter a friendly word about relatives or friends, whose hands they had grasped only yesterday, but who had been arrested overnight. On the contrary, men seemed fanatically slavish, some out of baseness and others, even worse, for no reason at all. Women alone took no part in this disgraceful denial of their dear ones – just as once, only women had stood by the cross and by the bloodied guillotine. The exiles' wives were deprived of all their civil rights; abandoning their wealth and their social position, they faced a lifetime of imprisonment in the terrible climate of eastern Siberia, under the even more terrible Siberian police. Sisters, who had not been allowed to follow their condemned brothers, left the court, many of them left Russia; most of them keeping alive their love for those who had suffered. Not so the men: fear had destroyed all feeling in their hearts; none of them dared to utter a word on behalf of the *unfortunate*.[14]

Society was deeply shocked by the revolt and the sentences, in part because people had grown unused to such things. During Alexander's reign political persecution had been rare. Apart from Pushkin only Labzin, Secretary of the Academy of Fine Arts, had been exiled. Herzen recalled the reason for his exile with his usual witty irreverence:

When the President had proposed the election of Arakhcheev to the Academy, Labzin asked what Arakhcheev had ever done for the Arts. He was close to the Tsar, was the somewhat lame reply. Well, in that case Labzin suggested, they should elect Ilya Baykov, the Tsar's coachman – 'He is not only close to the Tsar but sits in front of him!'[15]

The Tsar was not amused.

Meanwhile, there was no word from Sergei Volkonsky's wife Maria. Her father, furious with his son-in-law for putting his wife and child at such risk, afraid that she might be tempted to make a romantic gesture, suspicious above all of the influence of 'the Volkonsky women' on his beloved 'Mashenka', had contrived to keep her in the country and to keep all news from her. She did not know that Sergei had been sent off immediately after the trial, since all letters from the Volkonskys were intercepted. The Volkonskys, meanwhile, aware of the immediate departure of Princess Trubetskoy who had decided to join her husband in his Siberian exile, and the fact that several other wives had also decided to follow, were upset that Maria had not even tried to get in touch with them.

Old Princess Volkonsky, who had refused to visit her son in prison in St Petersburg, now talked of going to Siberia herself to give him her blessing. 'Grandmama cried a great deal yesterday and hardly slept today. – The Empress had been to see her and comfort her. – She says that she wishes to go to Siberia to see her son,' wrote her granddaughter Alina.[16] The family were, apparently, not against the idea. Indeed Charlotte Disbrowe reported:

Princess Zeneide V. talks of it as nothing extraordinary of having a tent pitched on the Steps or Desert, a physician to attend her, that the climate is better than at St Petersburg, and that in the winter the trainage [travel by sleigh] will avoid the great fatigue of bad roads, etc.

However, Mrs Disbrowe believed that 'The Imperial family, who were much attached to the old princess, will contrive to prevent it'.[17] Perhaps Zinaida was not too sorry to send her mother-in-law thousands of miles away. Sophia, who was particularly close to Sergei, had just received a pathetic letter from him, smuggled out of prison. Knowing of the decision of some of the wives to follow their husbands into exile, he wondered:

Will I enjoy the same happiness? Will my beloved wife deny me this comfort? I have no doubt that her kind heart would sacrifice everything to me, but I am afraid of the influence of others [Maria's family], and I know that they will keep her away from you all in order to put more pressure on her. Will my wife give me the consolation which others are already assured of? I understand what her duty is to our son, and of course I wouldn't wish to separate her for ever from that unfortunate child.[18]

At the beginning of September 1826, within two weeks of the coronation, Alexander Pushkin was allowed to return from his exile. He had been confined to his family estate of Mikhailovskoe in the province of Pskov for almost two years. Pushkin's exile had been providential. He had too many friends among the Decembrists and would certainly have been caught up in the revolt. He was taken straight to the new Tsar. Nicholas had dismissed Arakhcheev after the sentencing of the Decembrists. Now it was time for a liberal gesture. What better than to lift the sentence from Russia's favourite poet? Would Pushkin have taken part in the Decembrist plot had he been free, the Tsar asked him? Yes, he would have joined his friends on Senate Square, replied the poet. For the future, however, the poet did give his word of honour as a Russian nobleman 'to conduct himself in an honourable and decent manner'. With the words 'I myself will be your censor,' the Tsar dismissed him. He was now free to travel in Russia and free to publish.[19]

On leaving school the young poet, whose exceptional talent had already been noticed, had soon won universal admiration and acclaim for his famous epic poem *Ruslan and Ludmilla*. At the same time his poems 'Derevn'ya' ('In the Country'), 'Vol'nost' ('Ode to Liberty') and 'Noel', with their ringing indictment of serfdom, their sympathy for tyrannicide and their all-too-obvious targeting of the Tsar and Arakhcheev (about whom, for good measure, Pushkin had written a stinging epigram), were circulating in St Petersburg in manuscript. Not surprisingly, when they came into the Tsar's hands Pushkin had been exiled. 'We ought to send Pushkin to Siberia', Alexander had said. 'He has flooded Russia with his revolutionary verse, all our youth know it by heart.'[20] It was only thanks to his friends, particularly the poet Zhukovsky and the historian Karamzin, that the Tsar was prevailed upon to send him to the staff of General Inzov in Moldavia, rather than to Siberia. He was barely twenty-one when he left but already his poems had signalled a genius, as clear to his friends and mentors as it was to his enemies. The true reason for the banishment of 'the vast phenomenon of Pushkin', as Herzen was to call him, was indeed the influence which his poems had already had on his generation. The Tsar had been right. After the Decembrist coup, Zhukovsky wrote to Pushkin, 'Your poems were found among the papers of every single one of the activists.'[21]

As a result of this exile Pushkin had avoided active involvement with the Decembrists, although most of them were his friends and he had certainly met Pestel while at Kishinev. The truth was, they had not invited him to join the conspiracy, considering him too unreliable and perhaps realising that Pushkin was first and foremost a poet not a revolutionary. Nevertheless, at the time of the Decembrists' trial, Pushkin had feared the worst, convinced that he too would be sent for at any moment. While in the south, he had met the Raevskys, Maria Volkonsky's family, and was more or less adopted by them, travelling with them to the Caucasus. Maria's brothers became close friends, while the young poet fell in love with each sister in turn.

Pushkin's return to Moscow was greeted with universal joy. He was almost mobbed in the streets and when he visited the theatre all eyes were on him rather than on the stage. Count Tolstoy recalled, 'Pushkin's return and pardon were the great news of the time.'[22] At first he stayed not far from Zinaida's palace on the Tverskaya, at the house of Prince Gagarin, later moving to Sobolevsky's house. Sobolevsky was a charming and cultivated man about town and an habitué of Zinaida's salon. At her request, he brought Pushkin to Zinaida's house towards the end of September. Prince Viazemsky, who had himself just returned to Moscow, was there at their first meeting: 'I can remember and still hear how at their first meeting she greeted him by singing his poem "Iug" ["South"] which had been set to music by Henishta.'[23] Pushkin was deeply touched by such a graceful compliment. As her lovely voice rose, singing his elegy 'Now is the light of day extinguished / And evening mists fall on the dark blue sea,' he blushed to the roots of his hair, as he always did when moved in any way. He was also very flattered by the attentions of his beautiful and talented hostess.[24]

Soon after, Zinaida wrote to Prince Viazemsky:

Do not fail to come to supper on Sunday. I shall be reading something which you will like I hope. If you can catch that butterfly, Pushkin, do bring him too. Perhaps he thinks that he will find a big crowd here as before. Tell him he is wrong and do bring him. I am sure that he will like what I mean to read.[25]

In October, tired of being lionised, Pushkin left for his estate of Mikhailovskoe, writing to Viazemsky: 'Moscow has made an unpleasant impression on me.'[26] Before his departure Zinaida gave a literary dinner in his honour at which he listened rapt as Mickiewicz demonstrated his unique talent for poetic improvisation. Viazemsky recalled the evening and how they had all been immensely impressed by the Pole's talent. Pushkin maintained that he himself was nothing compared with Mickiewicz and called him a genius.[27]

Zinaida sent him her opera, *Giovanna d'Arco*, with a lithograph of a portrait of her as Joan by Bruni. '*Giovanna* was written for my own theatre,' she explains in the accompanying letter:

> I had played the part myself and wanted to turn it into an opera; I had to end it in the middle of Schiller's play. You will be getting a lithograph of my portrait (a head) painted by Bruni. Add it to the first page and sometimes think of me.

Zinaida goes on to praise Pushkin with such a lack of restraint as the young man may have found embarrassing. Comparing him to Shakespeare, Byron, Ariosto and Anacreon, she begs:

> Come back to us. The air of Moscow is easier to breathe. A great Russian poet must write either among the steppes or in the shadow of the Kremlin. The creator of *Boris Godunov* belongs in the city of the Tsars.[28]

In return Pushkin sent Zinaida a copy of his poem *Tsigany* (*The Gypsies*) together with some charming verses addressed to her. Paying tribute to her as one who, among the whist tables and noisy ballrooms of Moscow, prefers Apollo's games, the poem ends by begging her to accept the humble gift of a poet she has enslaved, ending with the stanzas:

> And in your tender hand you hold, the magic sceptre of inspiration – Twice wreathed with genius is your pensive brow, – Oh Queen of all the Muses and of Beauty.[29]

Pushkin soon returned to Moscow, to find himself lionised more than ever. Although he was not always in the mood for social life

and was known to dislike having to read his work in public, he
remained a frequent guest at Zinaida's salon. Sometimes their evenings
were more light-hearted and they would play charades. On one
occasion Pushkin, representing a rock in the desert during the passage
of the Israelites, covered himself entirely in a red shawl until he was
tapped by Moses's rod (Zinaida's fan), when he poured water on the
floor from a decanter.[30] Count Benckendorff, the head of the secret
police, must have been disappointed to receive this report on the
suspect poet from his informer Bibikov:

> I've been following Pushkin as much as possible. The houses where
> he is most often seen are those of Princess Zinaida Volkonsky and
> Prince Viazemsky. Discussions there are mainly about literature.[31]

Maria Volkonsky had waited in vain all through the summer and
autumn of 1826 for news of Sergei's fate. Together with her baby,
she was kept on her aunt's estate, closely watched over by her brother
Alexander. When he left for Odessa in October 1826, forbidding her
to move until his return, she seized her chance to go back to
St Petersburg. There she found her parents. Family loyalty prevented
Maria from explaining to the Volkonskys that her brother had intercepted all letters to her. With no money of her own, caught between
the cold disapproval of the Volkonskys and the fury and anguish of
her own family, she decided to follow her husband into exile. Maria
knew that she was breaking her father's heart; the thought of parting
with his favourite child in such circumstances was intolerable to him.
He had done all in his power to keep her away from 'those Volkonsky
women'; now he used his considerable influence to ensure that permission to follow her husband, which she had sought from the Tsar
through Count Benckendorff, would not be granted. Though barely
twenty, Maria pawned her diamonds, paid off some of her husband's
debts, and wrote to the Tsar directly. She received Nicholas's answer
on 21 December 1826:

> I have received your letter of the 15th of this month, Princess, and
> was pleased to read the expression of your feelings of gratitude to

me for my interest in your welfare, but in the name of that interest, I feel it to be my duty to once again repeat my warning as to what awaits you once you cross the line beyond Irkutsk. I leave it to you to decide on whatever course of action seems most fitting.[32]

Years later, in a memoir in which Maria described her Siberian exile, she recalled the painful parting with her father:

During all that time my father was in a black mood and quite unapproachable. But I had to tell him that I was leaving and to ask him to be the guardian of my poor baby, whom I was not allowed to take with me. So I showed him His Majesty's letter, whereupon my poor father lost all control. Raising his fists he shouted, I will curse you if you are not back within a year. I said nothing, threw myself on the sofa and hid my face in a cushion.

Maria left St Petersburg that very night, afraid to delay any longer. She had first gone to see her mother-in-law, who ordered that Maria should be given only as much money as was required to pay for horses as far as Irkutsk. Her brother-in-law, Prince Peter, had come to collect her to take her to lunch with Sophia. He asked her if she was sure she would return. 'I have no wish to return unless it is with Sergei,' Maria had replied, 'but for God's sake don't tell my father.' Far from cursing her, her father had blessed her, turning away silently. They were both unable to utter a word.

Before leaving, Maria spent the whole evening with her baby who, she later recalled, had played with the big red seal of the Tsar's letter, the very letter which had given his mother permission to part with him for ever. She spent a long time on her knees, praying beside his cot, before leaving him in the care of the Volkonskys. It was the last time that she would ever see her beloved Nikolenka. Adored by the entire family, he died at the age of two, on 17 January 1828. Pushkin wrote the epitaph which Maria's father sent her, with the news of the child's death: 'In heaven's radiance and in eternal peace/ Beside the throne of the Eternal Creator/ He smiles down at their earthly exile/Blessing his mother, praying for his father.' Maria wrote that she had been moved and comforted by these verses.[33]

Just before Maria's departure, old Princess Volkonsky once again wrote to Barbieri. Begging his pardon for not having paid 180 roubles, which she owed him for making her a silver snuffbox with a copy of a painting by Van Dyck on it, commissioned as a gift for her son Nikita, she enclosed a letter for Zinaida:

ask her to read it as soon as may be. It is essential that she does so and I count on you to make sure of this. I wish you a happy New Year, which is almost upon us, and beg you to believe in my respect and friendship. Yours etc. Princess Volkonsky, née Princess Repnin.

It seems probable that the letter was about Maria's imminent departure to Siberia. The Princess would have been unwilling to trust it to the post. That she sent it through Barbieri shows the degree of trust he enjoyed.[34]

On her way to Siberia, Maria felt morally obliged to visit the wives and families of other Siberian exiles in Moscow. Although she had not yet met Zinaida, there was no question where she would stay. Zinaida's warm-hearted support of the relatives and friends of the Decembrists was well known and she had always been close to Sergei. As soon as she arrived in Moscow, Maria went to Zinaida's house where she was welcomed 'with a warmth and goodness that I can never forget. She surrounded me with care and attention; full of love and sympathy.' Knowing how much Maria loved music, Zinaida had invited all the best singers in Moscow, including Italians, to sing at a farewell party which she organised for her sister-in-law on the eve of her departure for Siberia. Maria was thrilled by the beauty of their voices. The thought that she might be hearing such music for the last time made the pleasure even more intense. She longed to sing too, but she had almost lost her voice as a result of a cold. Pushkin, who was at the party, never left Maria's side all evening. He had once been in love with her, although, Maria wrote, 'he was only truly in love with his muse,' adding affectionately that in any case, 'as a poet he believed it to be his duty to be in love with all the pretty girls and young women of his acquaintance.' She recalled how once, when she was fifteen, they had stopped by the sea and she had playfully chased the waves in her bare feet. Pushkin had been so touched that he had celebrated the scene in a poem in which he declared himself to be jealous of the waves which were allowed to kiss her feet. Later he also celebrated Maria's famously beautiful dark eyes in one of his poems of the south, *The Fountain of Bakhchiserai*: 'Your captivating eyes,/clearer than day, darker than night.'

That evening at Zinaida's party Pushkin was sad, but also filled with an exulting admiration for the courage of the Decembrists and the heroism of their wives. He had wanted to present Maria with a poem he was writing for them all, but it was not quite ready. He sent it later with Alexandra Muraviev: 'In the depths of the Siberian mines, keep that proud courage alive.' Pushkin also dedicated his long narrative poem *Poltava* to Maria:

> To you, – but will you hear the voice of the dark muse,/ and will your modest soul admit my heart's direction/ or like the love which once no answer found,/ you won't accept the poet's dedication? But hear at least the sounds once dear to you,/and think that on that day of final parting/ Your lonely desert,/ the last sound of your voice,/ remain in my inconstant fate/ my soul's one love,/ the single treasure and the shrine.

Now, as Maria sat outside the main drawing-room, unable to cope with the many guests, Zinaida ran back and forth to her, thinking only of how she could please her. While singing an aria from Paer's *Agnese*, Zinaida broke down in tears as she came to the point where the unhappy daughter begs for her father's blessing. She quickly left the room, and the two women cried together. At last, most of the guests left, and only a circle of intimate friends remained. Zinaida tried to lift the general gloom by playing the piano. Maria could not tear herself away, asking each of her friends to sing so that she could take with her the memory of their voices. At length Zinaida asked for supper to be served. They all tried to be cheerful but no one had the heart for laughter. Pushkin sat close to Maria in deep silence. Alexei Venevitinov, who left at two in the morning, 'my heart overflowing', described the evening in a letter to his brother, the poet Dimitry.[35]

Maria's sister Ekaterina Orlov had come to say goodbye, bringing quantities of books, paper, drawings and tapestry wool. She also brought a bearskin rug, and, seeing that Maria had no fur, took her fur-lined pelisse off her own shoulders and gave it to her. Maria left Moscow on 27 December at four o'clock in the morning. Her sister's presents, and the many parcels and letters given to her by the relatives of those already in Siberia, made it necessary to hire an extra *kibitka* (a tilt-cart). Zinaida had a little clavichord strapped to it secretly, just before Maria set off.

The two women had forged strong ties of friendship in their brief time together. Zinaida's admiration for Maria's heroic self-sacrifice, her pity for her youth and bleak future, were matched by Maria's gratitude and admiration for Zinaida's lack of concern for herself. She was particularly grateful for Zinaida's loving care, her warm sympathy and understanding, which had been lacking in her own family and the other Volkonskys. Zinaida never forgot Maria. Recalling her slender, dark and graceful form, 'like a daughter of the Ganges', Zinaida wrote: 'You who came to stay with me; you whom I had only known for three days, but whom I called my friend; your image is imprinted on my soul.'[36]

Maria was to remain in Siberia for thirty years, but the two women never lost touch. Zinaida sent letters, music and drawings and later seeds from her Roman garden which enabled Maria to plant a garden in Siberia. They would meet again as old women, in Rome, in 1859, three years after Maria and Sergei's return from exile.

Dimitry Venevitinov, to whom his brother Alexei wrote the moving account of Maria's last night in Moscow, was a talented poet, and translator of Byron, Schiller and Goethe, as well as other works of literature and philosophy. Although only twenty – sixteen years younger than Zinaida – he was a much-loved member of her inner circle of friends and a constant guest at her salon. He was considered to have exceptional promise. Like Zinaida he was drawn to all the arts and was also a talented musician and painter. It was Venevitinov who had brought the German composer and musician Henishta into Zinaida's circle and who had introduced the composer Glinka to her.

Poor Venevitinov was hopelessly in love with her. Zinaida, although deeply fond of him and of all his family, kept him at arm's length, hoping that a young man's romantic passion would eventually change into friendship.

She was, in any case, already involved in a new love affair. Soon after her arrival in Moscow in 1824, Zinaida met the Riccis. Count Miniato Ricci, an impoverished Florentine nobleman, had come to Russia as a result of his marriage to Ekaterina Lunin, the daughter of a Russian general, whom he had met while she was completing her musical and voice-training studies at the Philharmonic Academy in Bologna. The Riccis had returned to Russia in 1819 and settled in the Lunins' grand Moscow house, on the corner of the Tverskaya not far from the Beloselsky Palace.

Some ten years younger than his wife, the strikingly handsome Count was well known both in his native Italy and in Russia as a singer, as well as a poet and translator of some of Russia's best poets. His bass voice was neither very clear nor very strong, but he sang with great style and ability. Although not very effective on stage, he was an excellent chamber concert singer, particularly adept at singing romantic songs of his own composition in French, then very popular in Moscow.[37] Both Riccis often took leading parts in the operas and concerts staged by Zinaida between 1826 and 1828.[38] Soon the romantic duets which Zinaida and the Count sang so beautifully turned into a love affair. The affair was much more serious than that between Zinaida and Barbieri, who stayed on as a valued member of her household until she left Russia in 1829. Ricci was nearly her own age (he was born in 1792), and of her world. Doubtless, he made her feel closer to Italy. There was constant contact between them, not only at the parties and concerts where they sang together. Prince Shalikov recalled an evening at Princess Volkonsky's where 'all the arias sung by Zinaida Alexandrovna Volkonsky, all the duets which she sang with both Count and Countess Ricci and with Barbieri, entirely captivated, astonished and thrilled the large audience.'[39] Ricci also drew close to Zinaida through his work as a translator, Zinaida suggesting works he might translate into Italian. Venevitinov must have known of the affair. Certainly his unrequited love caused him great anguish, and inspired some fine poems full of romantic longing and despair. In the autumn of 1826 Venevitinov was transferred to St Petersburg where, with Zinaida's help, he had won a place at the college of Foreign Affairs. Before he left he wrote a short play, *Fête Impromptue*, in honour of Zinaida's name day which was on 11 October, in which he celebrated his goddess.[40] As a parting gift, Zinaida gave him a ring, found in Herculaneum. It became a talisman, as well as the subject of a poem in which he prophetically writes of his death, asking that the ring be buried with him.

At the time of Venevitinov's departure with his friend Khomyakov, Zinaida was sheltering a Decembrist sympathiser, Charles Auguste Vaucher, in her house. He was the Swiss librarian of Prince Laval, whose daughter Katasha, Zinaida's cousin, had married the Decembrist Prince Trubetskoy. Vaucher had just returned from accompanying her to Siberia. Knowing that everyone connected with the Decembrists was under surveillance and afraid that Vaucher might run into trouble on his way to St Petersburg, Zinaida had asked Venevitinov and Khomyakov if they would mind taking him with them. No sooner had they arrived in St Petersburg than Venevitinov was arrested and interrogated, spending three days in a damp cell before managing to convince the authorities of his innocence. This episode undermined the poet's already fragile health, and increased his depression. He wrote plaintively to Zinaida saying that he hardly went out. He missed Moscow and his friends, and had no heart for sightseeing. Above all, he missed Zinaida, asking for news of her in his letters to his family and sending his love through friends.[41] Zinaida had sent the young poet to her friend, the blind poet Kozlov, who was delighted with the young man, and with Zinaida's letters, which he described as being 'like those pots of flowers one places in prisoners' windows'. (Kozlov was evidently unfamiliar with the Tsar's prisons.) Kozlov, who knew Zinaida's stepmother well, through her sent Zinaida a copy of a recent publication of his translation of Byron's *The Bride of Abydos*. In his letter he refers to Princess Sophia's illness. She had taken Sergei's exile very hard and had been seriously ill all summer. Kozlov refers to Pushkin's *Boris Godunov* which friends were reading to him. Zinaida had been to an early reading of it by Pushkin himself at the Viazemskys'.[42]

By March, Dimitry Venevitinov had recovered his spirits sufficiently to go to a few balls. After one such late night, he caught a cold which soon turned into pneumonia. He died in the arms of his friend Khomyakov on 15 March 1827. To the end he murmured Zinaida's name, asking for the ring she had given him, which he always wore on a chain around his neck. When it was slipped on his finger, he thought in his delirium that they were getting married.

Zinaida's relationship with Venevitinov had a strange and romantic postscript. Venevitinov was buried in Moscow at the Simonov monastery. In 1930 the monastery was destroyed by the Soviet government and turned into a Palace of Culture. When his body was exhumed and buried again in the Novodevichi cemetery, on 22 July 1930, Zinaida's ring was still on the poet's finger. In his poem 'To My Ring', Venevitinov had imagined that, years after his death, someone might 'trouble his ashes', find the ring, 'and once again hear the whisper of his timid love'.[43] Venevitinov's untimely death deprived Russia of a fine poet. '*Comment donc vous l'avez laissé mourir?*' ('How could you let him die?'), Pushkin wrote to his friends. Venevitinov was so much loved by them that they met annually for the next fifty years, in honour of his memory. When news of his death reached Zinaida in Moscow she was deeply moved, visiting his mother daily and writing a poem in his memory.[44] Many years later she placed a memorial tablet to him in the Allée des Mémoires of her garden in Rome.

Throughout her years in Moscow, Zinaida continued to write and to take a serious interest in cultural life in Russia. Poems and extracts from her travel notebooks in Italy were published in the *Moscow Herald* in 1827.[45] She attempted to launch a society, the 'Pat>rioticheskaya Beseda', intended to promote mutual exchanges on arts and sciences between Russia and the West, under the auspices of the Society of History and Russian Antiquities. Her salon remained at the centre of Moscow's cultural life throughout the years 1824–29. Her husband Nikita's name never appears in any of the many contemporary accounts of Zinaida, or in letters to or about her. He remains in the shadows. Although Zinaida was then in her late thirties, almost middle-aged by the standards of the time, all her contemporaries wrote of her beauty, her warmth and vitality, her intellectual energy. Her distant relative and a great friend of her brother Muraviev, thought Zinaida the 'personification of grace and beauty'. On one occassion at one of the many evenings at Zinaida's, Muraviev knocked over a huge statue of Apollo, breaking its arm, which led to Pushkin composing a witty epigram at Muraviev's expense.[46] Many years later, Maria and Sergei Volkonsky's grandson, also Sergei, in a memoir about the Decembrists based on family papers and letters, described Zinaida as:

a beauty, a woman with an enchanting mind, exceptional artistic talents. A friend of Pushkin, Gogol and Venevitinov, she has made a mark on the history of our artistic and literary development. Much has been written about her, and yet, not enough. The full enchantment of her character has not come down to posterity, a character as lively and multifaceted as it was passionate. Everything about her was warmed by the flame of her deeply felt love of art, of her country and, above all, of people. She knew how to welcome, how to make much of people. She would surround them with the emotional, physical and practical support which they needed for their work, their inspiration.[47]

Ricci's love affair with Zinaida was serious enough for him to leave his wife in 1827. He returned to Italy in 1828, to be followed soon after by Zinaida herself.[48] Zinaida's decision, in 1828, to return to Italy was perhaps precipitated by Ricci's departure. While he had been with her, she had ignored the gossip. All their contemporaries knew of the affair. Certainly Pushkin did. In January 1829, just before Zinaida's final departure from Russia, Pushkin, writing to Prince Viazemsky from St Petersburg in a mood of self-disgust mentions the affair:

I've been here barely a week. All of society is here, in full swing. They are out to have fun till they drop, e.g. at the routs [large receptions, not unlike the modern cocktail party] which have become all the rage here. We should have discovered them long since, we are made for routs, they require neither wit, gaiety, nor general conversation, neither politics nor literature. One steps on carpets and people's feet indiscriminately, apologises, and this passes for conversation. As for me, I am delighted with the routs, and recovering from Zinaida's damned dinners. (May God grant her neither bottom nor cover, i.e. neither Italy nor Count Ricci!)[49]

Pushkin's less than friendly remark about Zinaida's dinners was puzzling for one who had spent a great deal of time at her house, but it may be that the poet felt under pressure from her frequent invitations, and had had a surfeit of being lionised. Like all artists he needed solitude for his work, and Zinaida could be too pressing. Pushkin was moody and well known for the vehemence with which he often expressed himself in letters to friends. Pushkin's friendship with Zinaida certainly influenced his writing. In his sketch 'The Guests were Assembling at the Dacha' the heroine is called Zinaida Volskaya, as is the young woman in another sketch, 'An Evening at the Dacha'. Although not entirely true to Zinaida's life, there are enough similarities for them to have been based on it. In his story 'Roslavlev', set in 1812, at the time of Madame de Staël's visit to Russia, Napoleon's invasion and the burning of Moscow, the heroine Paulina receives a letter from Madame de Staël. This episode is probably based on Madame de Staël's letter to Zinaida, when she was recovering from a nervous breakdown. Zinaida would almost certainly have shown the letter to Pushkin. Although the circumstances in the real and fictional letter are a little different, there can be little doubt that it was Zinaida's letter which inspired the story.[50]

Zinaida herself had once again gone through one of her periodic bouts of depression. Deeply religious as she was, her irregular life and perhaps her role in the break-up of the Riccis' marriage, as well as all the gossip surrounding them, had begun to prey on her. Haunted by guilt and a fear of death, she turned to the Orthodox Church for help for the last time, writing to the Archimandrite Pavsky, a priest and theologian. The only two of his letters to her to survive show that she must have been in a state of fear and confusion. His recommendations are stern and unsympathetic, reprimanding her for her way of life. They obviously failed to help. Once again her inner malaise made her restless. Russia felt like a prison and she began to look for ways of escape.[51] A longing for Italy, the country of her childhood, began to overwhelm her, not least because Ricci had returned there.

On 3 December 1828, Zinaida's thirty-ninth birthday, her closest friends came to her house in Moscow for the last time, to bid farewell to the 'Queen of the Muses'. Viazemsky, Baratinsky, Shevyrev, Pavlov and Kireevsky together composed couplets to commemorate the occasion, celebrating the Princess's many gifts. Baratinsky wrote a poem entitled 'Away from the Kingdom of Winter and of Whist' which ends with the thought that Zinaida will be happier among the beauties of the southern landscape.[52] Before leaving Russia, Zinaida was obliged to go, once again, to St Petersburg where she stayed for over a month. She had to take leave of the Tsar and there were many members of her family and friends to see as well as the Tsar's permission for Nikita to join her to be obtained.

Zinaida left Russia on 28 February 1829, never to live there again although she returned twice. She was accompanied by her elder sister Madeleine, who had came to live with Zinaida soon after her return to Russia, remaining with her until her own death in 1857. Madeleine was Zinaida's total opposite. Plump and unattractive, she was simple and home-loving, a Martha to Zinaida's Mary. The two sisters were nevertheless devoted to one another, Madeleine taking over the management of the household, which left Zinaida free for her artistic, intellectual and, later, religious pursuits. 'Sorella dolcissima, to whom I owe all my life, happiness, tranquillity, and shelter,' Madeleine later wrote in Zinaida's album.[53] With Zinaida also went her seventeen-year-old son Alexander, Vladimir Pavey, Stepan Shevyrev, professor at Moscow University whom Zinaida had persuaded to come to Rome as her son's tutor, and Barbieri, who left her household on arrival in Italy. She also took four of her Russian servants and a girl, Lisanka, from an institution.[54] Her husband Nikita, having failed to obtain the Tsar's permission to leave, remained in Moscow for the time being.

PART III

The Villa and the Church

10

Rome: The Villa Volkonsky

'What bliss to be streaming towards Italy'

ZINAIDA VOLKONSKY

Russia was still covered in winter snow and ice and in the grip of the other 'iron winter of Nicholas's reign', which had been forecast by the poet Tuutchev, when Zinaida left, on 28 February 1829. She left Russia with relief. She disliked Nicholas, the new Tsar, and all he represented as much as she had loved his brother Alexander, who was enshrined in her memory as he had been when she first met him. Everything about Nicholas's repressive, militarist and authoritarian nature was foreign to her. For her, change was a psychological necessity, and travel, as she expressed it in her diary, 'a source of endless riches for reflection'. She loved Russia and always considered herself Russian, but she belonged to a generation and a class nurtured by the French Enlightenment, accustomed to European travel.

> Home [she wrote in her travel notes], a sacred word and a sacred place; fatherland, you are our native land, but our friends and brothers are everywhere – wherever life flows and hearts beat. Slavs! be proud of your land, give your lives to it, but stretch out your hand to everyone, because a greater family unites on earth all those who love the eternal truth of the Creator and the beauty of His Creation.

Zinaida's travel notes, written in a style high-flown even by the standards of that time, demonstrate a highly strung, emotional nature and a romantic imagination, but they are also a testimony to her acute and sensitive eye, and her ability to communicate her experiences vividly.

The Princess travelled in the leisurely style of the time. The journey to Rome, which was intended as part of her son's education, followed the traditional itinerary of the Grand Tour. After a visit to Potsdam they spent the whole of April in Berlin, going on to Leipzig and then Dresden, Zinaida's birthplace, where the art gallery delighted her as much as it had once delighted her father. In May, Zinaida visited Goethe in Weimar, accompanied by her son's tutor Shevyrev, and Rozhalin, the Russian translator of Goethe's *The Sorrows of Young Werther*. They had encountered Rozhalin in Leipzig and had persuaded him to come to Italy as a second tutor for young Prince Alexander. To Zinaida, the visit to Goethe was a pilgrimage. After five years at the hub of Russia's cultural life, she believed it to be a sacred duty to visit a man whose influence in Russia had been so great. She had last met him in May 1813, in Teplitz – it must have seemed a lifetime ago – when she had been travelling through the newly liberated German lands in the Tsar's suite. After Alexander's death she had arranged for a copy of her cantata, 'To Alexander I', to be sent to Goethe, writing to a friend in Weimar, 'These verses are not worthy perhaps of the great poet's notice, but the feelings they express are.'[1]

The grand old man of European letters received her kindly, although he had been startled by the visit, and listened with interest as she told him of his influence in Russia, of Russia's poets, particularly Pushkin, and of life under the new regime. Shevyrev and Rozhalin sat in silence, struck dumb by the great man's presence. Goethe had shown them a painting, a present from Zhukovsky, on the theme of his *Helen*, which had pleased him very much. His daughter-in-law Ottilia and her baby son were present. Ottilia had trouble in pronouncing Pushkin's name, and the child had put his arms around his grandfather's grey head.[2] Zinaida recalled this scene in her travel notes, when she was in Vicenza, where Palladio's architecture reminded her of her meeting with the great German poet:

Only eternally young nature with her tender hand covers the delicate lines [of fallen stones and carvings among the ruins] much as the great thinker Goethe's young grandson had caressed him and wound his child's hands around the grey head.[3]

Four days after Zinaida's visit Goethe sent her two silver medals, as he noted in his diary (16 May). There was an exchange of letters and messages between Zinaida and Goethe after she settled in Rome. On 30 January 1830 Goethe noted the arrival of a parcel from Princess Volkonsky. In March of that year, Goethe's daughter-in-law Ottilia, in a letter to the Polish poet Mickiewicz who was then staying with Zinaida in Rome, wrote:

My father-in-law is well thank God, and entirely occupied with the second half of *Faust*. He has charged me to send not only the warmest greetings to you, but asked me to beg you to pass on his thanks to Princess Volkonsky for her letter and present, with which she honoured him and which made him most happy. Please add from me that I was so sorry that her visit to us had been so brief.[4]

Zinaida had a great ability to get on with people. She was loved not only by her friends, by those closest to her, but by many others from outside her social circle – no mean achievement in those days of rigid social division and etiquette. Above all, she had a genuine rapport with artists. And yet she failed to be loved by two of the greatest writers of her time, the two she most admired – Pushkin and Goethe. Pushkin actually expressed irritation with her before her departure, as we have seen, and there are no letters from him, nor any record that they saw each other again when Zinaida returned to Russia briefly in 1836, although she saw all their mutual friends and Pushkin was living in St Petersburg while she was there. Goethe, too, seems to have kept her at a distance, although, of course, it would have been natural for a very old man engaged on the completion of his greatest work to save his energies. The answer probably lies in Zinaida's excessive admiration for them as artists. Her normal affectionate warmth and sensitivity were blunted in the case of these two men by her adoration of their talent. That reverence, probably expressed in exalted terms, made them feel uneasily like monuments in their lifetime. Pushkin, however much he may have been flattered by her attention at first, grew tired of it and was too young to enjoy being a monument. Goethe, aged eighty and nearing the end of his life (he died at the age of eighty-two in March 1832), may well have preferred not to be reminded that he almost was one.

Zinaida's letter to Pushkin, and even more her travel notes, in which she likens Goethe to the town of Weimar, clearly demonstrate her worshipful attitude:

> That pantheon of great German writers. There, everything breathes of science, poetry, reason and respect for genius. There I visited Goethe. Such a universal poet may be compared to that ancient, exquisite, populous town, where the clarity of style of Greek temples, with their pure harmonious lines and their marble statues, stands side by side with Gothic churches, dark and secretive, their transparent steeples carved like lace; their tombs of medieval knights. I see Goethe in the image of this ideal town.

Zinaida commemorated him in her private pantheon, the Allée des Mémoires, where a plaque beside an amphora, now broken, reads: '*Il fut l'auréole de sa patrie.*' ('He was his country's glory.')

From Weimar Zinaida's party travelled on to Munich, through Bavaria and into the Bavarian Tyrol. In the town of Berneck the Pearl River, flowing beneath the castle of the Vallenrods, Knights of the Order of the Virgin Mary, led to some reflections on the lot of women, providing an insight into the frustrations any intelligent woman might have felt then: 'Notice the similarity between a woman's favourite adornment and tears. Are pearls not created to remind our sex of our fate, even when we are festively dressed?' But there is a perceptible lightening of mood as they approach her beloved Italy:

> What bliss to be streaming towards Italy, to leave behind the cold winds, the dry sandy earth, the sluggish nature of the north! What heaven to breathe spring air after a long illness! – Is winter itself not an illness? It wipes out all colours, turning them pale, dries up all the sources of life; even hot tears freeze into drops of ice.

Happy the land where flowers bloom in a continuous garland from spring to spring. Of course the winter garland is not so full, so bright, so many-hued, so sweet-scented as during the reign of the sun and of love. Cold winds may rock it, but do not tear it: just as the heart's passions sometimes calm down, but do not disappear quite. They are beyond the reach of anxiety, illness or old age.

Zinaida was perhaps thinking of her reunion with Count Ricci, whose departure from Russia had left a large gap in her life.

The Alps, which they had just left behind (on 22 May), seemed to her

to be towering behind us, looking down severely on the beauty of the Italian lands, like the Goths and Vandals when they swooped down in iron waves from those rocky crests. The passage from the Tyrol into Italy makes me think of the change from the harshness of the Middle Ages into the exquisite age of the Medici. Dry, angular contours give way to rounded voluptuousness; in this formative land, Nature is the prime teacher of grace.[5]

Zinaida and her companions visited almost every major town in Italy and many smaller ones, as is clear not only from her travel notes but also from Shevyrev's letters and her own. Vicenza, Venice, Padua, Milan, Bologna, Parma, Genoa, Turin and finally Naples and Ischia, where they spent the summer, all appear in their descriptions.[6] At last, in the autumn of 1829, they were in Rome. Zinaida first settled into the Palazzo Ferucci in Via Monte Brianza, close to the Tiber. Later she took a long lease on apartments at the Palazzo Poli which backed on to the Trevi Fountain. This remained her winter home for many years.

In Rome, Zinaida wrote again to Viazemsky:

My first letter is dated from Pompeii. – I repeat my invitation. Come to Italy – the sea shortens distances. – Come and collect marbles, lava, memories, poetry, above all come and reflect under this cloudless sky. – This country in which I have lived altogether for four years, is my second home: I have real friends here who have welcomed me with joy such as I could never value enough. I have been recognised and welcomed by ordinary people. Today I was visited by a woman who had travelled forty kilometres to see me for a moment. Everything is a friend to me in Rome; the arts, the monuments, the air, my memories.[7]

In Rome she was reunited with Miniato Ricci. For the next five years he was constantly with her, acting as her administrator and man of business. This, of course, provided an excuse for his constant presence, but in any case all Zinaida's lovers, including the Tsar, were expected to make themselves useful to her, perhaps because her husband was so much the opposite. When writing to her, Zinaida's Russian friends invariably sent their respects to Ricci, so it is clear that he was very much with her. Zinaida was, however, well on her way to conversion to the Catholic faith and increasingly preoccupied with religion and sin.

For all her joy at being in Italy once again, Zinaida was nevertheless homesick for Russia at first, and longed for news. Her letters, particularly in the first two years, are full of questions. She begs Viazemsky to tell her all about their Moscow friends, especially Pushkin and Baratinsky, as well as about the journal *Literaturnaya Gazeta*, which Pushkin had started, of which she wanted copies. 'Please put me on the subscription list for your journal, and Zhukovsky's, Delvig's and Pushkin's, and give them to my husband for me,' she writes in March 1830, and later in August:

We've all been reading the Literary Gazette, with genuine interest, and you are quite wrong to think it colourless. – On the contrary it is a very pretty and elegant lady, with good manners and the *bon ton* of civilised Russia, endlessly witty, with good judgement and freshness, which makes it *geniale* (an Italian expression which I adore). Please go on sending it to me. Shevyrev and Alexander also beg this kindness of you. It is important that we all read it, but especially those of us who are far from our native land, in Rome. I can't think of anything which might be better. – Pushkin does very well to get married.[8]

During the first few years, letters and books, many of them dedicated to the Princess by their authors, found their way to Rome.
Pushkin's poems, his *Tales of Belkin* and *Boris Godunov*, both published
in 1831, and later Zhukovsky's *Undine* were sent to her. Nikolai Melgunov, a Moscow intellectual, who was a minor composer and a noted
music critic, as well as journalist and translator, sent her, via Shevyrev,
a copy of Griboyedov's *Gore ot Uma* (*Woe from Wit*), which must have
been read in her Moscow salon when it was circulating in manuscript
form. He complains that their friend Sobolevsky, then in Rome, staying
with Zinaida, had managed to lose the first copy. He also sent two songs
especially composed for Zinaida's voice. The Princess 'must be sure
that she is remembered by all those who knew her ... Come back to
Moscow,' he begs Shevyrev. Zinaida's voice and her musical salon were
sorely missed by everyone. Writing to Shevyrev, Viazemsky asks:

What about Princess Zinaida's voice? Has she kept it in spite of her
illnesses? Here we no longer have that musical world which used to
exist in her Moscow house. – Her house was like the magic castle of
a musical fairy: no sooner had one's foot crossed the threshold than
one heard harmonies; whatever one might touch a thousand harmonious echoes replied. The very walls sang there; there thoughts,
feelings, conversation, movement, everything, was song.[9]

Melgunov and Pogodin, who was also a professor at Moscow University
and a colleague of Shevyrev, continued to beg Shevyrev to come back
and bring the Princess with him. Knowing of her love of the South,
Pogodin wonders whether she might consider settling in the Crimea?[10]
   Zinaida had resumed her musical activities as soon as she arrived
in Rome. In 1830 she set Zhukovsky's poem 'Dubrava Shumit'
('Sounds of the Forest') to music. She also began to hold musical
evenings. Shevyrev described one such evening where Russian songs
had made them all homesick, adding, 'You know that with her even
the deaf and dumb sing.'[11] Shevyrev, who had been reluctant to leave
Russia but had been persuaded by his friends that travel with the
Princess was an opportunity not to be missed, was now absolutely
devoted to Zinaida: 'The better you know her the more you love her
and respect her,' he wrote to Alexei Venevitinov. 'You can only really

understand the Princess when you see her in her own salon, and then you want to go more often. How can one compare her to others? She is so much greater than them!' Shevyrev was otherwise quite hard on those Russians whom he considered 'Frenchified', and determined that 'my prince Alexander Nikitich' (Zinaida's son and his charge) would be thoroughly Russian.[12]

Before she left Russia, Zinaida had put forward a project to the University of Moscow. Her idea, which was to found a Museum of Fine Arts in association with the university, based on the one in Naples, was published in the journal *Teleskop* in 1831.[13] She suggests that the museum would 'acquire plaster casts and marble copies of outstanding sculpture, copies of the finest examples of classical painting, prints of ancient and medieval architecture and monuments and models of the artifacts of ancient times.' The Princess intended to be very much involved, choosing works personally, which her artist friends in Italy – Canova, Thorvaldsen, Camucini and Vernet – would have good copies made of, at reasonable prices. Shevyrev was very enthusiastic about the idea and sent copies to Prince Nikita in St Petersburg, with whom he was in regular correspondence, as well as to his friends Melgunov and Pogodin in Moscow. Nikita was sceptical:

> The idea is noble, splendid, great, but you didn't mention how you intended to achieve your aims: bear in mind that there [i.e. in Moscow] they hardly care about the origins of Apollo or Minerva. You will need more than five thousand [roubles] to start with.

However, Nikita adds, when the court goes to Warsaw shortly, he hopes to be able to go to Moscow himself, where he will be in a better position to judge the possibilities.[14] Melgunov was also doubtful that they would be able to raise sufficient funds. Pogodin, on the other hand, was wildly enthusiastic, his enthusiasm probably not unmixed with the hope that the university might choose him to go to Rome for six months, as he explains in his joyful reply to Shevyrev: 'Long live the Princess! She will write her name in diamond letters in the annals of Moscow and of all Russia!' But, he wonders, where will the Princess find time to travel all over Italy to choose the works of art, and order copies to be made?

If she would care to invite me for six months – brilliant thought! – say from September to February, I could deal with the meetings with artists under her direction, with making enquiries, packing, despatch, help with placing the objects in Moscow, or even do it all myself?

Completely carried away by such a delightful prospect, Pogodin suggests 'a plan of action' – to whom she should write, etc. The Princess should request 'an official from the university [Pogodin perhaps], who is known to me and therefore the most suitable.' He adds, 'I am starting Italian lessons again as from tomorrow . . .'[15]

Poor Pogodin didn't get his tour of Italy, though he did travel there later. Zinaida's plan was turned down by the university's governing body for lack of funds. However, eighty years later, in 1912, Ivan Vladimirovich Tsvetsaev, father of the poet Marina Tsvetsaeva, founded the museum – today the Pushkin Museum of Fine Arts. In his inaugural address, Tsvetsaev acknowledged Zinaida as the originator of the idea.[16]

In 1830, Zinaida bought the Vigna Falcone, a large and beautiful piece of land within the Aurelian walls, between the Basilica of St John Lateran, the Church of Santa Croce in Gerusaleme and the Porta Maggiore. The land was divided from east to west by a Neronian spur of the first-century Claudian aqueduct, built by Nero originally to bring water to his Domus Aurea (Golden House). This part of the city had been largely uninhabited – although there had been a medieval church there in the eighth century, the S. Nicolo del'Ospitale, with a hospital attached, which records suggest had survived until the end of the fourteenth century. No trace remained of these however. Since that time the land had been used for vineyards and pasture.

Zinaida immediately set about repairing the crumbling aqueduct, managing to convince the papal government to undertake the repairs at their expense. In 1830, she commissioned a Roman architect, Giovanni Azzurri, to design her a summer villa. The villa, of a vaguely Renaissance aspect, was a small two-storey structure into which he incorporated three of the aqueduct's bays. While the building was being completed, Zinaida began to create a garden. Standing on a small hill, the grounds of her villa rolled away across vineyards to ravishing views of the Roman Campagna, and beyond to the Alban and Sabine hills. The garden soon took shape. Fragments of Roman sculpture, found in the grounds, were set into the walls of the house and the aqueduct and placed in small, cool grottoes formed from the aqueduct's buried lower arches. From the staircase of her house, and from the terraces on top of the aqueduct, there was a splendid view of the saints on top of the Basilica of San Giovanni, towering dramatically against the setting sun.

It was here that Zinaida began to create her Allée des Mémoires. First she placed a bust of her beloved Tsar Alexander on a granite column,[17] to be followed by memorials to the Empress Dowager Maria Feodorovna, her parents, her grandparents, her two sisters, her nurse and her teacher, three of her father's servants, Peter, Kolmar and Pimen, and several of her friends. A column to Capo d'Istria, an urn to Goethe, memorials to Byron and Venevitinov were to be followed by memorials to Walter Scott, Pushkin, Baratinsky and Zhukovsky. 'Corinne-Zénéide took me around her charming villa,' wrote her friend, the indefatigable traveller, Alexander Turgenev, who came to Rome in December 1832.

> She has brought this wilderness of her villa to life with memories of the living and dead. – There stands an urn to the Emperor Alexander, a Greek vase bears the name of Capo d'Istria, and there is a French epitaph to her nurse.[18]

Here too she placed the huge amphorae, gifts from her beloved Cardinal Consalvi, who had died soon after she had left Rome in 1824. Now the amphorae, inscribed with his name, were constant reminders of their friendship and of her promise to him that she would return.

Fanny Mendelssohn, sister of the composer, described Zinaida's garden a few years later:

> The villa itself is not a palace, but a dwelling house built in the delightfully irregular style of Italian architecture. The staircase is

quite open, and can be seen from the outside. Through the garden lengthways run the ruins of an aqueduct, which they have turned to account in various ways, building steps outside the arches, putting seats at the top and filling vacant places in the ivy-mantled walls with statues and busts. Roses climb up as high as they can find support, and aloes, Indian fig-trees and palms run wild among capitals of columns, ancient vases and fragments of all kinds. As for the roses there are millions of them, in bushes and trees, arbours and hedges, all flourishing luxuriantly; but never more lovely and poetic than when clinging to the dark cypress-trees. The beauty here is of a serious and touching type, with nothing small and 'pretty'.

Augustus Hare, who saw the garden in the 1870s, when it was already famous, described it as 'a most beautiful garden, running along the edge of the hill, intersected by the broken arches of the Aqua Claudia and possessing exquisite views over the Campagna, with its lines of aqueducts, to the Alban and Sabine mountains.'[19]

Here and at the Palazzo Poli, Zinaida entertained her friends and many distinguished foreign travellers. Perhaps the most famous was Sir Walter Scott. In the autumn of 1831, it was decided that Scott, who had suffered a violent stroke in the previous spring, would not survive another Scottish winter. Accompanied by several members of his family, he left on board a British warship, on which he had been given free passage, for Malta, from where he was bound for Naples. He was still writing, although his mind was beginning to cloud: 'I am perhaps setting – like a day that has been admired as a fine one the light of it sets down amidst mists and storms,' he wrote in his journal.[20] He recovered sufficiently in Naples to consider a journey to Greece, and a detour to Weimar to see Goethe on the way home, but Goethe died on 22 March. In April, the Scotts were in Rome and it was then that he visited Zinaida. At the villa, he met her great friend, the Russian painter Karl Bruilov who painted one of the last portraits of the Scottish writer. Walter Scott was particularly loved and appreciated by the Russians of his time. Bruilov had also painted Zinaida. Shortly before his death, Walter Scott had stood for more than an hour before Bruilov's painting *The Last Day of Pompeii.*

The painter, he said, had created not just a painting but a true poem. Zinaida commemorated him not only in her Allée des Mémoires, where she had inscribed, 'The quiet lamp of our conversations has been extinguished,' but also in an essay about him, which was later published:

> Walter Scott, our lovely dream of spring, our summer's shade, our autumn's rest, our long winter evenings, our castle in Spain, always ready and complete: Walter Scott, the vagabond minstrel, to whom the gatekeeper's daughter will always open the door before he need knock! How much the people owe him, for having interested them without tiring them, instructed them without boring, amused them with no shame, for having frightened them, for having made them laugh and cry, while not making them blush for their tears, their laughter or their fears. Walter Scott, gentleman and popular writer, an aristocrat who loved the people, was one of them, wore their mourning, drank their wine, laughed with their happiness, spoke their language, loved with their love, sat carefree at their table, who fought, felt, was transported and then quiet again like them.[21]

Bruilov, who had lived in Zinaida's house when he first came to Rome, was a very close friend. Almost twenty years later, in 1850, Bruilov returned to Rome. He was ill and only two years away from death. When he and Zinaida met again after a long parting, it was 'with such an explosion of joy, such a reunion of common interests, that all present felt they were set apart, that they were merely chance, outside witnesses of another life.'[22]

Another visitor was Gaetano Donizetti, who looked so much like the painter Schedrin that the two were frequently taken for brothers. Donizetti had been so moved by the story of the Decembrists that he wrote *The Siberian Captives*. The composer Mikhail Ivanovich Glinka came to Rome in October 1831. He had already met Zinaida in Moscow, through their mutual friend Melgunov, who was one of the composer's closest friends. Zinaida's nephew Grigory Volkonsky, a passionate music lover and himself the possessor of a magnificent basso profundo, knew Glinka well and had just sent his aunt an album of music published by Glinka, and containing some of his own compositions.[23]

The son of a rich landowner, Glinka had already spent almost a year in Milan, where he had studied Italian music and met Donizetti who, together with Bellini, were an important influence on one who later came to be known as the father of Russian music. Glinka loved Italy although throughout his time there his fragile nerves and strong inclination to depression had prostrated him with constant illness, so much so that before his arrival in Rome there had even been rumours of his death. Glinka was all the more warmly welcomed by Zinaida who well understood the debilitating effects of depression. Glinka and his friend Ivanov, a promising young singer who had come from Russia with him, remained in Rome for two weeks where, as he wrote in his memoirs many years later, 'Shevyrev was my cicerone, explaining all the important sights to me.' They were on their way to Naples, where musical life around the San Carlo Opera was particularly important. There, recommended no doubt by Zinaida, Glinka met the painter Karl Bruilov, with whom he forged a lifelong friendship and an important artistic collaboration.

While in Rome Glinka composed his song 'Venetian Nights', in which he set to music a poem by Kozlov. It is more than likely that Zinaida suggested this. The blind poet had been dear to her, and had noted in his diary that he had read this poem to Zinaida in St Petersburg. He had been very ill when Zinaida left Russia. Writing to him from Moscow at the time, Prince Viazemsky told him that he had read 'your sonnets at a dinner given by Princess Zinaida who heard them with great pleasure. She is about to come to St Petersburg so she will tell you so herself.'[24] After her departure for Rome, Kozlov sent her another poem, 'Song of the Nightingale', in which he wishes he could fly after her to the distant country of his dreams.[25] Zinaida in her turn had sent him a poem to comfort him beginning with the words, 'You are the harp of suffering,/ You are the harp of endurance,/You are the harp of love,' ending with the encouraging thought that he will be rewarded as his harp rings with hope and promises paradise.[26] Kozlov had replied with another poem playing on the same theme: 'You are the harp of expectation,/You are the harp of love,' ending with the thought that she burns in the heavens like 'a beautiful star,/like a lovely and eternal angel.' Kozlov died two years after this last poetic exchange with the Princess.[27]

Writing to Shevyrev, Glinka sent his 'most profound thanks to the Princess Zinaida Alexandrovna' for the way she had looked after them. Glinka was not happy in Naples which at first he thought detestable, and which reminded him, he said, of St Petersburg, although he was very happy to meet Donizetti and Bellini as well as other important figures in Neapolitan musical life such as the celebrated Italian tenor Nozzari. Among those he liked was Zinaida's sister-in-law Sophia, who was living there at the time.

Glinka remained in Naples until illness and depression drove him away, in February 1832. He intended to stop in Rome on his way to Milan, as is apparent from a letter which he wrote to Zinaida a few days before his departure on 23 February 1832.

My health has suffered from the changeable climate here to the point where I have had to abandon my harpsichord completely, and I am at present quite unable to accept the honour you do me of suggesting that I play at the Philharmonic Society,

he writes, adding that he would love to take part in making music at her house. He ends with greetings to Zinaida's sister and several others including Count Ricci and the painter, Bruni.[28]

Several members of the family were living in Italy at that time. Sophia Volkonsky, Zinaida's sister-in-law, her friend and companion of the campaigning years with Tsar Alexander, who was temporarily living in Naples, was already beginning to show signs of the eccentricity for which she was famous in old age. She was the absolute opposite of her father and two of her brothers, Nikita and Sergei, who were generous to the point of madness, and her stinginess would eventually turn into kleptomania. When paying visits, she would fill her bag, with the deftness of a magician, with candle ends, oranges, matches and pencils, as her nephew recalled. She became impossibly mean, scolding her maids for using a match instead of lighting one candle from another. On one occasion, when returning to Russia, she had asked the Repnins to look after a trunk for her. After several years of trailing the trunk around and seeing that it had become very battered, they decided to open it. It was full of firewood. Too mean to employ a lady's maid, she would cross the town every morning when she was living in Florence to have her hair done by her niece's maid. She always slept in her stays, which would be laced by her butler. The hotels knew her as 'the Princess with a Cossack for a lady's maid'. Towards the end of her life, nothing was safe from her. Knowing this, the family would patiently wait while she helped herself to whatever caught her fancy, and then hunt around her room to retrieve their belongings. She had always been very good company, however. Never a beauty, her lively dark eyes and strong personality had given her, as she herself put it, a *je ne sais quoi* which had made her attractive to men. Her grand-nephew recalled how she used to boast coyly that a tea service, a present to her from King George IV, 'was not a present from a king but a present from a man to a woman'. An indefatigable and adventurous traveller to the end of her days, she had journeyed all over Europe by public stagecoach. On one occasion in Switzerland, she was arrested because she was carrying a large number of diamonds in a stocking and nobody would believe that she had not stolen them. A great lady simply did not travel in this way. She raised hell, threatening to write to all the crowned heads of Europe, and was finally released. She was indeed in correspondence with half the statesmen and many of the crowned heads of Europe. Later she travelled by train – always in third class – 'to learn about local customs', as she put it. In Siberia in 1854 to see her brother Sergei, she went all the way to the Chinese borders, visiting every Buddhist monastery with the object of finding the Grand Lama, who was then ill. Not at all put out, she continued her search until she found him. 'I am going to see him, dead or alive.' In spite of her eccentricities, Sophia retained a sharp sense of humour and an amusing turn of phrase to the end of her days, making her popular with successive generations.[29]

Also in Italy, living first in Frascati at the Villa Muti, and later in Florence at the Palazzo Torigniani, were Prince and Princess Repnin, Nikita's eldest brother and his wife. Prince Repnin had left Russia after accusations that he had misappropriated government funds intended for an institution in Poltava where he had his estates. His name was only cleared two months after his death, after a protracted court case.

Zinaida was one of the few members of the family to write regularly to Maria Volkonsky in Siberia. Her warm affectionate letters and thoughtful presents meant a great deal. Vegetable and flower seeds, waterproof stockings for Sergei, sheaves of Italian music for Maria all somehow found their way from Rome to Siberia. Sergei had become a passionate gardener. He adored working on the land in Chita and was proud of the vegetables and flowers he grew in his garden. Maria never lost her love of music. The little clavichord which Zinaida had given her, so hastily and secretly strapped on to the back of the sleigh on the evening of Maria's departure from Moscow, had been one of her chief consolations and delights in Siberia. Maria too wrote often to Zinaida. In spite of censorship and long delays, their correspondence continued until the end. In July 1830 Maria had given birth to her second child, a girl christened Sophia, who died the same day. At last good news came: in 1832, a son Mikhail (Misha) was born, followed two years later by Elena, or Nellie as she was known. In 1835, when old Princess Volkonsky knew that she was dying, she wrote to the Tsar begging him to allow her son to return. Nicholas refused, but out of respect for the memory of one who had been so close to his family for over fifty years, he cut short Sergei's twenty-year term of forced labour, allowing the family to move to the little village of Urik, near Irkutsk, where they were to live out their exile.

Zinaida's husband Nikita continued to live in St Petersburg during the next few years, visiting Rome only occasionally. But he corresponded regularly with his wife and with Shevyrev about his son's education. Alexander was due to sit his university entrance exams and Shevyrev hoped that, in preparation for them, they might go to Paris to attend lectures on law at the university. The July Revolution of 1830, in which the Bourbon monarchy had been finally overthrown, had made that inadvisable. Writing to Shevyrev to give his consent to a new plan to go to Switzerland and Germany instead, Nikita was full of paternal concern and tenderness, asking for a report on Alexander's interests and character – 'his tendencies, both good and bad. At the age of twenty', he wrote, it is more important to pay attention to character and morals than to learning; the first turns the soul towards goodness, the second develops the mind. It would be good to see them develop equally but this doesn't always happen. Learning often destroys a simplicity of spirit; there are many such examples around. For God's sake take care of my young man, don't let him become headstrong. The spirit of Voltaire and Boileau is still strong, especially in Geneva.

Unlike his brother Sergei, Nikita was conservative and anxious that his son should not be exposed to any revolutionary ideas.[30] While Zinaida was prepared to consult her husband on their son's education, reports that her mother-in-law had views regarding the subject got on her nerves. The old Princess had wanted her grandson to sit his exams in St Petersburg, so that she might keep him near her, and perhaps near his father, apparently with Nikita's approval. Nikita had also suggested the University of Berlin as a possibility. When Zinaida, to whom St Petersburg, the court and probably her mother-in-law were anathema, heard of these plans, she sent off a furious letter to Nikita, announcing that Alexander would be arriving with Shevyrev at the beginning of September to sit his exams in Moscow. The Prince, who usually left all decisions to her – perhaps, given his passive nature, he had very little choice in the matter – caved in immediately. He could not understand why his wife was so upset, he wrote to Shevyrev in a letter which also congratulates Alexander on passing his exams. Mildly aggrieved, he supposed that somebody must have told her that it had been decided that Alexander was to take his exams in St Petersburg rather than Moscow. It had been no more than a conversation in the family, but the Princess had written angrily about his mother's interference. He hopes that Shevyrev will help to calm her down. In the same letter, and sounding very much like a man between two immovable forces, the Prince also admits to 'finding myself, in the extraordinary and ridiculous position of having no money, which has never happened before.' Would Shevyrev borrow 1000 roubles (to be paid back in the following month with gratitude and interest) and bring Alexander up to St Petersburg, so that his grandmother might embrace him and express her congratulations on his exam results in person?[31] In fact, poor Nikita was constantly in financial trouble. He was not good with money, and it was Zinaida who was obliged to take on responsibility for their financial affairs. Although the Prince loved his son, he apparently did not visit Alexander once during his years in Moscow, either out of financial embarrassment or laziness, or perhaps a combination of both.

Shevyrev and his charge left Rome for Geneva at the end of 1831, from where, after a few months, they were to go on to Russia. Zinaida knew that this, her first parting with her son, was also the beginning of his new life, a watershed for them both. The idea threw her into despair. In May she travelled to Switzerland to see him, intending to accompany him back to Russia. On the way, in Bolzano, she suffered a serious nervous breakdown for the second time in her life. Her illness seriously alarmed her friends. Prince Viazemsky wrote five letters to his wife about Zinaida's 'temporary madness', reporting that she had once again suffered uncontrollable fits during which she had bitten through her tongue and lip and had called for a priest, making her confession to a Greek priest from whom she also received communion. Zinaida's fits might almost suggest that she suffered from a mild form of epilepsy but in fact, since they were associated with extreme mental agitation, were more likely to be hysterical. Although she was often depressed she seems to have had no more than two such fits in her life.

In Dresden, Adam Mickiewicz received a letter from Zinaida's son with a postscript from her: 'I am dying – eternity begins for your friend.'[32] 'I cannot find an explanation for your terrible silence, which I can bear no longer,' he wrote back in extreme agitation a few days later, after sending off a hurried note to ask about her:

I've been counting the days, calculating the distance, and I feel that I should already have had a letter from that wretched Bolzano. Perhaps you misunderstood my last note? I know that it was scarcely legible – I was writing in the most terrible anxiety. Nonetheless, my instinct, which rarely lets me down, tells me that the dark foreboding which you expressed in those few lines you added to Alexander's letter will not be fulfilled and that Heaven will preserve you and lengthen your days, which are so precious to us all. If you are still ill, please dictate a few words, but sign them in your own hand. Please send the letter to Strasbourg. I remained

Princess Zinaida Volkonsky at the time of her Moscow salon

The Beloselsky Palace on Tversky Street where Zinaida held her Moscow salon 1825-

Alexander Sergeivich Pushkin by
I.I. Vivien 1826

imitry Venevitnov by
F. Sokolov 1827

Zinaida at the ball, in her Moscow salon

A ball at Zinaida's Moscow house in the late 1820's

Party at the Villa Volkonsky, Rome, in the late 1830's,
by G. Gagrin one of Karl Bruilov's students

Sketch of Gogol at the Villa Volkonsky, attributed to F. Bruni

Zinaida Volkonsky in 1822 and 1855

Zinaida's original villa in Rome, as it is today

Memorial to Zinaida, erected by her son, in the garden of the Villa Volkonsky, Rome

Cardinal Consalvi

Memorial tablet to Zinaida,
Nikita Volkonsky and Maria
Vlasova at the church of San
Vincenzo and Anerslasio in
Rome where they were buried

in Dresden for two months with the sole hope of seeing you on your way through; it was impossible to wait any longer. – I am going to France. – As soon as you are able to travel I beg that you forget your gloomy intention of burying yourself once again in the snows of Russia. Go back to Rome. Perhaps one of these days I shall make one more pilgrimage there.[33]

Mickiewicz's mind was put at rest by Shevyrev who wrote to tell him that the Princess was recovering. Zinaida herself also wrote, announcing that she was

in Rome as you had wished. – I was dying as you know. They had given me up. – I was so much comforted during my illness by our Heavenly Father that my death seemed sweet to me and I no longer sought to live. – My illness was the bridge between myself and God.[34]

Mickiewicz had spent the winters of 1829–30 and 1830–31 in Rome, a great deal of the time with Zinaida. There he had presented her with his own translation of 'The Greek Room' ('Pokoi Grecki'), which he had written about her house in Moscow, which begins: 'I moved towards the shadows where I saw her shining eyes, and followed her white dress which floated over the ebony tiles.'[35] He also translated a sonnet for her from the Polish into French so that she could understand it. The poem reflects his frustration at the language barrier in poetry: 'O Poetry, Yours is not the art of Painting / Yours is not the art of singing.'[36]

The Polish rising, which had broken out in November 1830 and lasted almost a year before being crushed by Russian troops, was a painful reminder to them both of the Decembrist uprising a few years before. The result was a tragedy for Poland. The constitution of 1815 was abrogated, the Church brought under secular control, while the brutal Marshal Paskevich, Nicholas's viceroy, proceeded with a programme of Russification at every level. Mickiewicz, who had not taken part in the rising but had felt it so deeply that he had fallen into deep depresssion and even contemplated suicide, now gave himself wholly to the twin calls of his country and his faith. Like Zinaida, he was becoming more absorbed by religion and mysticism. In the spring of

1832 he left for Dresden which was then full of exiled Poles.

While Zinaida's nervous breakdown was triggered by her unhappiness over the departure of her son, she had suffered intermittently from depression for the previous three years. Perhaps her return to Italy, which she had hoped would restore her to health, had proved less than perfect. Her inner anguish was not so easily left behind. Her reunion with Ricci provided no solutions, indeed it probably added to her growing sense of guilt. Her own explanation, confided to a French bishop, Monsignor Luquet, many years later, in 1851, was that a tormenting period of inward struggle had preceded her breakdown in Bolzano, during which she had once again experienced a strong religious call, similar to the one which she had felt early in her life and which she had rejected. Zinaida herself seemed to associate her hysterical fits and nervous collapse with profound spiritual experiences. Because of her breakdown Zinaida did not go to Russia, returning instead to Rome in July, where, with the loving support of her sister Madeleine, she recovered her health and her spirits. However deeply Zinaida may have been attracted to the Catholic Church, she did not take her conversion lightly. Even in Bolzano she had asked to see an Orthodox priest.[37] It is very likely that Zinaida was received into the Catholic Church sometime during Lent 1833, although her name, together with those of her sister Madeleine, Vladimir Pavey and five of her servants (who were all received into the Catholic Chuch at the same time), does not appear in the parish register of the church of Sts Vincenzo and Anastasio as a communicant until 1836.[38]

Music was once again heard in the drawing-room at the Palazzo Poli. One of Zinaida's first new friendships after her move to the Palazzo was with the Roman popular poet, Giuseppe Gioachino Belli, who lived a few doors away at 91 Via Poli. His brother-in-law, the writer Jacopo Ferreti, and his wife Teresa Terziani lived in the same buiding. Teresa, who was an accomplished pianist and singer, became a close friend, often going to the concerts of the Rome Philharmonic Society with Zinaida.

In spite of her own troubles, Zinaida did not forget her friends. After the fall of the Bourbons in the July Revolution, Sosthène de La Rochefoucauld, as an extreme Ultra, found himself in the prison of Sainte-Pélagie. Zinaida wrote to him as soon as she heard.

My dear Viscount, I could not but express my concern about your present situation. I believe that your enthusiasm will support you in all your trials, and that there is a consolation in the knowledge that one is suffering for those one loves. The thought of your dear wife, of your father, of the unhealthy air of a prison full of people, all this makes me think with pain of your captivity. I should like you to know that my friendship follows you everywhere, and that I shall never forget the proof you have given me of yours. May you soon find, in the bosom of a loving family, that peace which is so needed in this time of upheaval. May God grant you patience and good health. With all good wishes to you and yours, devotedly, Zinaida Volkonsky.

La Rochefoucauld later included this letter in his memoirs, writing that he had not been surprised that the Princess, 'with the grace which was natural to her', should have written to him as soon as she learned of his misfortune.[39]

At the same time Alexander Turgenev, brother of the Decembrist Nicolai Turgenev (and distant relation of the novelist), was in Rome and trying to persuade his dear Corinne – as he invariably called Zinaida – to contribute another travel article for Pushkin's journal *Severnii Tsveti* (*Northern Flowers*).[40] He had also asked her sister Madeleine to write a description of Zinaida's new villa. Zinaida contributed two poems instead. In the same letter he thanks her 'for Zhukovsky'. The poet Zhukovsky was recovering from illness in Switzerland at the time and Turgenev had been trying to persuade him to come to Rome. Zinaida had added her pleas to his letter. Zhukovsky arrived in Rome in the spring of 1833, travelling on to Naples with Turgenev. While in Rome they saw much of the Princess.[41] An old friend from her childhood, her music teacher, the French composer Boieldieu, also came to Rome in what was to be the last year of his life. Writing to her with his New Year wishes, he recalls the gardens of her villa: 'How happy I would be if I were your gardener! What lovely flowers I would bring you every week, winter and summer!'[42]

The end of 1834 brought one of Zinaida's closest friends to Rome. Apart from his time in Poland this was to be Prince Viazemsky's first journey abroad, though he had often made plans to travel before. He had been planning it with Zhukovsky, Pushkin, Krylov and Griboyedov. But the constellation of Russian writers never got there.[43] Now, together with his wife and three daughters, he was travelling in search of a cure for his daughter Praskovia's (known as Pashenka or Polina) consumption. 'The Viazemskys are here,' wrote Pushkin to his wife.[44] 'Poor Polina is very weak and pale. It is sad to look at her father. He is quite destroyed. They are all to go abroad. God willing the climate will help her.'[45]

The Viazemskys went first to Hanau to visit a Dr Kopp, strongly recommended to them by Zhukovsky. From Hanau Viazemsky wrote to Zinaida. Polina was recovering after three weeks of treatment, and Dr Kopp advised wintering in Rome, so Viazemsky was asking for her help and advice as well as that of Count Ricci, to find four sunny and not too expensive rooms in a salubrious part of town. After a number of practical questions regarding their itinerary – he trusts Zinaida more than the military adviser to the Duke of Saxe-Gotha, he says – Viazemsky writes that he longs 'to breathe freely and warmly near you and to be able to "de-Germanise" and "de-potato" [*déger-maniser* and *dépomme-de-terriser*] myself in "the land where the lemon trees bloom"' (a reference to Goethe's famous poem 'Kennst du das Land . . .' about Italy). In spite of his sadness and anxiety for his daughter, his letter is full of literary allusions and amusing word play common to both of them, in several languages; it is a letter to a friend with whom he has everything in common. He ends with his respects to Zinaida's sister and to Count Ricci.[46]

Zinaida's reply was immediate, answering all his questions about travel. Large and beautiful quarters at the Palazzo Conti in the Piazza Minerva were quickly arranged, so that when the Viazemskys arrived in Rome in December 1834 after being delayed by bad weather they found that Zinaida had prepared everything for them, 'like a loving sister, or tender mother'. They immediately felt so much at home that Viazemsky rushed off to see the Colosseum by moonlight that same night.[47] The Prince was anxious to settle his family since he had only four months' leave of absence from his post at the Ministry of Finance and he needed his job. He nevertheless extended his leave, spending five months in Rome, during which time he met all the Russians of note as well as many interesting Romans.

Soon after their arrival, Zinaida gave a party in Viazemsky's honour where he met the poets Belli and Ferreti. Belli was 'the poet of the people' writing in Romanesco, the Roman dialect. He believed that only in the simplicity and irreverence of popular dialect could one find true feeling. Zinaida had asked him to demonstrate his poetry:

> I was invited to a dinner by Her Highness, Princess Zinaida Volkonsky, together with the Russian poet Viazemsky. After dinner while I was thanking her, I was asked to show the Prince an example of my Roman style. I began with the following lines:

> Sor Artezza Zenavida Voroschi,
> Perché lei me vo'espone a sti du'rischi
> O che gnisun cristiano me capischi
> O me capischi troppo e me conoschi?
> La mi Musa è de casa Miseroschi
> Dunque come volete che finischi?
> Io già la vedo che finischi a fischi
> Si la scampo dar zugo de li boschi.[48]

On 13 January, Zinaida invited the Viazemskys to celebrate the Russian New Year, but they were unable to attend because they did not wish to leave their sick daughter alone. Once again Belli was invited to compose a poem, this time in honour of Count Ricci.[49]

Cardinal Mezzofanti, one of the wonders of Rome, fluent in thirty languages, was another friend Zinaida introduced to Viazemsky. Through her he also met Horace Vernet, in whose studio he spent many happy hours, and Stendhal, who was then consul in Civitavecchia. Viazemsky had so much admired *Le Rouge et le Noir*, but had been rather surprised by Stendhal's undistinguished appearance. Another guest at the villa was the American novelist and political thinker, James Fennimore Cooper. A great friend of Mickiewicz's, who had sent him to Zinaida, Cooper had been closely involved in European liberal politics, the ideals of which had led to the July Revolution in France, the Reform Bill in England and the Polish uprisings. Cooper was very pleased with the Russians he met at the house of the 'very kind and intelligent Princess Zinaida Volkonsky'.[50]

Zinaida surrounded Viazemsky and his family with love and care, delighted to have them in Rome and often visiting poor Pashenka, whose condition had at first improved. She even arranged to sing at the girl's bedside. But in the spring, Pashenka's condition suddenly took a turn for the worse. She died on 23 March 1835, and was buried in Rome. After the funeral the Viazemskys left for Naples with Alexander Turgenev, entrusting their younger daughter to Zinaida's care. They left Italy a month later. 'The whole journey seems to me to have been a terrible dream,' Prince Viazemsky wrote to Alexander Turgenev on his return to Russia. His passionately longed-for visit to Italy was to be forever associated with tragedy.[51]

Zinaida commemorated Pashenka's death in a moving poem, 'On the Death of his Daughter',[52] in which she assures her friend that, although he must leave, he is leaving his daughter's grave to her care and it will not be 'orphaned' by his absence. Zinaida kept her word. Three years later she took Nicolai Gogol to visit it. Afterwards he wrote to Viazemsky: 'The grave, so dear to your heart, is covered with roses. I am happy to say that it is not orphaned (abandoned).'[53]

Prince Alexander, Zinaida's son, finished his studies in Moscow in 1834. He entered the diplomatic service and was soon posted to Warsaw. Before leaving he had written an article, 'Arguments on Religions', which Odoevsky published in the journal *Soveremennik* (*The Contemporary*), together with a letter from Zhukovsky. 'The letter', wrote Nikita proudly to Shevyrev, 'not only praised the article but expressed amazement that a young man brought up abroad wrote with such facility in Russian.'[54]

Several matters were worrying Zinaida at this time. In 1835 Count Ricci was suddenly stricken with a serious eye disease. His relationship with Zinaida was in any case changing. The combination of his illness and her religious convictions gradually transformed their love affair into a warm friendship and he remained very close to her although much altered by his illness.[55] Zinaida's relationship with Ricci was her last love affair. Her search had always been more spiritual than physical and her romantic entanglements, with Tsar Alexander, with Barbieri and with Ricci, while exciting for a while, had given her no permanent happiness, indeed her lasting friendships with them all had proved more satisfying than the love affairs. She was also concerned, in 1834, about the passing in Russia of a new law which placed the estates of all Russians living abroad under the tutelage of the state. Nikita had written to Shevyrev about the problem, and had set about transferring their estates to his son. Zinaida finally decided that she must go to Russia herself. She met her son on the way and they travelled together to St Petersburg, ariving on 20 June 1836. She was presented at court on the following day. She must have arrived in St Petersburg with her usual mixed feelings. Many of her friends were there but there was also a great deal of business which awaited her, and she could not be sure of her reception. Princess Sophia Volkonsky, who was there at the time, wrote that Zinaida was well received but everyone had found her greatly changed. Zinaida had indeed changed. She was now almost forty-seven. In the seven years since the days of her Moscow salon, when she had been universally admired as the still-young and lovely Queen of the Muses, she had turned into a middle-aged woman. Her voice, still strong and musical, now caused surprise as well as admiration. After a concert at the Venevitinovs', where Zinaida sang accompanied by Glinka, Pavel Durnovo, her niece Alina's husband, wrote, 'The Princess is still singing well in spite of her years, Glinka played wonderfully.'[56]

The court itself had been transformed since her debut there. What had not changed was the Russian love of lavish entertainment. On 1 July, Zinaida went to Peterhof for the festivities to celebrate the Empress's birthday accompanied by the painter Bruni, at which supper was served for 5000 persons, amid splendid illuminations with all the fountains playing. She had intended to go on to Moscow at the end of July, as soon as she decently could, but the unexpected illness of her son kept her in St Petersburg until the middle of August.[57] She left Moscow on 1 October, stopping in Paris for a month. On the way back to Rome, in November, she stopped at the Grand Séminaire in Langres, where she had meetings with several theologians with whom she must have discussed attitudes towards Catholic converts in Russia and her own spiritual concerns.[58] At last Zinaida returned to Rome. Her travelling days were almost over. She was to see her own country only one more time.

11

Rome: Dead Souls and Souls Reborn

'He who has been to Italy may bid goodbye to other countries. He who has been to heaven will not wish to return to earth.'

NIKOLAI GOGOL

The year 1837 began with an event which shook St Petersburg and indeed all Russia. Alexander Pushkin died on 29 January, aged only thirty-eight. Zinaida had recognised his exceptional talent at once and they had many of the closest friends in common. Had she seen Pushkin during her visit to St Petersburg in the previous year? Probably not. He was in an unhappy mood and most likely kept away from society as much as he could. Zinaida would certainly have known through their mutual close friends, the Viazemskys, the Odoevskys, Venevitinov, Alexander Turgenev and Zhukovsky, all of whom she did see, that rumours were growing stronger concerning Pushkin's wife Natalia and d'Anthès, the adopted son of the Dutch ambassador. A great beauty, with an insatiable appetite for social life, Natalia was a star at Nicholas's court. In order to keep her there, the Tsar had made Pushkin a page, a humiliating absurdity at his age. For some time, Pushkin had been trying to extricate himself from court duties, which bored and exhausted him. He was in a bitter and angry mood when, goaded by an anonymous letter about his wife's infidelity, he addressed d'Anthès in terms so insulting that it was impossible for him not to challenge Pushkin to a duel. The duel, in which Pushkin was mortally wounded, took place on 27 January 1837. For two days, St Petersburg waited while the Viazemskys, the Karamzins, Alexander Turgenev and Zhukovsky kept vigil around his bed. Conscious almost to the end, Pushkin was able to say goodbye to all his closest friends. In an age when few Russians were literate, a silent crowd of 50,000 had gathered outside the house of the great poet.

The next day, glowing tributes to 'our people's glory' appeared in Russia's journals. Afraid of a public backlash, the Tsar ordered that Pushkin's body be taken to a small church close to his house, rather than to St Isaac's Cathedral. Soon excoriating verses, written on the day of his death by a twenty-two-year-old cavalary officer, Mikhail Lermontov, were circulating in St Petersburg. Outraged by what he saw as the connivance of the authorities in Pushkin's death, Lermontov wrote a famous postscript to his passionate 'Death of a Poet', for which he was exiled to the Caucasus:

> *And you the proud and shameless progeny*
> *Of fathers famous for their infamy,*
> *You, who with servile heel have trampled down,*
> *The fragments of great names laid low by chance,*
> *You, hungry crowd that swarms about the throne,*
> *Butchers of freedom, genius and glory,*
> *You hide behind the shelter of the law.*
> *Before you right and justice must be dumb!*
> *But, parasites of vice, there's God's assize;*
> *There is an awful court of law that waits.*
> *You cannot reach it with the sound of gold;*
> *It knows your thoughts beforehand and your deeds;*
> *And vainly you shall call the lying witness;*
> *That shall not help you any more;*
> *And not with all the filth of all your gore,*
> *Shall you wash out the poet's righteous blood.*[1]

Lermontov's bitterness was due to a common belief that Pushkin had been driven to his death by a repressive regime which had considered him a radical and his journal *Sovremennik* a hotbed of liberal thought.

Soon after the news of Pushkin's death another young Russian writer arrived in Rome. Nikolai Gogol had left Russia the previous year, angry at the stupidity, the lack of critical faculty or principle of the 'patriotic' press (i.e. rabid supporters of the Tsar's regime). He came with a letter of introduction to Zinaida from their mutual friend Viazemsky. Before his departure Gogol had shredded the reputations of the editors of the two most popular St Petersburg journals, Faddei Bulgarin of the *Northern Bee* and Osip Senkovsky of *The Reader's Library*. He was furious at the way his play, *The Government Inspector*, had been performed and received. With the exception of Prince Viazemsky (writing in *Sovremennik*) the St Petersburg press had been highly critical. 'There are so many vile faces in Russia, that I could not bear to look at them any longer,' Gogol wrote to the historian Pogodin after leaving Russia. Before he came to Rome, Gogol spent some months in Paris where he was already immersed in writing his masterpiece, *Dead Souls*. There he saw Alexander Turgenev and also met Adam Mickiewicz, both of whom must have recommended him to their friend Zinaida in Rome. Gogol, too, had been absolutely devastated by the news of Pushkin's death. 'All the joy of my life has disappeared together with him,' he wrote to his friend Pletyanov from Rome:

> I never undertook anything without his advice. I never wrote a single line without imagining him before me. – My present work was suggested by him. I owe it entirely to him. I can't go on. – I am broken-hearted.[2]

In Rome, Gogol first took rooms in the Via San Isidoro, not far from Zinaida's house. In June 1837 he moved to a top-floor flat in the Via Sistina, then called the Via Felice, near the Spanish Steps, where he remained until 1843. He loved Rome, although it had seemed small to him at first. 'But the longer I am here, the bigger it seems, the buildings are bigger, the views more beautiful, the sky lovelier and there are enough paintings, ruins, and ancient monuments to look at for a lifetime. You fall in love with Rome slowly and gradually, but for as long as you live . . .'[3]

Zinaida and Gogol felt an immediate rapport. Both were deeply spiritual and inclined to melancholy and excess, and they shared friends and interests as well as an abiding love of Rome. Gogol now spent days at Zinaida's villa, plotting his work on *Dead Souls*, lying for hours on the terrace on top of the aqueduct like a lizard, his back against the warm brick, silently gazing at the blue sky or across at the Roman Campagna.[4] He became very fond of Zinaida's sister Madeleine, with whom he used to discuss cooking. A short piece he wrote in her album begins:

> How stupid the turkeycock is, how stupid the Russian who has gone abroad and regrets the absence of his serfs, how stupid is uniform and evening dress two of the the most absurd inventions of the 19th century, but all of them put together are no stupider than my head. I simply can't dig anything out of it for you Maria Alexandrovna. It is full of nonsense and wildness, similar to a Russian provincial town; pointless like rooms on the day after a party, with which the host himself was dissatisfied, which his guests joked about, and after which all that was left to him was broken crockery, dirty floors and the sleepy mugs of his footmen. This is what I'd like to say to you, although I wish to say something better and I am very grateful to you for your kindness. Gogol[5]

This short sketch written casually in a friend's album is unmistakably 'Gogolian', bearing many of the images employed by Gogol, such as the turkeycock, the hated uniforms and evening dress, in *Dead Souls* and in his shorter stories.

Zinaida introduced Gogol to all the Russian painters living in Rome, most of whom he disliked. 'Terrible bores,' he wrote to his friend Danilevsky, 'each one of them is absolutely sure that he has great talent.'[6] But he nevertheless became particularly close to Alexander Ivanov. The most respected of the group, Ivanov had arrived in Rome in 1830 in search of a new style in art. In common with most Russian thinkers of his generation, he was then beginning to see the artist as having a great social responsibility. At first he painted biblical and mythological subjects, but he had just embarked on his *magnum opus*, a single enormous canvas, *The Appearance of Christ before the People*, which today hangs in the Russian Museum in St Petersburg. He intended it as an icon of the new age of Russian art, which he believed was dawning. Gogol later wrote an admiring essay, 'The Portrait', about this huge canvas and Ivanov's ideas of the function of art. Ivanov was openly homosexual, filling his canvases with naked boys. In one of two studies for this painting, a naked figure of a man has

Gogol's head, as does that of a crouching slave. It seems very likely that this sexual orientation was shared by Gogol himself, who tried to repress it. He had always been uncomfortable with women, except for his mother, and his strong religious beliefs had produced deep and abiding feelings of guilt in him.[7]

Recently converted to Catholicism, Zinaida espoused her religion with zeal, and set about trying to convert her friends and family. Evidently Gogol was no exception. News of her activities must have reached Russia, obliging Gogol to deny any such possibility to his anxious mother, herself an ardent Orthodox. 'Our religion', he wrote, 'is in no way different from the Catholic religion, and there is therefore no need to change one for the other. Both are true.'[8] Two exiled Polish priests, Hieronim Kajsiewicz and Piotr Semenenko, friends of Mickiewicz, had arrived in Rome in the meantime, and Zinaida had co-opted them in her attempt to persuade Gogol. 'He [Gogol] has a noble heart,' wrote one of them, 'and he is still young. If we succeed in influencing him more deeply later on, he will not be deaf to the truth and will turn to it with all his heart. The Princess cherishes this hope.'[9] The two young idealists had themselves come back to the Church and eventually to the priesthood through the influence of Mickiewicz who then lived in Paris. They had been persecuted by the Russian government as a result.

The arrival of the two Polish priests began a new period in Zinaida's life, dividing her loyalties. Her son, now a Russian diplomat, had been posted to Poland where he was working for Marshal Paskevich, the *de facto* and much-hated governor of Poland. As a Catholic, she was anxious to support the Church without betraying Russian interests. She maintained a patriotic front to the priests, but at the same time wrote to Prince Koslovsky for funds to help Polish pilgrims and to repair the Polish church of St Stanislas in Rome, pointing out that this building was now the responsibility of the Russian crown.[10] At the same time Zinaida took the exiles under her wing, introducing them to prominent members of the Curia, among them the Vatican's Secretary of State, Cardinal Lambruschini. The two priests wanted to set up a Polish centre for the religious fugitives who were now steadily trickling to Rome. As always, Zinaida threw herself whole-heartedly into the cause of the Poles, pleading for them before Pope Gregory

XVI himself who granted them an audience in 1840. This resulted, in 1843, in the establishment of a new order, the Congregation of the Resurrection.

Zinaida's salon continued to be an artistic and intellectual centre to which all the Russians in Rome gravitated. It was there that Gogol first met Belli. Gogol had been very impressed by Belli's work, particularly his *Sonetti Romaneschi*. Other frequent visitors at her salon were the poet Jacopo Feretti, the Dante scholar Frédéric Ozanam, painters and sculptors such as Horace Vernet, Cammucini, Tenerani and Thorvaldsen, as well as leading Catholic intellectuals, including Cardinal Mezzofanti, with whom Gogol became very friendly, and the musical and worldly Cardinal Albani. French liberal Catholics such as the priest and writer Félicité de Lammenais and his followers, the great preacher Father Lacordaire and the Romantic medievalist Comte Montalembert, who were also friends of Mickiewicz, were regular guests. After the July Revolution, which had, in part, been sparked by the issue of clericalism versus secularism, the three Frenchmen had striven to reconcile religion and liberty, founding a paper, *L'Avenir*, in which they had advocated the separation of Church and state and argued for universal suffrage and the abolition of censorship, until they were prevented by the Pope's encyclical of 1832 (*Mirari Vos*). The missionary Bishop Luquet was another of this group, and the Abbé Gerbet, who was also Zinaida's confessor.

In December 1837, the young Crown Prince of Russia, the future Alexander II, arrived in Rome as part of a Grand Tour which had already included Germany, Austria and northern Italy. He was accompanied by the poet Zhukovsky, his tutor since 1826. Zhukovsky's first visit to Italy had been in 1833, and he had often visited Zinaida since then.[11] A good artist himself, Zhukovsky was forever sketching, often in Zinaida's garden where he made several sketches of Zinaida and Gogol, with whom he spent most of his time. 'He makes excellent sketches a dozen a minute,' wrote Gogol.[12] Together the two poets visited many of the artists' studios, including those of Ingres, Vernet, Cammucini and Henry Williams, and spent hours in churches and walking all over Rome which both loved. 'Gogol is like a flash of lightning, he lives and breathes Italy,' Zhukovsky wrote in his diary. Together they celebrated Gogol's name day with Zinaida who, as always, arranged a dinner with music, where she sang with Ricci.

Zhukovsky seems to have been rather a negligent tutor – he did not accompany the Crown Prince on a visit to Naples during the two months they were in Rome, spending much of his time in the pursuit of his own pleasures. Between 16 December 1838 and 13 February 1839, his notes to Zinaida show that they saw each other frequently. 'We are here until Wednesday. I can't come with you today [on a visit to Palocardo as we see from his diary] because I am to see the Pope, and then at three o'clock to the Corso. Would it be possible to arrange to have dinner with you on Saturday or Sunday? Let me know which. Sunday might be better as that would be after the Corso,' Zhukovsky wrote at the end of January when the Crown Prince's party had been watch the carnival processions on the Corso for six out of the eight days.

Zhukovsky's last note to Zinaida, dated 11 February 1839, refers to her poem, 'To My Son and Friend: Four Angels', which had been published in 1836 in *Moskovski Nabludatel* (*Moscow Observer*).

Your corrections are excellent. I am sending back your *Angels*, with a few extra corrections. They are worthy of their name. Goodbye, I hope to see you here [i.e in this world] and not on the side of the angels.[13]

During the Crown Prince's visit, in whose wake there were countless important Russians in Rome, Zinaida agreed to organise a reception at the villa for a public reading of *The Inspector General* by Gogol himself, for which tickets were sold at a high price. The idea had been Ivanov's and the evening was to be in aid of one of the young painters then working in Rome, a poor fellow Ukrainian, Shapovalenko. In spite of his low opinion of his compatriot's talents, Gogol had agreed.

The Crown Prince, his entourage and all the Russians of note in Rome duly assembled at the villa for the reading. The usually taciturn and unfriendly Ivanov had advertised the event widely, telling everyone how well Gogol would read. Zinaida had provided delicious food and refreshment (even ice-cream!), wrote the artist Iordan admiringly. The evening began well. Gogol, however, seated at a small table on platform, framed by two candles, with a glass of sweetened water before him, was uneasy, scowled throughout and read badly. The Crown Prince looked bored, the audience grew restive, failing to applaud at the end of the first act. Someone was heard to remark that Gogol had already served them up this dull rubbish in St Petersburg. Poor Zinaida tried desperately to keep her guests seated, but the royal party soon left, followed by most of the rest of the audience.

Finally only the group of painters and a small circle of Zinaida's friends and family, who had stayed on for her sake, surrounded the by now outraged writer. It was a long time before Gogol could forget or forgive the shocking insult. Ivanov on the other hand was unperturbed as the money had already been collected, enabling his protégé to remain in Rome long enough to finish his work.[14]

One of the original members of the Crown Prince's Grand Tour was Prince Iosif Vielhorsky, whose father, Prince Michael, a courtier and talented musician, was a friend of Zinaida's. So, when the young man was discovered to have tuberculosis, it was decided that after treatment in Germany he would winter in Rome with Zinaida. It was at Zinaida's villa that Gogol met young Vielhorsky on 20 December 1838. Gogol was immediately drawn to the serious young man who was working on a bibliography of Russian history. Before long he was completely in love with Iosif, and at last, here was someone who fully reciprocated his affections. They were together all winter but, in the spring, Iosif's health suddenly took a turn for the worse. Zinaida, perfectly aware of how much the relationship meant to both, invited Gogol to come and live at the villa. Whatever she may have thought of their relationship, she could not but help her friends. Perhaps she also cherished the thought of converting two souls at once. Gogol was grief-stricken, as he wrote to Shevyrev: 'I spend my days and nights at the bedside of the sick Iosif, of my Vielhorsky. The poor boy cannot bear a minute without me beside him.' To another friend, and former pupil, Maria Balabina, he wrote: 'I catch his every minute. His smile or an expression of momentary happiness represents an epoch to me, an event in my monotonous day.'[15]

Gogol kept a detailed diary of Iosif's last days at the Villa Volkon-sky, later found in his friend Pogodin's archive and published in Russia under the title *Nights at the Villa*, as if it were part of a work of fiction.

They were sweet and tormenting, those sleepless nights. He sat ill, in the armchair. I was with him. It was sweet to sit near him, to look at him. For two nights already we have been saying 'thou' to each other,

he wrote in the first entry. After several nights without sleep, Gogol went home to rest. The next day he was back, racked with guilt. On another occasion, leaving the sickroom for a while to prepare some-thing for Iosif, he was gone for an hour. When he returned, Gogol writes:

'My saviour,' he said to me. They still sound in my ears those words. 'My angel! did you miss me?' I kissed him on the shoulder. He offered his cheek. We kissed; he was still pressing my hand.

In spite of Gogol's and Madeleine's devoted nursing, Iosif Vielhor-sky died at the villa on 21 May 1839. 'The wind had wafted the scent of blossoming wild jasmine and white acacia, which it mingled with whirling rose petals. – I watched you my precious, tender flower,' wrote the distraught poet. Gogol had rushed out to find an Orthodox priest to administer extreme unction, when swept in Zinaida followed by a Catholic priest, the Abbé Gerbert. Her niece Varvara Repnina, who had been present, reported that Zinaida urged the Abbé, 'Now is the time to receive him into the Church.' He had hushed her, insisting that there must be peace and quiet in the room of a dying man. Vielhorsky then tried to take off his ring and give it to those looking after him – perhaps he meant it for Gogol – whereupon Zinaida had exclaimed that it was immoral, perhaps because one shouldn't be thinking of worldly things at the hour of death. As she bent over the dying boy, she cried out, 'I saw his soul leaving his body and it was a Catholic soul!'[16]

Zinaida's zealous but ill-judged attempt at a last-minute conversion caused a rift between her and Gogol. Both were still angry when Gogol left Rome with Iosif's father, at the beginning of June, to meet his mother who had arrived too late to see him.

A few days ago I buried my friend, one whom fate gave me at a time when friends are no longer given, I mean my Iosif Vielhorsky. We have long been attached to each other, have long respected one another, but we became united intimately, indissolubly and absolutely fraternally, only during his illness, alas. He was a man who would have adorned the reign of Alexander II. The rest of those who surround him haven't a grain of talent. The great and beautiful must perish, as all that is great and beautiful must perish in Russia,

Gogol wrote bitterly to Danilevsky, on 5 June.[17]

Prince Nikita, now nearly sixty but still a member of the Tsar's household, obtained leave to come to Rome in 1839. Here he pottered around writing bad poetry which he pressed his friend Shevyrev to try and get published. New laws concerning property rights had been passed in Russia meanwhile, but Zinaida knew that it was no use leaving things to her husband who had already squandered and mismanaged a large part of their fortune. She knew she would have to return to Russia and deal with the matter herself. She was depressed, consoled only by the thought of being able to see their son on the way, in Warsaw. To her great sorrow, when she arrived in Warsaw after leaving Rome in December 1839, she found her son still away on a mission to Constantinople and, although she waited in Warsaw for almost two months, she was unable to see him until her return journey to Rome in the following summer.

Although she had converted to the Catholic Church, Zinaida's reception in St Petersburg was not as bad as she had expected. She stayed with her half-sister Ketty, from whose house she wrote to Madeleine and 'mes amis de Roma', who were her familiars – her husband Nikita, Count Ricci, Shevyrev who was then in Rome, Marietta

Capalti and the Abbé Gerbet. Her rather disjointed letter was written apparently while a ball was in full swing.

My good sister, I write these words to you in a small grove covered with ivy. My friends from Roma [sic], it seems to me to be both original and consoling to chat to you here, while people gossip in one corner, play [cards] further on and dance in another room. It is very amusing. I picked up my pen to write to Viazemsky, [but had not something] which Ketty has forgotten that I am waiting for. I therefore pick up another piece of paper to talk to you from such a distance and in such a different environment. What *toilettes*, how many floating dresses and floating wits. The Emperor has already gone. He was quite charming to me. He spoke with a depth of feeling about himself at a time when his wife, son and daughter were all ill. I have been surrounded [with affection] and embraced and I am very touched by several sincere proofs [of friendship]. The Grand Duke Mikhail was delighted to see me again. The E. [Emperor] wishes to present me to his wife, so I shall see her soon. Perhaps I will be able to do something about this sad case [presumably their financial affairs]. Dear Miniato [she teases Count Ricci], I saw your beauty again, – the widow Saltikov. Zinaida has been dancing, but why are you not here, Marietta? Shevyrev, my friend, where are you? Only the dear Abbé might feel uncomfortable here, but I would find him a quiet spot. Everyone, dear Nikita, is so glad to know that your health has improved. I told the Emperor about my son's accident at sea. I miss him and wish he were near me. [To her sister she continues] I look at the house opposite, my dear friend, and I recall my father and hear him speak of his love for us, and tears come into my eyes.[18]

Although the Tsar had been kind and the Empress had presented her with a bracelet, Nicholas was not likely to exempt Zinaida from the new law regarding Roman Catholics. In addition to restrictions of property rights, Nicholas had decreed more severe measures against Russian converts, such as separation from any under-age children and a mandatory spell in a monastery for a period of penitence and, presumably, counter-indoctrination.

Knowing of Zinaida's conversion and of her proselytising activities among the Russians in Rome, an attempt was indeed made to persuade her to return to Russia and to Orthodoxy. This she categorically refused to do and, greatly overwrought, suffered another of her hysterical fits. While she was prostrated, letters flew between various members of the family. 'She has had another attack of her old illness, a kind of insanity,' wrote her niece Alina's husband, Pavel Durnovo, 'they are torturing her. The Synod wants to confine her to a monastery.'[19] Her niece Varvara Repnina later described these events briefly:

When the news of Princess Zinaida Volkonsky's conversion to Catholicism reached the Emperor Nicolai Pavlovich, His Majesty wished to bring her to reason and sent a priest to her for this purpose. But she had a *crise de nerfs* and convulsions. The Emperor allowed her to leave Russia and she chose Rome as her dwelling place. There she was soon called 'beata'.[20]

Was Zinaida's well-timed fit of hysterics simulated? She was, after all, an excellent actress. There were at that time, however, quite enough problems in her life to test the nerves even of a woman much less highly strung; she was, moreover, at a very vulnerable age. The pressures from her family, the imperative – for all their power and influence – not to offend the Tsar unduly, her concern for her son, now a diplomat with all his career before him, and finally financial worries as well as the possible loss of all their properties: all these considerations were pulling against deeply held religious convictions, as well as an independent and imperious nature. The combined pressure was quite enough to drive her into hysteria. Her predicament was much talked about, even as far away as Paris, where Count Rudolph Apponyi, ambassador of Austria-Hungary and the son of her friend the former ambassador in Rome, who himself knew Zinaida only by repute, wrote:

There has been much talk here of Princess Volkonsky, who is said to be intelligent and learned, but a bit strange and very excitable. The Emperor of Russia has ordered her to return to Orthodoxy;

when she refused she was sent into exile, and her lands con-
fiscated.[21]

Zinaida's exile was, in fact, self-imposed, though her conversion would
have made it very difficult to remain in Russia. It seems, however,
that she never had any intention of doing so. Her properties were
successfully transferred to her son, who managed to remain loyal to
his mother, to his country and to his religion.

Zinaida returned to Rome, arriving without warning on 10 June
1840, her sister's birthday. She had been happily reunited with her
son, in Warsaw, on the way home.

> I hasten to tell you of an unexpected joy. Tears poured from my
> eyes and I offered my most sincere thanks to the Almighty as her
> health, thank God, has much improved. I give you these details,
> knowing of your interest in my family. I have also just received an
> unexpected command from the Imperial Court to return to Russia
> at once,[22]

wrote Nikita to Shevyrev. The unexpected recall to Russia was because
the Tsar was afraid, not without foundation, that Zinaida would try
to convert her husband too. Nikita was, however, allowed to return
to Rome a year later. He had managed to get the Tsar's consent to
join his wife and remained in Rome until his death. He was now old
and probably considered harmless. In any case, the Prince was unlikely
to be missed in St Petersburg where his post at court had been due
to family connections rather than any merit of his own.

The Volkonskys' last years together were quite amicable although
there were recurring financial worries, particularly for the Prince. In
one of his many letters to Shevyrev at this time, the Prince complains
that their man of business, Emilianov, had again delayed payments
of his income, which, Nikita said, they needed. A telling postscript
from Zinaida makes clear her resigned and even affectionate tolerance
of Nikita's hopelessness with money. Shevyrev should ignore what
the Prince writes about Emilianov, who is a perfectly honest man,
she writes:

It is just that the Prince is worried about his income always being late, but this money serves only to pay for his carriage in my household, and only because he wishes it, and for nothing more; but he loves to give presents and gives whole fistfuls of money to the poor. He has already set aside a present of more than 600 roubles for my Alexander. He has always been like this. What is a great consolation to me is that he speaks of eternity, of God. He is searching for the Saviour, looks with repentance at the crucifixion and is generally becoming kinder and purer. I offer him up, and everyone, and myself, to the wounded breast of Jesus Christ. I am expecting my son here, and I bless him and pray for him, I bless you too. Soon Alexander will be here to console me.[23]

'My household', 'my son' – Zinaida had no doubts as to who had been in control from the start. She had long known her husband to be lazy and ineffectual. Now her only hope was to convert him to the Catholic faith. As for Nikita, he relied on her for everything, bowed to her superior mind and strength and seemed to adore her. That he was unhappy with his life, and suffered from a sense of futility and inadequacy, is clear, however, from some of the poems which he still sent to Shevyrev. One, composed to mark his sixtieth birthday, reads, 'I am still in this world/what is the point of living? / there is no happiness here/ our whole life is as nothing,' and more in the same vein.

There was a great deal of happiness for them both, however, in a visit from their son Alexander, although he wasn't able to stay for long.

Alexander is here with us. He is as clever and as good as it's possible to be. He is to return to Warsaw soon. I couldn't be more unhappy. My age and infirmity do not permit me to wish him *au revoir.*[24]

In his next letter to Shevyrev he writes:

Alexander has left for Warsaw, my wife is accompanying him as far as Livorno. I have stayed behind because of the weakness in my legs. My son is wonderful! I thank God for his existence, and you and my wife for his education!^{25}

Alexander was indeed all that his parents could have wished. He had inherited his mother's intelligence and thoughtfulness, her kindness and sincerity, as well as some of his father's softness of manner. Loyal to both his parents, he seems to have been stable and trustworthy and was well liked in Russia and abroad. Not as artistically gifted as his mother, he nevertheless wrote well, producing several treatises on philosophy, religion and literary criticism. In 1845, he married a young Frenchwoman, Louise de Lilien – to Zinaida's delight, a Catholic. 'My son is not yet a son of the Church! He has a good Catholic wife and a little daughter called Zinaida like me,' she wrote to her friend Mother Maria de Matthias.^{26} Although devoted to his mother and knowing it to be her dearest wish, Alexander never converted to the Catholic Church himself, but he unfailingly helped Zinaida in her charitable activities and carried out her wishes after her death to the letter. The Prince and his wife had no natural children of their own, but adopted two Russian children of their friends, the Illins, Zinaida and Nadezhda.

Zinaida's life after her return from Russia went on much as before. She continued to see her friends and those members of her family also living in Rome. Among them was Nikita's nephew, Grigory Volkonsky, son of his sister Sophia and Prince Peter. He and his sister Alina had always been close to Zinaida. As a member of the Russian mission to the Vatican, Grigory lived for many years with his family at the Palazzo Salviati, on the Corso. He was bohemian by nature and musically gifted; his was the only private house in which Pope Pius IX would allow the choristers of the Sistine Chapel to sing. Zinaida was a frequent and welcome guest there. Grigory, like his uncle Nikita, was excessively generous, in contrast to his mother Sophia. The whole Volkonsky clan seemed to have had a truly Russian capacity for excess.

Zinaida's own drawing-room was now more often filled with her religious rather than her artistic friends, many of whom were put off by her religious zeal. 'She has reached the extreme limits of fanaticism and is constantly surrounded by abbots,' wrote Andrei Muraviev, who had not escaped from Zinaida's efforts to convert her friends. 'It was odd to see her adopted son Pavey, first English, then Orthodox, now a Catholic and a Chamberlain at the Papal Court,' Muraviev continues.[27] Vladimir Pavey, always known in Rome as the Cavaliere Pavey, had considerable influence as a result of his post. Very little is known about him; he was never mentioned by either Zinaida or Nikita in their letters, nor was any more light thrown on his origins. He had been educated with Alexander and was at home in several languages. A poem to Zinaida's sister Madeleine in French shows his affection for her. He remained absolutely devoted to Zinaida, who obviously relied on him. Soon after Nikita's death Pavey went to Russia to sort out the Volkonskys' financial affairs, which had been left in complete disorder by the Prince. He managed them very efficiently, paying off all their debts over the next few years.

However, until her husband's death Zinaida still enjoyed and played music, went for drives and even occasionally to the theatre. 'Her love of the arts had not entirely left her, while her villa, built into the ancient Neronian aqueduct, breathed with the poetry of her past,' wrote Muraviev.[28] The Volkonskys continued to travel within Italy, although their journeys now usually had a religious focus. In his last letter to Shevyrev, still accompanied by his indifferent verse, poor Nikita writes of his failing health, although Zinaida's, he says, is not too bad.[29] Although Zinaida was becoming more and more immersed in her religion, from which she drew great comfort, she was still prey to bouts of melancholy and depression. She succeeded in her aim to convert her husband. The Prince was received into the Catholic Church in the last year of his life by their friend, the Abbé Gerbet. Soon afterwards the Volkonskys journeyed to Assisi, and it was there, on 6 December 1844, that Nikita died. His body was brought back to Rome for burial in their parish church of Sts Vincenzo and Anastasio, opposite the Trevi fountain.

Gogol had returned to Rome in 1840, intending to stay for two years and to finish *Dead Souls*. He had promised to return to Moscow in the following year with the first part of *Dead Souls* ready for publication. Before he left, his precarious emotional balance had been noticed by all his friends in Moscow. In Vienna, on his way to Rome, Gogol had fallen into severe depression as a result of several months of writer's block which had followed a bout of manic creativity. In Rome, Gogol and Zinaida once again resumed their former friendship. Gogol's young friend Annenkov, who lived with him in Rome and spent two months copying the first part of *Dead Souls* to Gogol's dictation, recalled how elated the writer would be after he finished dictating a particularly satirical passage, often at top speed, but also his great fear of being alone. He recalled too, the beginnings of Gogol's 'spiritual education' when he would spend hours on Zinaida's terrace, gazing at the sky.[30] In Rome, in January 1843, Alexandra Smirnova Rosset found Gogol anxious and unable to write. Determined to show her the city, 'Gogol was mostly silent. He would walk at a distance from us, picking up pebbles, tearing at the grass and waving his arms about, stumbling into trees and bushes. Sometimes he would stretch out on the ground, crying "Let's forget everything. Just look at the sky!"'[31] Gogol's 'spiritual education', a subject he had often discussed with Zinaida, had a disastrous effect on his writing. Back in Rome in January 1845, after travels in Europe and another visit to Russia, he was in a state of near nervous collapse although his final breakdown did not come until that summer. At the end of June he burnt all that he had written of the second volume of *Dead Souls*. That autumn he had recovered sufficiently to write to Alexandra Smirnov: 'God is merciful and my spirits will revive and my strength will be restored to me.'[32]

Early in the following year, 1846, Gogol began work on *Dead Souls* once again but put it aside to concentrate on a set of essays which were published at the end of that year. He no longer saw Zinaida. Her religious mania was alienating most of her former friends, very few of whom now came to the villa. Zinaida now turned almost entirely to charitable work and soon to the personal spiritual quest of a true Christian mystic. Gogol's own religious mania took a different form. He began to see his work as part of a process of Russia's redemption and of her special mission in the general regeneration of the world. This conviction had resulted in a book entitled *Selected Passages from Correspondence with Friends*, published at the end of 1846, in which he expounded his views on death, and the role of art and

literature. Exhorting his fellow Russians to repent, he urged submission and the acceptance of the existing order of things as willed
by God.

The book caused an uproar. Most of Russia's intellectuals, by now
divided into Westerners and Slavophiles, with divergent views of their
country's future development, had one thing in common: a belief in
social reform and the need for the abolition of serfdom. And now,
here was Gogol, defending serfdom, the autocracy and the entire
status quo – the very things he had formerly ridiculed to such effect!
The fiercest attack came from the most influential critic of his time.
Outraged by Gogol's volte-face, Belinsky felt personally betrayed as
he lambasted the book and its author in *Sovremennik*. Gogol, deeply
wounded and annoyed, wrote in protest to the by then dying Belinsky.
A further, furious blast came in reply:

> You are either ill, in which case consult your doctors, or a preacher
> of the knout, apostle of ignorance, champion of superstition and
> obscurantism. Russia has no need of sermons (she has had her fill
> of them!), nor of prayers (she knows them by heart), rather of the
> awakening in people of a sense of human dignity. She needs laws
> and rights compatible not with the doctrines of the Church, but
> with justice and common sense.

What really mattered was the abolition of serfdom, Belinsky raged,
and yet a great writer, who through his wonderful works of art had
greatly helped Russia in the period of her self-realisation, now comes
out with a book in which, instead of writing that the peasants are his
brothers in Christ and cannot be used as slaves, he teaches the barbarian landowner, in the name of Christ and the Church, to make
more money out of his peasants.[33] Although Gogol's friends loyally
tried to support him, even Viazemsky, one of his closest friends,
could only manage a lame remark that Gogol had a right to express
his views.

Zinaida, too, now saw salvation only through religion, but for her
that meant the Catholic Church. She must have harangued her friends
constantly, for even her faithful friend and admirer Shevyrev, who
was also Gogol's literary executor, when writing to Gogol about his

book, could only say that while he agreed with his ideas he objected to the 'ecstatic way', like Princess Volkonsky's, in which they had been expressed. Was Gogol perhaps a closet Catholic? Gogol wrote a swift denial.

> Your comparison of me with Princess Volkonsky and your suggestion of symptoms of Catholicism in me are unfounded. I haven't seen Princess Volkonsky for a long time, nor have I probed into her soul. As for Catholicism – I can only say that I have come to Christ in a Protestant rather than a Catholic way.[34]

As Shevyrev, who knew both of them well, had noticed, both Zinaida and Gogol had travelled a very long way.

12

The Beata

'Her great desire was to work for God; she sought every
means of doing good.'

DON G. MERLINI

It would be easy to dismiss Zinaida Volkonsky, as no doubt many
did in her own day, as an unstable woman or a religious fanatic. She
was both of course, but there was much more. As Zinaida approached
the age of sixty, old age in those days, her lifelong spiritual quest, her
longing for illumination and peace, which neither the arts which she
had adored nor the men she had loved had given her, brought her
to the Roman Catholic Church. She could have become a quietly
devout Catholic like her sister Madeleine, but Zinaida's passionate,
striving nature took her on a final, arduous pilgrimage.

Soon after her husband's death, Zinaida turned her attention to
her Polish friends. She had been instrumental in the establishment
of the Congregation of the Resurrection in 1843. When later some
Polish ladies arrived in Rome in the hope of setting up a female
branch of the order, Zinaida took them under her wing, encouraging
them and putting them up in her own house. In return the Poles
loved and admired her, indeed thought her saintly. She actively promoted their cause with several of her influential friends among the
clergy, including Don Luigi Marchetti, rector of the Collegium Ghisli-
eri, Don Vincenzo Pallotti, who was in charge of the organisation of
orphanages and the founder of the society of missions, and, more
importantly for her personally, Don Biagio Valentini of the Congregation of the Adorers of the Most Precious Blood. Although she was

extremely busy with practical work for the Church, Zinaida had, from the start, eagerly sought spiritual perfection. After a visit to Naples where she met the nun and mystic, Maria Luisa of Jesus, she became an oblate of the Serve di Maria on 31 July 1845.

Zinaida's activities on behalf of the Poles had not endeared her to the Russian court. By 1845, when the Emperor Nicholas visited Rome and had an audience with the Pope, the rift with Zinaida was complete. Zinaida had openly approved of the Pope's pronouncement in June 1842 against the treatment of Catholics in Russia, and now whole-heartedly supported the Catholic Poles. The Tsar was in Rome to discuss some form of mutual recognition with the Pope, but the visit was not a success. Although Nicholas was accompanied to Rome by Zinaida's brother-in-law Prince Peter Volkonsky, who was still his Chamberlain, and in spite of the fact that Prince Grigory Volkonsky, her nephew, was a member of the Russian mission to the Vatican, there is no record of Zinaida having been invited to the reception in the Tsar's honour, nor, more surprisingly, did she attend the gala performance at the opera at which Ivanov, the young singer who had accompanied Glinka to Rome, sang.

Zinaida was now immersed in a different kind of life. A young Belgian laywoman, who later became Sister Mary of the Sacred Heart, was a frequent visitor at Zinaida's house in those years and has left a vivid description of Zinaida's activities and the daily rhythm of her life.

The hours were divided so that different groups could meet without embarrassment. In the morning between ten o'clock and midday, queues would form of collectors for good causes, beggars, the poor, people looking for work and those who merely sought advice and comfort. At midday the Princess would ask us to accompany her to some church or other for the last Mass of the morning or to a Benediction, followed by a walk on the Pincio.

She dined at two. This was the hour for her relations, of whom there were many in the embassy; fashionable society would arrive then, for they were sure to find her at home, and everyone was welcome at the dinner where her intimates had their places; the Abbé Gerbet, Monsignor Luquet, the Abbé Martet. Many Frenchmen would present themselves then, preferring to keep their evenings free for society.

She was at home on Tuesdays. Catholic celebrities who were in Rome would use her house as a rallying point. She was happy to bring them together, to hold discussions, to try and help them to reach agreement on all the topical questions which were such burning issues at the time. How many such encounters took place! Old friends who had been seminarians together, returning from distant missions, would recognise each other with great emotion.[1]

From the very begining Zinaida was no mere benefactress of the poor. She had a proselytising spirit, and a genuinely mystical side to her nature, which at times led to an over-zealous search for miracles. She could be high-handed, as only one born to power, in her impatience for signs and results. Of course this brought ridicule on her head from former friends, but also irritation among the more level-headed clergy whom she was now seeing regularly and trying to assist in their various tasks.

In January 1842, while she was trying hard to support the Poles, Zinaida's interest in religious orders was unexpectedly, and, as she saw it, miraculously, channelled into a new field – the conversion of the Jews. A young French Jew, Alphonse Ratisbonne, who was visiting Rome had been shown the sights by a friend of Zinaida's, one Baron de Bussières. On the way to visit the Princess at the Villa Volkonsky, they stopped at the nearby Scala Santa. This flight of marble steps is believed to be the one on which Christ was scourged before his Passion. It had been brought to Rome from Jerusalem, reputedly by St Helena, mother of the Emperor Constantine, and the first great collector of holy relics. As they approached the staircase, the Baron made Ratisbonne laugh by exclaiming loudly, 'Hail Holy steps!' When they entered the lovely gardens of the Villa Volkonsky, Ratisbonne in his turn shouted, 'Hail true marvel! It is before you and not before a flight of steps that one should prostrate oneself.' No more was thought of the incident. On the day following the visit to the Princess, while visiting a church, Ratisbonne had a vision of the Virgin Mary and was converted to the Roman Catholic faith.[2]

In 1847, Alphonse Ratisbonne and his brother Theodore founded the Congregation of Our Lady of Sion in Paris, which was devoted to the conversion of the Jews. By then, Zinaida had assumed responsibility for a school of a different order in Rome. She again intervened with the Pope to obtain a house in Rome for the new Congregation as well as offering help and hospitality to the three sisters who were to teach in the city. She was excited by Ratisbonne's miracle and, as always, impatient to get things moving. The founders, however, wanted to move forward more slowly. Perhaps to encourage them still further, Zinaida journeyed to Paris where she visited the Congregation and stood godmother to a Jewish woman who had converted. She managed to give a party for poor Jewish children in their school, and busied herself making the Congregation known to some of her influential friends. She was so enthusiastic about this mission that she was eager to rent a house in the ghetto in Rome at once and live there herself with the teachers.[3] (She had left the grand apartments of the Palazzo Poli soon after Nikita's death, moving into a smaller house nearby in the Via degli Avignonesi.)

The Princess's own spiritual odyssey must be seen against the background of a great and general religious revival in Europe. In some countries, such as Poland, popular piety was closely associated with national resistance. In others, particularly in Protestant Europe, but also in Catholic France, churchmen tried to provide social leadership in response to industrialisation and the growing mass of urban poor. The revolutionary wave of the 1830s in Europe was accompanied by strong missionary activity which no longer looked only to distant lands, but concentrated on the new urban proletariat. The effects of this renewed interest in religion in the Romantic age were reflected in music and art as well as in social attitudes, especially in Protestant northern Europe. The Pre-Raphaelites in England, the Nazarenes in Germany, the neo-Gothic style in art, as well as the attitudes of the Russian Slavophiles, were all part of a general reaction to the Age of Reason. Roman Catholic intellectuals like Lammenais, Montalembert, Lacordaire and Ernest Renan had not been immune from these changes, but the response of the Vatican hierarchy had been one of ultra-conservative reaction and it was not until the late 1870s that the Church began to move closer to contemporary thinking on social and political issues.

Nurtured in a spirit of European civilisation, Zinaida had always instinctively rejected a purely nationalist point of view. Throughout her life and in all her endeavours, whether artistic or social, she was a bridge builder. Now she turned all her energies into similar enterprises within the Church. What had attracted her especially about the Roman Catholic Church was its universality. Close to the new Pope, Pius IX, for whom she had a special devotion, although he could hardly be described as a liberal, she was in a position to intervene on behalf of the many causes dear to her heart, writing him long letters about her hopes and projects. Zinaida never hesitated to go right to the top when she needed help.

One of her religious projects came about as a result of her close friendship with Monsignor Luquet, a missionary who had recently returned from India. Twenty years her junior, he became something of a son, saying Mass for her and later acting as chaplain to one of her schools. Luquet helped to focus Zinaida's missionary zeal. She financially supported a journal he had founded, and intervened on his behalf with the Pope from whom she obtained a subsidy which enabled Monsignor Luquet to organise worldwide hostels for missionaries, as well as 'holy postes restantes' to make it easier for them to correspond more frequently and easily. The latter idea was Zinaida's. She was always anxious to help the poor, and extended her support to Frédéric Ozanam, the Dante scholar who had set up a lay foundation with this aim. She encouraged Dom Guéranger in his ideas of a liturgical revival. But the cause closest to her heart in the late forties was the Oriental Society. Founded in June 1847 and based on the idea of a reconciliation between the Eastern and Western rites, the society was promoted by her two closest clergymen friends, the Abbé Gerbet and Monsignor Luquet, and had been the result of a general disappointment in the Concordat which the Pope had just signed with the Tsar. After the Tsar's visit in 1845, the Pope had privately expressed his misgivings about his intentions to Zinaida, who had answered, 'Make Russia into a field of missions;' the Concordat was nonetheless signed largely on Russia's terms. Writing on behalf of the Oriental Society, in her best hand, quite unlike her usual scrawl, Zinaida wrote to the Pope: 'Most blessèd Father, I who am humbly prostrated at your Holiness's feet in the desire to co-operate in whichever way I might in the propagation of the faith among our brothers, who have been blinded by the errors of the Schism . . .'[4] As well as writing to the Pope, Zinaida brought in Monsignor Bussi, secretary of the Congregation of Extraordinary Ecclesiastical Affairs at the Vatican, its under-secretary Ferrari and the Pope's own confessor, Graziozi, and offered her house for meetings.

The society did not deal with doctrinal issues, but concentrated rather on preserving the Eastern rite among Uniates (Russian Catholics). Archimandrite Vladimir Treletsky, a Russian Uniate missionary, acted as secretary on the Russian side while Prince Lichnowski, himself a Polish priest, dealt with Latin questions. Treletsky, who had arrived in Rome penniless and found a room near the Russian Uniate church, was quickly taken under Zinaida's wing. 'I had no money to live on,' he wrote. 'Luckily Princess Volkonsky who had learnt of my poverty suggested that I give Russian lessons to two Italian monks who were teaching in one of the schools founded by her, for which I was paid 15 roubles a month. This was enough to keep me from dying of hunger.'[5] In a letter addressed 'To the Eastern Christians' in January 1848, the Pope promised to safeguard the Eastern rite and urged them towards reunion. Zinaida offered to return to the Eastern rite herself, if it would be helpful to the Catholic Church. Although the Oriental Society had not been consulted, and the response from the Russian Orthodox Church was negative, it was believed that the society had done much to raise interest in the question.[6]

In April 1847, Zinaida met a woman who was to be of major importance for the rest of her life. Maria de Mattias was a young girl in the small town of Vallecorsa in southern Lazio when, in 1822, after hearing a sermon preached by fathers of the Adorers of the Most Precious Blood, she had felt a call to form a female branch of the missionary order. The order itself had only just been founded by Don Gaspere di Bufalo. Its mission lay mainly in the poorest part of the Papal States, the country to the south of Rome known as the Ciociaria. Don Gaspere had been greatly assisted in his task by other young priests, among whom were Don Biagio Valentini and Don Giovanni Merlini. Maria de Mattias, after great opposition from a conservative Curia, succeeded in her task and the Order of Sisters, Adorers of the Most Precious Blood, was duly founded in the village of Acuto in the diocese of Anagni, on 4 March 1834. Its task was to preach and organise schools for girls in the country.

After Don Gaspere di Bufalo's death on 28 December 1837, his tomb at Albano began to attract pilgrims and there were even rumours of miraculous happenings. Always attracted to miracles, Zinaida went to see for herself, and there she met Don Biagio Valentini who had succeeded Don Gaspere as head of the order. Don Biagio became her spiritual guide and confessor, and after his death his successor, Don Giovanni Merlini, became her confessor too. Don Merlini was also Maria de Mattias's confessor and it was through him Zinaida met Mother de Mattias in 1847.

The two women already knew of each other through Merlini, indeed Zinaida had written to the nun in December 1845 asking if there were any girls in Acuto who might be sent to Mother Maria Luisa in Naples, to whose order Zinaida had dedicated herself as an oblate. When they met in April 1847, Zinaida knew that Maria de Mattias wanted to open a school for working-class girls in Rome, and suggested that she found one, beginning with a few nuns, in Zinaida's own house in the Via degli Avignonesi. Zinaida had hoped to merge Maria de Mattias's order with Mother Maria Luisa's in Naples, but the idea was strongly rejected by Maria de Mattias.

Among the founding sisters of the Order of the Adorers of the Most Precious Blood were four sisters, Teresa, Carolina, Agnese and Rosa, daughters of a devout provincial doctor, Gioacchino de Sanctis, from the town of Patrica in lower Lazio. Zinaida needed someone with experience to start her school in Rome and asked for Carolina who was soon followed by her sisters. It is from her letters home that we have something of the flavour of Zinaida's house at this period. The little nun wrote, round-eyed:

I am in the house of a Princess of Russia, and she is a saintly woman. She has a son who is very far from Rome, and who is not yet a Catholic, but she hopes by recommending him to the Lord that he will come round. The Princess has servants it is true, but they mostly serve nuns and priests and other clergy who come to see her and who constitute her noble court. In all the rooms, staircases and everywhere, all you see are pictures of the Virgin

Mary, saints, crosses and crucifixes, with votive candles around them.[7]

Zinaida, always prone to exaggeration, embraced her religion with fanatical zeal. Her relationship with Mother de Mattias was not always smooth. Both were very strong personalities, with imperious wills and often differing views. Don Merlini's diplomatic skills, as he advised and soothed them both, were often needed. The school opened in December 1847 with forty pupils and was an immediate success, doubling the number in slightly more than a year. Letters went back and forth between Mother de Mattias and Zinaida, sometimes tense and sharp. Zinaida had become particularly attached to Gioacchino de Sanctis's youngest daughter, Rosa, and corresponded with him about his daughters and their role in her school. At this point, however, the whole enterprise came under serious threat for different reasons. In 1848 Italy rose in revolt and the school had to be closed.

The year 1848 was a watershed in the whole of Europe, as revolution spread from France to all the major countries except Britain and Russia. In Italy, 'the year of revolutions' began with demonstrations in Milan, Rome, Bologna and Naples, but the revolution proper actually began in Palermo. By the end of January the Bourbon King of the Two Sicilies had been forced to grant a constitution. He was followed by the ruler of Tuscany and by the Pope, as temporal ruler of the Papal States, who towards the end of that year was forced to leave Rome and flee to Gaeta, in the Kingdom of Naples. Zinaida and Madeleine also left Rome, now ruled by a triumvirate which included Mazzini. The Risorgimento was greatly strengthened by the courage with which his Republican government held out in Rome against the combined armies of Austria, France, Spain and Naples. A Roman assembly, which was elected by universal suffrage at the beginning of 1849, in spite of papal prohibition, immediately abolished the Inquisition and instituted a free press. In July, having defended Rome for over two months, Garibaldi surrendered the city to the French, leading his army to the Alban hills with the ringing cry, 'Let all who love their country follow me.' By the end of 1849 the revolution was over. Escorted by French troops, the Pope returned in state to Rome, entering the city through the Lateran gate to take up residence at the Vatican.

In 1850 Zinaida's school could reopen. She was impatient to get it started and unwilling to allow some of the nuns to return to the Mother House in Acuto, causing some annoyance to Maria de Mattias:

> I know how good your heart is and that you really love me, I thank you for this love and for the love you bear our institute and for everything you do for it. May God reward you with his blessing. The Rome house will flourish when the Lord wills it. As I am responsible to God, I beg you in the name of the love which you bear the Divine Blood to give me the freedom to bring back the Adorer nuns now in Rome, at least for a while. It is necessary for their spiritual purification. Believe me, Madame, this is no whim of mine or anything else. Should you not agree to my request I shall be at peace in the Heart of Jesus. If you will be so kind as to do this for me, I will send you capable others [nuns] who will do good, and it will become clear that it is God who does good, not we ourselves who are but miserable instruments of his will.

Mother de Mattias adds for good measure that it was the devil who, jealous of their success, was behind the political disturbances which had led to the closure of the school during the revolution of 1849, but that God had triumphed in the end.[8]

The school duly reopened. It provided a basic course of reading, writing, sewing and embroidery, as well as religious instruction. It was so immediately popular that two daily shifts of teaching had to be organised, catering to a wide age range, from little girls of five to adult women. Zinaida soon opened another school in the Via Rasella, between the Colosseum and San Giovanni in Laterano, then a very poor quarter. The new school, which was not far from her summer villa, was from the outset working at full capacity. The schools, while always financially insecure and short of staff, were a great success and a lasting monument to the Princess. The nuns who taught there were even referred to as the 'Volkonsky nuns'. Zinaida had set an example which was soon followed by others. A similar school, set up by the Marchese Gianpietro Campana and his English wife Emilia Rowles, was opened in the Via Babuino.

Although Zinaida had full permission from the Vatican for her charitable works, her relationship with Maria de Mattias was dogged by constant friction. Maria was often irritated by Zinaida's interference in the life of the nuns and the teaching programme which sometimes undermined her authority as Mother Superior, while the Bishop of Anagni – the order was in his diocese – was displeased because he had not been consulted. The two women were united by the success of their schools, however, and needed each other. Zinaida also raised money for similar schools in the provinces and for other community projects, and encouraged the establishment of a novitiate of the order in Rome, where, indeed, one was needed and later established. For all her mysticism and lapses into fanaticism, Zinaida was an intensely practical, capable and active person. Nor was she only interested in grand schemes. Don Merlini wrote that when she heard that the nuns in Narni were absolutely destitute and had not even enough money to pay for the oil in the votive lamps, Zinaida at once turned to her son who, hating to see her unhappy, gave her twelve scudi, which she joyfully sent to them.[9]

The Princess's direct links with the Pope were tremendously useful to the order. Just as in the past Zinaida had never hesitated to write to the Tsar when she needed help, so now she wrote to the Pope whenever she thought it right to do so. Her confessor, Don Merlini, who began to keep notes with a view to writing her life, recorded that when the Princess realised that parts of the Roman Campagna were only served by itinerant priests, who merely celebrated Mass, 'She suggested to the Holy Father that the best thing would be to establish mission posts where priests could also preach and hear confessions.' The Pope was apparently delighted to comply with what he clearly thought an excellent idea. He provided several chapels and up to a hundred priests for this work. Zinaida herself occasionally sent a priest to preach to country people at her own expense.[10] Concerned at the state of repair of some churches and their general cleanliness, she once asked the Pope to arrange for the cleaning of the Scala Santa, which pilgrims would climb, then as now, on their knees.[11]

Another of Zinaida's causes was the Instituto of San Giuseppe, founded in 1850, where boys were taught arts and crafts as well as agriculture. The Pope himself gave the school a vineyard, known as the Vigna Pia.[12] Don Merlini recalled Zinaida's other initiatives to promote moral action among fathers of families, and also a scheme to give financial assistance to girls who were unable to marry for lack of a dowry, and to those who wished to enter the religious life.[13]

Maria de Mattias was twice received by the Pope in 1853. In the following year, the rule of the female branch of Adorers of the Most Precious Blood was established. Zinaida, Don Merlini recorded, had been very upset that she did not have enough money to give the order her own house. She had already started to turn to her son Alexander whenever she was short of funds. Now she begged him to complete her work. Her family was increasingly worried for her but, as always, Alexander did not let her down. He was a very loving son and tried to look after his mother as best he could. Madeleine also remained entirely devoted to 'my incomparable sister', as is clear from a letter to Mother de Mattias which she wrote on 20 August 1852, in which she tells her that her 'angelic sister' was away for a few days in Naples, where she had gone to keep her daughter-in-law company while Alexander took sea baths at Castellamare.[14] Zinaida was very fond of her son's wife, showering her with blessings, praising her kind heart and calling her her dear daughter, on the many occasions that Luisa helped her out with clothes and other gifts to the poor.

Although religion and her charitable activities, which were now her whole life, gave Zinaida a sense of purpose and some comfort, she still remained prone to depression. Sometimes, unhappy because she couldn't do as much as she wanted to, she would make herself ill. 'Princess, do not distress yourself,' Don Merlini would console her, listing all her achievements;

> the nuns have become known in Rome through you, who brought them here. They are known to the Holy Father who had blessed and accepted them because of you. It was because of you that the Marchese Campana made his move and sought permission to open his school on 21 August 1851, and is determined to open another in Civitavecchia, which has been especially blessed by God. Thanks

to you, having heard of the nuns' good conduct, the Holy Father, through the offices of Monsignor Francesco Saverio de Merode, has given them the house of San Luigi, with a school attached to it, which he has endowed, as well as the obligation to look after a poor woman who sleeps there every night. Even if your school were to come to nothing you have done great good and the institute will be eternally grateful.[15]

In her last years Zinaida lived a truly ascetic life, taking vows of poverty in Naples, in 1853, after becoming a tertiary of the Franciscan order of her friend Mother Maria del Gesú. She now lived entirely among the poor. The plight of the old worried her and she dreamed of turning her house into a hospice, but it was already crowded enough with the school. She took in a poor old woman, however, to whom she gave a room. This gave her great joy, for in her she recognised Christ, as she told Merlini. He was more and more worried for her. Her natural generosity as well as her whole-heartedness led to a desire to keep nothing for herself.

She often gave away not only alms, but also her own clothes, so that she herself looked like a beggar. I often had to tell her to dress a little better not only out of a sense of decorum but out of necessity, especially in the winter when she felt the cold very much. Not satisfied with depriving herself of clothes, she also gave away her portion of food every day, but very tactfully, so as to conceal her mortification.

Don Merlini, worried about her health, would urge her to eat more:

Those suffering from their nerves are weakened even more by abstinence. To this she replied that eating was bad for her and that she could not digest food, that the little she ate was quite enough, but at the same time she would suffer the fear that she had eaten too much. Mostly, all she ate was handfuls of greens, and bread, which she was fond of.[16]

Zinaida had a special love for her servants. She was far more concerned for their welfare than for her own, only recommending them to fear God. She would believe no ill of them and, if warned to put away her money, she would look displeased and reply that there were only trustworthy people in her house. The plight of other people's servants also worried her. When the butler of the Russian ambassador to the Vatican fell ill, Zinaida visited him every day.

Tsar Nicholas died in 1855, but by then Zinaida's life was one of such religious intensity that she probably hardly noticed, as she had not noticed the Crimean War in her native country. However, for two members of her family, once so dear to her, the Tsar's death changed their lives. On the morning of the new Tsar Alexander II's coronation in the summer of 1856, Sergei Volkonsky was pardoned for his part in the Decembrist uprising. Maria and Sergei were now free to leave Siberia and return to Moscow. In 1859 they travelled to Europe, spending some time in Paris and Rome before going on to Geneva for the wedding of their son Mikhail, to the granddaughter of Princess Sophia Volkonsky. They stayed with Prince Alexander and his wife at the Villa Volkonsky, travelled to Frascati to visit Maria's mother's grave, and visited her sister's grave at the Testaccio cemetery. The meeting with Zinaida had been very touching, as her son recorded. Zinaida had been a constant friend throughout the bitter years of exile. What can they have thought and felt – the two old women and the upright, silver-haired and still handsome former Decembrist? Did Zinaida recognise the lovely, dark-eyed, 'daughter of the Ganges' as she herself had called Maria in the woman so sorely tried by years of Siberian exile? Could Maria see anything of the once radiant Queen of the Muses who had bidden her farewell on her journey to Siberia in that freezing December morning in Moscow so long ago, in the painfully thin old woman dressed like a beggar? Maria, above all, who understood the nature of sacrifice, would have understood how Zinaida was now able to give up everything she had once loved for the love of God. Maria's own sacrifice and Sergei's had not been in vain. In less than two years, during a church service in Paris on 3 March 1861, Sergei heard the Tsar's manifesto was read out announcing the emancipation of the serfs, the Decembrists' most cherished aim.[17]

Madeleine, Zinaida's beloved and closest companion and devoted elder sister, died in 1857. For the past thirty years, she had taken over

all the burdens of running their household, more than happy to live
in the shadow of her brilliant younger sister. Her kind-hearted, simple
ways had endeared her to all their friends and family, including
Zinaida's husband Nikita, who probably found her easier and less
intimidating than his talented and highly strung wife. Vladimir Pavey
too saw in Madeleine a maternal figure. One of the few traces of him
in the life of his adopted family is a charming translation into French
of a poem by Byron, dedicated to Madeleine, which she kept in her
album. This album is full of expressions of affection from their many
friends, among them Mickiewicz and Gogol. Zinaida repaid Madeleine's devotion by looking after her, but also by depending on her
utterly. She had her sister buried in the same tomb as Nikita, at their
parish church of Sts Vincenzo and Anastasio, where she herself would
join them in due course.

Count Miniato Ricci, Zinaida's former lover and friend, died in
1860. All the closest links with her past life were now severed – her
only link with her old world was through her son, who, although
devoted to her and ever ready to support her with money, was now
far away in Dresden, the city of his mother's birth. In 1858, he was
appointed to the same post of ambassador to Saxony which had
once been held by his maternal grandfather. Later he was also to be
ambassador to Spain. After Zinaida's death, Alexander kept his
promise and bought the house in which his mother had been living,
in the Via degli Avignonesi, and gave it to the sisters.[18]

After Madeleine's death Zinaida gave herself up entirely to a life
of poverty and prayer. For some years she had kept a spiritual diary,
her *scritti spirituali*, of which only those between 1852 and 1854 survive.
They show that, well before Madeleine's death, Zinaida was already
experiencing high levels of religious ecstasy, when the disturbance of
her thoughts was even reflected in her handwriting:

My visions continue; and on the eve of the feast of St Monica, I
saw an Augustine nun. I asked for the calendar, something I rarely
do, and I see 4 May, St Monica. So it was she who had called me
to prayer, therefore it must have been her that I saw and not
St Rita. Pius IX's angel makes up the third crown of rubies, martyrs
of the spirit. St Agnes help him! I feel that he will not live long.[19]

Sometimes she saw St Dominic crowned with a star, as in the painting by Fra Angelico. Sometimes Jesus appeared to her, dressed in red, with a lamb beside him. 'I said to him, Good Shepherd, I will follow you, in spite of my misery and my spiritual impoverishment.'[20] At other times she would write of her adoration of the Virgin, of the Sacred Heart of Jesus, or simply record her fervent prayers, her thanks to Jesus on Christmas Day, or her reflections on the state of her soul.

More lucidly, Zinaida explained in her spiritual notebooks that her love of music and beauty had never left her but that now it was channelled towards God.

> I was always sensitive to the beauties of nature; this never left me: it took the form of prayer. When I hear birdsong, I think of St Rose who used to say that their singing and even the hum of insects seemed to her to be the Creator's hymns. She was right: prayer fills the space of the love of God. It is the ladder up which angels come and go. And God is there in the Heavens and in our hearts. And the trees! How can we not love them? They have given us the Cross! Here is life: Here is the sap which never runs dry.[21]

One winter day, looking like a poor woman herself, Zinaida was slowly making her way home when she saw a beggar woman shivering in the bitter cold. Taking her into the shelter of a porch, Zinaida took off her warm petticoat and gave it to her, slowly continuing on her way home. Thoroughly chilled when she arrived, she soon caught a severe cold which was followed by a strong fever. On 5 February 1862, at the age of seventy-three, lovingly tended by the nuns she had called 'my daughters', Princess Zinaida Alexandrovna Volkonsky breathed her last.

As the little cortège left her modest house, among whom were princes and diplomats, cardinals and humble nuns, her family and friends, it was joined by more and more people. Out of the narrow streets they poured, most of them in rags, all weeping. The poor of Rome were following Zinaida to her last resting place, to the church of Sts Vincenzo and Anastasio, where she had been received into the Catholic Church and where she would be buried next to her sister and her husband. The ragged crowd was not following a princess, nor a great figure of the Church. Most of them did not even know who she was. They were following one who had loved them, and cared for them, and lived among them, and they called her '*beata*'.

Zinaida was never officially beatified by the Church. It would have been enough for her that the poor and dispossessed had called her blessed. That day, however, the Vatican newspaper, the *Giornale di Roma*, published her obituary on its front page:

> She was an example of most rare virtues, particularly of penitence and abstinence, whose death brought tears to the multitiude of the poor.[22]

In the garden of the Villa Volkonsky, shaded by trees and close to the monuments Zinaida had erected to the memory of those she had loved and admired, there is now another monument, a little larger than the rest, placed there by her son, Prince Alexander Volkonsky. The inscription reads:

> *Elle dédia le souvenir*
> *de cette alleé*
> *à la piété filiale*
> *à la reconnaissance*
> *à l'amitié.*
> *Le même hommage*
> *est offert*
> *à sa chère mémoire.*[23]

Appendix

Chapter 1, Note 5

Voltaire's verses to the Prince

Dans des climats glacés Ovide vit un jour
Une fille du tendre Orphée,
D'un beau feu leur âme exhausée
Fit des chansons, des vers, et surtout fit l'amour.

Les dieux bénirent leur tendresse.
Il nâquit un fils orné de leurs talents;
Vous en êtes issu; connaissez vos parents,
Et tous vos titres de noblesse.

Chapter 2, Note 25

A Madame de Staël en lui Renvoyant Corinne

Que j'aime à retrouver dans vos récits touchants
L'empreinte de ce feu qui pénètre Votre âme!
L'imagination de ses ailes de flamme
Traverse les climats qu'ont illustrés vos chants!
Salut! Belle Italie! à toi dont la parure
Réunit tous les dons épars dans la nature,
Et se compose tour à tour

De fléaux de souvenirs, de regrets et d'amour!
Corinne! je te suis dans ces ruines sombres
Au pied de ces volcans qui enivrent leur fureur
Alors que ton pinceau nous trace tes douleurs,
Et peuple ces déserts de magnifiques ombres!
Je n'ai point conne vous de ces bards enchanteurs
Eprouvé la noble influence,
Dans le sein des frimats s'écouls mon enfance,
Chez nous l'astre du jour n'est pas le Dieu de vers,
Le luth languit sans harmonie.
Aussi la fleur éclose au milieu des hivers
Exhale en s'entrouvrant un vain souffle de vie.
C'est à vous de chanter, à vous dont le génie
Sous un ciel libéral a pris un libre cours.
La gloire Vous réclame, et l'amitié fidèle
Qui voudroit seul occuper tous vos jours
Vous offre en soupirant une palme immortelle.

Chapter 5, Note 30

Hélas! ainsi que moi la pauvre hirondelle,
Prête à quitter les lieux où la flèche cruelle
Atteint son faible enfant, le perça de son dard . . .
Elle s'arrête . . . et croit dans sa douleur amère
Manquer au devoir d'une mère
En le privant de son regard.

Mais elle entend la voix de ses douces compagnes,
Qui l'invitent en choeur à franchir les montagnes:
Partons, lui disent-elles, profitons des instans!
Je les vois s'élancer vers la céleste plaine . . .
Fuyons aussi! fuyons la peine,
Elançons-nous vers le printemps!

Chapter 6, Note 24

A Mademoiselle Mars
(En lui envoyant une garniture de boules-de-neige et de roses le jour où elle devait jouer Le Secret du Ménage.*)*

> On dit que sur la terre une Muse est parue,
> Et sous un nom guerrier déguisant son vrai nom,
> Exerce en souriant sa puissance absolue,
> Et fait la guerre aux coeurs sans quartier, nous dit-on.
> Son âge est ignoré: selon sa fantaisie
> Elle est ce qu'elle veut, et toujours elle est bien.
> Après avoir aux dieux versé de l'ambroisie,
> De la sage raison elle prends le maintien.
> Puis saisissant un dard, sûre de sa conquête,
> Et jouissant tout bas du malheur des humains,
> Elle a l'esprit, le ton d'une franche coquette:
> Ses yeux sont tour à tour fiers, naïfs et malins.
> C'est Pallas, c'est Thalie, une Nymphe, une Grace,
> C'est le Palladium, le charme de Parnasse:
> Vous qui savez si bien deviner un secret,
> Vous seule qui pouvez achever ce portrait,
> Ah! déposez aux pieds de l'aimable immortelle
> Ces fleurs, qui dans le Nord sont écloses pour elle!

Notes

Chapter 1 Childhood: Her Father's Daughter

1. There have been some discrepancies in Zinaida's date of birth. According to a note written by her grandmother, Maria Dimitrievna Tatishchev (now in the Volkonsky archive of the Houghton Library, Harvard), the eldest daughter Maria was born in Dresden on 29 May 1784, Zinaida on 3 December 1789 and Natalia on 28 March 1791.
2. Ivan Bocharov and Yulia Glushakova, *Italianskaya Pushkiniana*, p.291.
3. The Prince's *Vademecum*, published by A. F. Alekseeva in *Zelyoni Albom*.
4. Bibliothèque Nationale, Paris, *Fonds des Manuscrits Français*, quoted by André Mazon in *Deux Russes Écrivains Français*, p.10.
5. See Appendix. The Prince's *Vademecum*.
6. Ibid.
7. Letter of 26 June, 7 July 1780. Foreign Policy Archives, Moscow. Relations between Russia and Saxony, 1780, File 199, 1–4, also quoted by Mazon, op.cit.
8. Ibid., File 203, 17–17.
9. *Épîtres aux Français, Épîtres aux Anglais* and *Épîtres aux habitants de la République de St Marin*. The poems were republished in 1789 under the title *Poésies françaises d'un Prince Étranger*.
10. *Circe: Cantate. L'avertissement par l'auteur de la Musique en Italie, Le Prince de Belosselsky*, Imprimerie de la Cour, Dresden, 1787.
11. Quoted by Bocharov and Glushakova, op.cit., p.205.
12. Kant's letter in Centralnyj Gosudarstvennyj, Archiv Literaturi i Isskustva, f. 172, op. 1, d. 153, also quoted by Mazon, op.cit., p.85.

13. Foreign Policy Archives, Moscow, Relations between Russia and the Kingdom of Sardinia, 1792, File 99.
14. A. Gulyaga, *Iz Zabitogo*, Nauka i Zhizn, Moscow, 1977, Vol.III, pp.104–7.
15. P. Cazzola, *Diplomatici Russi a Torino nel Settecento*.
16. All the Prince's despatches from Turin were published in French by Princess Lise Trubetskoy in *Un Ambassadeur Russe à Turin, Dépêches de SA le Prince Belosselsky de Bélozersk*. Also in Russki Archiv, 1877, Vol.VIII, pp.369–402, Vol.IX, pp.5–47.
17. *Archiv Literaturi i Isskustva*, f. 172, inv. 1 no. 155; also quoted by Mazon, op.cit, p.91.
18. The chapel no longer exists, but part of the funerary sculpture, a figure of a woman veiled in draperies by the Florentine sculptor Innocenzo Spinazzi, stands in the San Pietro in Vincoli cemetery in Turin.
19. Foreign Ministry Archives, 141, File 133/4.
20. Letter from Count Rostopchin to Count Vorontsov, Russki Archiv, 1878, Vol.VIII, p.293.
21. Published in *Galatea*, 1929, Vol.V, pp.21–31, together with a rather mystical essay by the Princess entitled 'Snovidenie' ('My Dream').
22. The ground floor of this palace has been occupied by the grocer Eliseev, the Russian 'Fortnum's', throughout this century.
23. Viazemsky, Complete Works, Vol.VII, p.96.
24. It was rebuilt in the mid-nineteenth century under the supervision of the architect Stackenshneider, and later still, in 1884, sold to Alexander II, who bought it for his son, the Grand Duke Sergei. In 1915 the palace, then known as the Dimitri Palace after Grand Duke Sergei's son Dimitri, was briefly the Anglo-Russian Hospital. Today it is the St Petersburg Municipal Cultural Centre, organising charity functions and national and international festivals, concerts and exhibitions, a role which both Zinaida and her father would have surely approved.
25. The Comte de Laval emigrated to Russia at the beginning of the French Revolution and married Alexandra Kozitsky, sister of Anna Grigorievna Volkonsky, Zinaida's stepmother. The letter is in the Prince's *Vademecum*, also quoted by Mazon, op.cit., p.108.
26. *Vademecum*.
27. Mary Berry, *Extracts of the Journals and Correspondence of Miss Berry*, vol.III, p.275.
28. Elizabeth Vigée-Lebrun, *Souvenirs de Madame Vigée-Lebrun*.
29. *Letters of E. I. Trubetskoy*, ed. I. Kologrivov, Frankfurt on Main, 1934.
30. Poem from *Iz Materialov Stroganovskoy Akademii*, *Literaturnoe Nasledstno* 33–34, pp.206–8.
31. Madame de Staël, *Dix Années d'Exil*.
32. Pushkin, *The Bronze Horseman*.

33. Ibid.
34. *The Russian Journals of Catherine and Martha Wilmot, 1803–8.*
35. Pushkin, *The Bronze Horseman.*

Chapter 2 At Court

1. Empress Elizabeth's letter to her mother of 13 March 1801, quoted by H. Troyat in *Alexandre Ier: Le Sphinx du Nord.*
2. Prince de Ligne, *Mémoires, lettres et pensées.*
3. Lists of Paul's ukases (orders) forbidding the use of certain words, clothes and behaviour, in *Russkaya Starina*, 1873, Vol.7, p.717, *RS* 1884, Vol.41, p.371, *RS* 1872, Vol.6, p.98.
4. Prince I. M. Dolgoruky, *Russkaya Starina*, 1874, Vol.2 p.177.
5. F. C. de La Harpe, *Correspondance de Frédéric-Cézar de La Harpe et Alexandre I.*
6. Alexander Herzen, *My Past and Thoughts*, Vol.IV, p.1519.
7. Adam Czartoryski, *Mémoires et Correspondance avec l'Empereur Alexandre Ier.* Grand Duke Nicholas Mikhailovich, *Le Comte Paul Stroganov.*
8. *Iz Materialov Stroganovskoy Akademii*, p.208.
9. Madame de Staël, op.cit.
10. G. Goyau, *La Pensée Religieuse de J. de Maistre*, quoted by James H. Billington in *The Icon and the Axe.*
11. *Iz Materialov Stroganovskoy Akademii*, pp.198–99.
12. Ibid., p.209.
13. Vigée-Lebrun, op.cit.
14. *Iz Materialov Stroganovskoy Akademii.*
15. Dorothea, Princess Lieven, *Letters.*
16. Grand Duke Nicholas Mikhailovich, ed., *Scenes from Russian Court Life: The Correspondence of Alexander I and his sister Catherine*, Letters of 15 and 20 September 1805.
17. John Quincy Adams, *Memoirs of J. Q. Adams Comprising Portions of his Diary 1795–1848.*
18. J. Bourgeat, *Napoléon: Lettres à Josephine.*
19. Prince Sergei M. Volkonsky, *Vospominanie o Dekabristakh po Semeinim Vospominaniam.*
20. Ibid.
21. A. N. Volkonsky, *Poezdka fligel-aiutanta Kniaza N. G. Volkonskogo k Napoleonu v 1808 om godu*, Russki Archiv, 1847, I, 1, pp.1047–50.
22. *Chastnie Pisma 1812 goda M. A. Volkovoy k V. I. Lanskoy*, Russki Archiv, 1872, pp 2388–9, 2395–7
23. Archive du Grand Séminaire de Langres: *Journal d'un Missionaire*, VII, pp.206–10, quoted by Nadezhda Gorodetsky in 'Zinaida Volkonsky as a Catholic'.

24. *Zapiski Grafa Buturlina*, Russki Archiv, 1897, IV, p.640. and Comtesse de Boigne, *Mémoires de la Comtesse de Boigne*, pp.18, 19.
25. See Appendix. *Iz Materialov Stroganovskoy Academii*, pp.33–34.
26. Volkonsky Archives, Houghton Library, Harvard.
27. Madame de Staël, op.cit.
28. Letter to Jacques Necker, 1803. Madame de Staël, *Oeuvres Complètes*.
29. Ibid.
30. Madame de Staël, *Dix Années d'Exil*.
31. Ibid.
32. Ibid.
33. Ibid.

Chapter 3 War: 'Our Knight and Angel'

1. Zinaida Volkonsky, *Oeuvres Choisies de la Princesse Zénéide Volkonsky*.
2. Letter to Grand Duchess Catherine, *Scenes from Russian Court Life*.
3. A. de Caulaincourt, *Mémoires du Général de Caulaincourt*, Vol.I, p.293.
4. Ibid., pp.293–4.
5. Comtesse de Choiseul-Gouffier, *Mémoires sur L'Empereur Alexandre I et sur L'Empereur Napoléon*.
6. Grand Duke Nicholas Mikhailovich, *L'Empereur Alexandre I*.
7. Caulaincourt, op.cit., p.354.
8. Thompson, *Napoleon's letters*, pp.268–70.
9. *Iz Zapisok Grafini Edling*, Russki Archiv, 1887.
10. Madame de Staël, *Dix Années d'Exil*.
11. Ibid.
12. Sir Robert Wilson, *Narrative of Events during the Invasion of Russia*.
13. Comtesse Edling, *Mémoires*.
14. *Archiv Brat'ev Turgenevyx*, Petrograd, 1921. Letter to P. Viazemsky.
15. Letter to Baron Mérian, Z. Volkonsky, *Oeuvres Choisies*.
16. S. M. Volkonsky, *Archiv Dekabrista*, 1918, I, xl.
17. Letter of 28 December 1813 from Kutuzov to E. M. Tiesenhausen, Starina i Novisna, 1874, X, p.377
18. Shishkov, *Zapiski mnenie i perepiska*, Berlin, 1870, pp.187–8.
19. S. M. Volkonsky, op.cit.
20. Ibid.
21. Shishkov, op.cit.
22. Letter of 16 April 1813, *Scenes from Russian Court Life*.
23. *Z. Volkonskaya i Goethe S. Durylin Russkie Pissateli u Goethe*, Literaturnoe Nasledstvo, 1932, IV-VI, p.477.
24. Volkonsky Archives, Houghton Library, Harvard: also commented by

B. Aroutunova, in *Lives in Letters: Princess Zinaida Volkonsky and her Correspondence*.

25. Chateaubriand, *Napoléon*.
26. Lady Burghersh, *Journal and Letters of Lady Burghersh*, p.677.
27. Letter of 8 August 1813, *Scenes from Russian Court Life*.
28. Burghersh, op.cit., p.146.
29. Burghersh, op.cit.
30. Letter 4 January, *Scenes from Russian Court Life*.
31. Burghersh, op.cit.
32. Metternich, *Mémoires*, Vol.I, p.223.
33. Castlereagh, *Correspondence, Despatches, and other Papers of Viscount Castlereagh*, Vol.IX, letter from Langres, 30 January, p.212.
34. Letter of 28 February, ibid., p.229.

Chapter 4 Peace: Paris and London

1. *Iz semeinikh vospominaniy* by Prince A. N. Volkonsky, Russki Archiv, 1874, Vol.IV, 1047–1050.
2. Boigne, op.cit., pp.327–29.
3. Ibid.
4. Burghersh, op.cit.
5. Boigne, op.cit.
6. Boigne, op.cit.
7. Boigne, op.cit., p.219.
8. Boigne, op.cit., pp.332–33.
9. Chateaubriand, op.cit., p.269.
10. Boigne, op.cit.
11. La Rochefoucauld, *Mémoires du Vicomte de la Rochefoucauld*, Vol.I, pp.37–38. Also Boigne, op.cit.
12. Chateaubriand, op.cit., p.270.
13. Madame de Staël, *Considérations sur la Revolution Française*, Part V, Ch.6.
14. Simone Balayé, *Madame de Staël: Lumières et Liberté*.
15. Castlereagh, op.cit., Vols IX and X.
16. Called the Place de la Révolution after the French Revolution, today it is the Place de la Concorde.
17. Boigne, op.cit., p.371.
18. Ibid., p.420.
19. Evangeline Bruce, *Napoleon and Josephine: An Improbable Marriage*.
20. Le Comte de la Villele, *Mémoires*, quoted by H. Troyat, op.cit.
21. *Scenes from Russian Court Life*, p.267.
22. Castlereagh, op.cit.
23. Boigne, op.cit., p.359.

24. Lieven, op.cit.
25. Chateaubriand, op.cit., p.271.
26. *Scenes from Russian Court Life*, p.234.
27. Louise de Cochelet, *Mémoires sur la Reine Hortense et la Famille Impériale*, Letters of 11 and 25 June 1814, Vol.II, p.15.
28. *Scenes from Russian Court Life*, p.207.
29. Ibid., p.268.
30. Ibid.
31. Also quoted by Arthur Bryant, *The Age of Elegance 1812–1822.*
32. Flora Fraser, *The Unruly Queen.*
33. Metternich, op.cit., Vol.I.
34. de Cochelet, op.cit., p.17.
35. Lieven, op.cit.
36. Thomas Creevey, *The Creevey Papers.*
37. M. D. Buturlin, *Zapiski*, Russki Archiv, 1897, I, 4, p.641.
38. de Cochelet, op.cit.
39. The painting of *The Allied Sovereigns at Petworth* by Thomas Phillips is part of the Egremont Collection at Petworth House.
40. Creevey, op.cit., pp.16, 17.
41. Metternich, op.cit, Vol.I.
42. de Cochelet, op.cit., letter of 11 June 1814.

Chapter 5 A New Europe: At the Congress of Vienna

1. de Cochelet, op.cit., pp.16–17.
2. V. K. Constantin Mikhailovich, *Pavlovsk Ocherki i Opisanie 1777–1877*, St Petersburg, 1877.
3. Commandant Weil, *Les dessous du Congrès de Vienne*. Also H. Nicolson, *The Congress of Vienna.*
4. La Garde Chambonas, *Souvenirs du Congrès de Vienne.*
5. Nicolson, op.cit.
6. Prince Sergei G. Volkonsky, *Mémoires.*
7. Jean Baptiste Isabey, 1767–1855. A pupil of David. During the Congress of Vienna he was officially attached to the French delegation.
8. Sergei G. Volkonsky & Nicolson, op.cit.
9. Sergei M. Volkonsky, *Vospominanie*, p.84.
10. H. C. Robbins, *Beethoven, His Life, Work and World*, also quoted by Gregor Dallas in *1815.*
11. Adrien Boudou, *Le Saint Siège et la Russie: Leurs relations diplomatiques au XIX siècle 1814–1847*, pp.38–39; P. Angelluci, *Il Grande Segretario della Santa Sede*, p.49; Boigne, op.cit., Vol.II, pp.280, 405; John. T. Ellis, *Cardinal Consalvi and Anglo-Papal Relations*, pp.21–33.

12. J. Crétineau-Joly, *Mémoires du Cardinal Consalvi*, I, p.65.

13. *Diario del Marchese di San Mazzano* (Ambassador of Piedmont) quoted by Illario Rinieri, in *La Russia e l'arbitrato della Santa Sede*, Civilta Cattolica, 1899.

14. Boudou, op.cit.

15. Ibid., pp.48–52.

16. Nicolson, op.cit.

17. Brian-Chaninov, *Alexandre I*, Paris, 1934, also quoted by H. Troyat, op.cit.

18. One result of Napoleon's blockade against Britain had been that, in retaliation, Britain had required that all neutral shipping to and from the enemy be licensed, pay customs and be checked for contraband in British ports. The British navy was strong enough to enforce this measure. American shipping suffered particularly as a result, forcing Madison's government to declare war on Britain in June 1812.

19. La Garde Chambonas, op.cit.

20. Castlereagh, op.cit., Vols IX and X.

21. Nicolson, op.cit.

22. Ibid. and Duff Cooper, *Talleyrand*, pp.255–56.

23. Sergei G. Volkonsky, op.cit., p.330–31 and Nicolson, op.cit.

24. La Garde Chambonas, op.cit.

25. From the programme of the Fête de la Paix drawn up by the inspector-general of the Royal Academy of Music. Note 81, Metternich, op.cit., Vol.I, and La Garde Chambonas, op.cit.

26. Sergei G. Volkonsky, op.cit, p.332.

27. Friedrich von Gentz, *Journal*, Leipzig, 1861.

28. Robbins, op.cit.

29. Sergei G. Volkonsky, op.cit, p.332.

30. See Appendix. Poem in the Volkonsky Archives, Houghton Library, Harvard, published and commented by N. Gorodetsky, 'Princess Zinaida Volkonsky'.

31. La Garde Chambonas, op.cit.

32. *Corrispondenza inedita dei Cardinali Consalvi e Pacca del tempo del Congresso di Vienna*, Torino, Unione Typografico, 1903.

33. Illario Rinieri, op.cit.

34. Metternich, op.cit., Vol.I.

35. *Napoleon on Napoleon*, p.243.

36. Quoted by Troyat, op.cit.

37. Castlereagh, op.cit.

38. Edling, op.cit., and E. Knapton, *The Lady of the Holy Alliance*, pp.125–91.

39. Ibid.

Chapter 6 Travels: Rome, Paris and 'the Mud of Odessa'

1. *Otryvki iz Putevykh Zapisok, Moskovskiy Vestnik*, 1830, II, pp.140–50.
2. de Cochelet, op.cit., Vol.II, pp.41–43.
3. Letter to Z. V. from Count Moscati, 23 April 1815, Volkonsky Archives, Houghton Library, Harvard.
4. M. Svistunov, ed. *Griboyedovskaya Moskva v pismakh M. A. Volkovoy k V. I. Lanskoy*, 'Vestnik Evropi,' 1875, VIII, p.679.
5. Stendhal, *Vie de Rossini*.
6. Creevey, op.cit.
7. Letter 28 June 1815 to Sir Charles Stewart, Castlereagh, op.cit.
8. Chateaubriand, *Mémoires d'Outre Tombe*, p.391.
9. It remains the residence of the British ambassador to France to this day.
10. Boigne, op.cit., Vol II.
11. Webster, ed., *British diplomacy, 1813–1815*.
12. Boigne, op.cit.
13. Frances, Lady Shelley, *Diary, 1787–1817*, Vol.I.
14. *Empaytaz, Notice sur Alexandre Ier*, quoted by Troyat, op.cit.
15. A copy of this document is in the Bibliothèque Nationale. Printed in full by Lacroix in *Madame de Krüdener*, pp.139–48. Quoted by Knapton, op.cit., p.157.
16. Castlereagh, op.cit.
17. Boigne, op.cit.
18. de Cochelet, op.cit., p 176.
19. Sergei G. Volkonsky, op.cit., pp.337–38.
20. Shelley, op.cit.
21. Sergei G. Volkonsky, op.cit., p.338.
22. Commentary of A. N. Volkonsky with six letters from the Emperor Alexander to Princess Z. Volkonsky in *Zbornik Russkogo Istoricheskogo Vestnika*, 1868, III, p.312.
23. Shelley, op.cit.
24. See Appendix. Volkonsky Archives, Houghton Library, Harvard.
25. Sergei G. Volkonsky, op.cit.
26. Ibid., p.381.
27. Ibid., p.379.
28. The Ultras were the party of rigid, reactionary legitimists who represented the purest ideas of the counter-revolution. Well to the right of the King, they followed his brother, the Comte d'Artois.
29. Boigne, op.cit.
30. Sergei G. Volkonsky, op.cit., p.379.
31. Boigne, op.cit.

32. Ibid.
33. Patricia Herlihy, *Odessa: A History, 1794–1914*.
34. Letter of 1 October, *Scenes from Russian Court life*.
35. Volkonsky Archives, Houghton Library, Harvard, Letter of 12–24 May 1816.
36. N. I. Turgenev, *Pisma k bratu S. I. Turgenevu*, Moskva, Ak.Nauk, SSSR, 1936, p.232.
37. Volkonsky Archives, Houghton Library, Harvard, Letter of 18/10/1817.
38. Letter from A. Bulgakov of 19 August 1818, Russki Archiv, 1900, III, p.129.
39. Volkovaya to Lanskaya op.cit. M. Svistunoved. Griboyeduvshaya, Moskva v pismakh MA Volkovoy k VI Lanskoy 'vestnik Europi' 1875, VIII, p.679.
40. Abbé Nicolle's notes on the education of Prince A. N. Volkonsky, Russki Archiv, 1896, Vol.IV, pp.486–96, mentioned by N. A. Belozerskaya, *Kniginia Zinaida Alexandrovna Volkonskaya*.
41. Quoted by Belozerskaya, op.cit.
42. Sergei G. Volkonsky, op.cit., pp 398–408.
43. Poem 'La Boue d'Odessa', Volkonsky Archives, Houghton Library, Harvard, also commented in N. Gorodetsky, '*Un Épisode de Romantisme Russe*'.
44. *Iz zapisok Kn.Repninoy*, Russki Archiv, 1897, II, 7, p.489.
45. Bulgakov, letter of 19 August 1818, to his brother. Russki Archiv, 1900, III, 9, p.129, also quoted by Aroutunova, op.cit.
46. *Quatres Nouvelles par la Princesse Zénéide Volkonsky* were published in Moscow in 1820 and after her death, in *Oeuvres Choisies*.
47. *Usadba Kn. Z. Volkonskoy v Rime*, Vremmenik Obschestvo Druzei Russ-knigi, Paris, 1938, IV, pp.163–65, quoted by Aroutunova, op.cit.
48. La Rochefoucauld, op.cit., Vol.I, pp.228–35.
49. Letter of 30 September 1819, in Ostafievsky Archiv, Kn.Viazemskikh, St Petersburg, 1886–1903.

Chapter 7 Rome, Verona and Paris

1. Letter to Baron de Mareste, 3 March 1820, Stendhal, *Correspondance*, Vol.V, p.299.
2. Belozerskaya, op.cit.,
3. Lieven, op.cit., letter of 8 February 1820
4. *Sculptor S. I. Galberg v ego Zagranichnikh Pismakh i Zapiskakh*, 'Vestnik Iziashnikh Isskustv', II, 5, pp.122–25, St Petersburg, 1884.
5. Ibid.
6. Berry, op.cit., pp.274–76.

7. R. E. Terebenina, *Zapiski o Pushkine etc. v dnevnike P. D. Durnovo*, 'Nauka', Leningrad, 1978, VIII, p.266.
8. Prince Sergei M. Volkonsky, *My Reminiscences*, Vol.I, pp.295–313.
9. Berry, op.cit., p.276.
10. V. M. Fridkin, *Propavshi Dnevnik Pushkina*, p.179.
11. Libretto of her opera *Giovanna d'Arco, Dramma per Musica ridotto da Schiller della Principessa Zeneide Volkonsky*, Presso Paolo Salviucci & Figlio, Rome, 1821.
12. Boigne, op.cit., Vol.I, pp.280–81.
13. Elizabeth Duchess of Devonshire to Lord Byron, letter of 17 August 1821, *The Two Duchesses*, London, 1898.
14. Stendhal, *Vie de Rossini*.
15. Volkonsky Archives, Houghton Library, Harvard.
16. Metternich, quoted by M. Paleologue, Paris, Plon, 1937.
17. Letter of 3 February 1821, Volkonsky Archives, Houghton Library, Harvard.
18. Berry, op.cit.
19. Letter of 13 February 1821, Volkonsky Archives, Houghton Library, Harvard.
20. Domenico Cimarosa 1749–1801. The opera was first performed at La Fenice in Venice on 26 December 1796.
21. Berry, op.cit., p.289.
22. Canning, who succeeded Castlereagh, was also unwilling to intervene, but had to give in. Greece won her independence with the help of both Russia and Britain. In 1828 Capo d'Istria became the first president of Greece. He was assasinated four years later.
23. Lieven, op.cit.
24. Letter of 24 November 1822, in *Princess Lieven*, by H. Montgomery Hyde, p.145.
25. La Rochefoucauld, op.cit., letter of 24 November 1822.
26. Letter to A. Benckendorff, 23 October 1822. Lieven, op.cit., p.57.
27. Temperley, *The Foreign Policy of Canning*, quoted by Wendy Hinde in *George Canning*.
28. Letter of 24 November 1824, Lieven, op.cit.
29. Chateaubriand, *Mémoires d'Outre Tombe*, Vol.IV, 'Alexandre'.
30. P. A. Viazemsky, Complete Works, II, p.107 and VII, pp.451–52, Commented by Aroutunova, op.cit.
31. Volkonsky Archives, Houghton Library, Harvard.
32. Letter from Visconti Archive, quoted by Fridkin, op.cit., p.177.
33. They were transferred later to the Villa Volkonsky, where they remain to this day.
34. J. Crétineau-Joly, op.cit.
35. Letter of 22 June 1823, Volkonsky Archives, Houghton Library, Harvard.

36. *Tableau Slave du Cinquième Siècle*, Paris, 1824, also in *Oeuvres Choisies*, pp.157–218.
37. No. 150, 30 May 1824, quoted by Belozerskaya, op.cit.
38. 31 May 1824. Ibid.
39. *Revue Encyclopédique*, VXXII, Paris, 1824, quoted ibid.
40. Talma was the greatest classical actor of his day in France. He died in 1826.
41. Berry, op.cit., p.345.
42. *Olga, Otryvok,* 'Moskovski Nabludatel', 1836, IX, pp.308–38, also *Oeuvres Choisies*.
43. Letter of 4 August 1823, Volkonsky Archives, Houghton Library, Harvard.
44. Letter of 10 October 1823, ibid.

Chapter 8 The End of an Era

1. Bulgakov, letter 28 July 1824, Russki Archiv, 1901, II, 5, p.74.
2. La Rochefoucauld, op.cit., I, pp.395–401.
3. Letter of 8 June 1824, Volkonsky Archives, Houghton Library, Harvard.
4. Note of August 1824, undated letter July-August 1824, Volkonsky Archives, Houghton Library, Harvard.
5. La Rochefoucauld, op.cit., pp.410–17.
6. Prince Shalikov in *Damski Journal*, 1827, I, p.48.
7. A. N. Muraviev, *Znakomstvo s Russkimi Poetami*, pp.11–14, also quoted by N. Gorodetsky in 'Princess Zinaida Volkonsky', p.97.
8. Maria Nikoleavna Volkonsky's *Zapiski*, in Sergei M. Volkonsky, op.cit., pp.248–87.
9. This referred to Prince Nikita's promotion to the rank of general.
10. Volkonsky Archives, Houghton Library, Harvard.
11. K. Grot, *Dnevnik Kozlova*, Starina i Novisna, 1906, p.46.
12. La Rochefoucauld, op.cit., pp.373–81.
13. Quoted by Belozerskaya, op.cit., p.952.
14. *Trudi i Letopis Obshestva Ist. i Drev. Rossii*, Part III, V. 2, 1827, quoted by Belozerskaya, op.cit., p.963.
15. Quoted by Bocharov and Glushakova, op.cit., p.210.
16. Charlotte Disbrowe, *Original Letters from Russia 1825–28*, pp.90–91.
17. Published in 1862 in the *Ladies Journal* and the *Moscow Telegraph*.
18. It is a Russian superstition that it is unlucky to light candles in daylight, because normally candles were only burned during the day around a coffin.
19. *Poslednie dni Zhizni Aleksandra I: Rasskazi Ochevidtsev Zapisanie Kn. Z. Volkonskoy*, 'Russkaya Starina', XXI, 1873, pp.139–50.

20. Letter of 2 February 1826, published as *Extraits d'une lettre au Baron Mérian en 1826*, in *Oeuvres Choisies*, pp.221–318.
21. Sergei G. Volkonsky, op.cit., p.408.
22. Mickiewicz, op.cit., also quoted by C. Sutherland in *Princess of Siberia*.
23. *Portrait de Mickiewicz*, in *Oeuvres Choisies*.
24. Mickiewicz, op.cit.
25. Disbrowe, op.cit.
26. Maria N. Volkonsky, op.cit., pp.248–87.
27. Quoted by Anatole Mazour, *The First Russian Revolution, 1825*.
28. Maria N. Volkonsky, op.cit.
29. Ibid.
30. Herzen, op.cit., Vol.I, pp.41–42.
31. *Issledovania i stat' i po Russkoi Literaturi i prosfesheniu*, M. I. Suknomilova, Vol.II, 1889, quoted by Belozerskaya, op.cit., p.965.
32. P. A. Viazemsky, *Complete Works*, Vol.9.

Chapter 9 A Salon in Moscow

1. Letter of 11 August 1826, quoted by R. E. Terebenina in *Pushkin and Zinaida Volkonsky,* Russkaya Literatura, 1975, Vol.II, pp.136–45.
2. Quoted by Fridkin, op.cit., pp.179–80.
3. Buturlin, op.cit.
4. Letter to Barbieri of 15 July 1825, Visconti Archive, quoted by Fridkin, op.cit. pp.178–79.
5. A. Y. Bulgakov to his brother, letter of 25 May 1825, Russki Archiv.
6. Mickiewicz, op.cit., also quoted in Sutherland, op.cit.
7. Herzen, op.cit., p.383.
8. Disbrowe, op.cit., pp.152–53
9. Ibid., p.148.
10. Ibid., pp.151–54
11. Ibid.
12. Ibid.
13. *Russkaya Starina*, 1881, no.9, p.191.
14. Herzen, op.cit., Vol.I, p.42.
15. Ibid.
16. Sergei M. Volkonsky, op.cit.
17. Disbrowe, op.cit. p.150.
18. Sergei M. Volkonsky, op.cit.
19. Repeated by Benckendorff to Pushkin in a letter of 30 September 1826, quoted in E. J. Simmons, *Pushkin*, p.295.
20. *History of the USSR*, Vol.II: *Russia in the 19th Century*, ed. M. B. Nechkin, 1949, p.123.

21. Letter of 12 April 1826, Terebenina, *Pushkin and Zinaida Volkonsky*.
22. Russki Archiv, 1901, Vol.II, p.250, and 1885, Vol.II, p.29.
23. Henishta was a talented German musician and composer who had done much to make German classical music known in Moscow.
24. *Pushkin v Vospominaniakh Sovremmenikov (Pushkin in Contemporary Memoirs)*, 1950, Gos. Izd. Khudozhestvennoi Lit., P. A. Viazemsky, p.92.
25. Lit. Nasledstvo, 1952, p.52, Z. A. Volkonskaya-P. A. Viazemsky, 20/9/1826–17/5/1827.
26. Letter of 9 November 1826, Viazemsky, *Complete Works*, Vol.X.
27. Viazemsky, *Complete Works*, Vol.VII, p.328, also quoted by Belozerskaya, op.cit., p.966.
28. Extracts from her letter to Pushkin, 29 October 1826, Pushkin, *Complete Works*, Vol.XIII, p.299.
29. Volkonsky Archives, Houghton Library, Harvard.
30. Quoted by Simmons, op.cit.
31. B. L. Modzalevsky, *Pushkin pod Tainim Nadsorom (Pushkin under secret surveillance)*, Vol.I, pp.31–32.
32. Maria N. Volkonsky, op.cit.
33. Ibid.
34. Letter of 21 December 1826, Visconti Archive, quoted by Fridkin, op.cit., pp.179–80.
35. A. V. Venevitinov, Russkaya Starina, 1875, Vol.XII, p.822.
36. *A la Princesse M. V., née R.*, Oeuvres Choisies.
37. Buturlin, op.cit., pp.178–79.
38. Russki Archiv, 1898, Vol.II, p.315.
39. Prince Shalikov, *Damski Journal*, 1827, I, pp.45–48, quoted by Belozerskaya, op.cit., p.970.
40. Found in the Venevitinov Archives, published in a Russian translation in 1934. French original published in 1940. See Gorodetsky, 'Un Épisode du Romantisme Russe'.
41. Letter to Pogodin, quoted by Belozerskaya, op.cit., p.968.
42. Letter of 25 November 1826, Volkonsky Archives, Houghton Library, Harvard: also commented by Aroutunova, op.cit.
43. Venevitinov 1934, p.422–23, M. Baranovskaya; also quoted by Gorodetsky, 'Un Épisode du Romantisme Russe'.
44. Gorodetsky, 'Un Épisode du Romantisme Russe'.
45. Russki Archiv, 1885, Vol.I, pp.113–31; also *Oeuvres Choisies*.
46. Muraviev, op.cit., quoted by Belozerskaya, op.cit., p.972.
47. Sergei M. Volkonsky, op.cit.
48. E. Dimitrieva, *Moi Vospominania*, Zvenya, Moscow, VIII, 1950, pp.789–95, also quoted by Gorodetsky.
49. Letter of 25 January 1829, Pushkin, *Complete Works*, Vol.XIV, p.38.
Wishing someone 'neither bottom nor cover' is to wish them bad luck. It

isn't clear whether Pushkin had seen Zinaida in St Petersburg, where she spent more than a month before leaving Russia. He certainly saw Shevyrev. The somewhat coarse reference to Ricci shows how well known the affair was.

50. Terebenina, op.cit., Vol.I, pp.143–44. Pushkin and Z. Volkonsky, 'Russkaya Literatura' 1975
51. Volkonsky Archives, Houghton Library, Harvard.
52. Ibid.
53. Ibid. Their younger full sister Natalia had died in 1815. There is a plaque to her memory in the garden of the Villa Volkonsky in Rome which reads: *'J'ai trop d'âme, disait elle pour vivre longtemps/ à vingt-trois ans elle reposait déjà dans l'humide terre.'*
54. Letter of 2 March 1829, quoted by Terebenina, op.cit.

Chapter 10 Rome: The Villa Volkonsky

1. Letter to Countess Caroline Eglofstein, Moscow, 31 January 1826, quoted by S. Durylin in *Russkiye Pissateli u Goethe*, 'Literanturnoe Nasledstvo', 1932, IV-VI, pp.477–86.
2. Russki Archiv, 1879, Vol.I, pp.138–39, Letter from Shevyrev to E. P. Elagina from Florence 29 May 1829.
3. *Otrivki iz Putevikh Zapisok (Extracts from Travel Notes)*, published in *Severnii Tsveti (Northern Flowers)*, Vol.VI, 1830, p.14.
4. Letter of 3 March 1830, quoted by Durylin, op.cit.
5. *Travel Notes*, Weimar, Bavaria and Tyrol.
6. Published in the journal *Galatea* 1829, V, pp.3–31, VI, pp.88–90, and in *Moskovskiy Vestnik (Moscow Herald)*, 1830, II, pp.140–51, also *Severnii Tsevti*, 1830, pp.216–27, 1831, pp.120–21.
7. Letter of 13 September 1829, *Lit. Nasledstvo*, op.cit, 1952.
8. Letter of 23 August 1830, ibid.
9. Letter from *Ostafievskiy Archiv, Kn. Viazemskikh*, 1899, Vol.III, p.223, also quoted by Y. Glushakova in *Russkaya Villa u Drevnikh sten Rima, in Mir Russkoi usad'be*, Nauka, 1995, p.284.
10. N. P. Barsukova, *Zhizn i Trudi Pogodina*, III, 1890, p.304.
11. Letter to Pogodin, ibid., II, 1889, pp.74–76.
12. Ibid., II, p.36, also quoted by Belozerskaya, op.cit.
13. Ibid., III, pp.385–99.
14. Letter of 2 April 1830, quoted by Belozerskaya, op.cit.
15. Barsukova, op.cit.
16. Sergei M Volkonsky, op.cit.
17. Taken from the same piece of granite as the Alexander column which stands on Senate Square, St Petersburg.

18. *Archiv Brateev Turgenevykh*, VI, Akademia Nauk, Petrograd, 1921, Letter from Rome 12/24 December 1832.

19. Augustus Hare, *Walks in Rome.*

20. Journals of Walter Scott, No.659.

21. *Oeuvres Choisies.*

22. Sergei M. Volkonsky, op.cit.

23. 'The Lyric Album of 1829', inscribed *'Offert à ma très chère tante par son très affectioné neveu G. V. à Rome le 16 avril vendredi 1830'*, is in the Volkonsky Archives, Houghton Library, Harvard.

24. Letter of 2 January 1828, A. Khomoutov, 1896, p.183.

25. Unpublished MS, Volkonsky Archives, Houghton Library, Harvard, quoted by Aroutunova, op.cit.

26. Published in *Utrenyaya Zarya (Dawn)* in 1839; Volkonsky Archives, Houghton Library, Harvard.

27. Kozlov, *Complete Works*, 1960, p.301.

28. M. I. Glinka, *Complete Works*, Moscow, Izdatelstvo Musica, 1973, I, pp.242–43.

29. Prince Sergei M. Volkonsky, op.cit.

30. Letter of 15 June 1831, quoted by Belozerskaya, op.cit.

31. Letter of 17 September 1832, ibid. *Zvenya*, 1951, LX, pp.369–71, 380, 386–87.

32. Letter of 3 March 1832, Mickiewicz's Literary Archive, XII, Warsaw, 1968, p.214.

33. Letter of 10 June 1832, ibid.

34. Letter in Mickiewicz, *Correspondence*, Vol.II.

35. Volkonsky Archives, Houghton Library, Harvard.

36. Ibid.

37. G. Barbero, 'La Principessa Zeneide Wolkonski', *Osservatore Romano*, No.28, p.3, 3 February 1950.

38. Gorodetsky, p.34 Aroutunova and 'Zinaida Volkonsky as a Catholic' op.cit., p.305. Slavonic + E. European Review, Vol XXXIX No 92 Dec 1960.

39. La Rochefoucauld, op.cit., Vol.I pp.291–92.

40. Archiv Brateev Turgenevikh.

41. Zhukovsky, *Dnevniki, (Diaries).*

42. Letter of 1 January 1834, quoted by Trofimoff in *La Princesse Zénéide Volkonsky.*

43. Letter PA to V. F. Viazemsky, 17 May 1828, *Drusia Pushkina*, Vol.I, Moscow, 1984, p.418.

44. He had married Natalia Goncharova in February 1831.

45. Letter of 3 August 1834, *Drusia Pushkina.*

46. Volkonsky Archives, Houghton Library, Harvard.

47. Letter 4–16 December 1834, quoted by N. Kauchtschviliin, *L'Italia nella*

vita e nell opera di P. A. Viazemskij, Milan, Soc. ed. Vita e Pensiero, 1964, p.265.

48. Your Highness Zinaida Volkonsky/ Why expose me to two risks?/ either that no Christian will understand me/ Or that they will understand me only too well./My Muse comes from a miserable home/ So how do you expect this to end?/I can see that it will end with catcalls/ If I escape, search for me in the woods.

49. Orioli, *Z. Wolkonski*, Palatino, 1966, No. 2, also L. P. Lemme, *Salotti Romani dell'Ottocento*, pp.80–103.

50. *Letters and Journals of James Fennimore Cooper*, Cambridge, Mass., 1960–68, ed. J. F. Beard jnr, Vol.1.

51. Viazemsky, *Complete Works*, p.267.

52. *Moskovski Nabludatel*, 1835, II, p.113.

53. Letter of 25 June 1838, Gogol, *Complete Works*, p.156.

54. Letter of 24 April 1835. MS at St. Petersburg Library, quoted by Belozerskaya op.cit.

55. O. G. Basankur, *Perevodchik Pushkina – Ricci*, (Pushkin's translator – Ricci), Pushkin, Vremmenik Pushkinskoi Komissii, Mos-Len, 1941, pp.424–29.

56. P. E. Terebenina, *Pushkin i Zinaida Volkonskaya*, Russkaya Literatura, 1975, Vol II, p.145.

57. Ibid.

58. N. Gorodesky, 'Zinaida Volkonsky as a Catholic'.

Chapter 11 Rome: Dead Souls and Souls Reborn

1. Translation by Maurice Baring, *Russian Literature*, 1914, Williams and Norgate, p.110.

2. Letter of 28 March 1837, Gogol, Complete Works.

3. Letter of 15 April 1837, ibid.

4. *Memoirs and Critical Works of A. P. Annenkov*, 1877.

5. Volkonsky Archives, Houghton Library, Harvard, commented by Roman Jacobson and B. Aroutunova, in 'An Unknown Album Page by Nikolaj Gogol', *Harvard Library Bulletin*, Cambridge, Mass., July 1972, XX,3.

6. Letter of 13 May 1838, Gogol, *Complete Works*.

7. For a scholarly analysis on Gogol's sexuality and its effects on his work, see Simon Karlinsky, *The Sexual Labyrinth of Nikolai Gogol*.

8. Letter of 22 December 1837, Gogol, *Complete Works*.

9. Letters of Hieronim Kajsiewicz and Piotr Semenenko, quoted in Gorodetsky, 'Zinaida Volkonsky as a Catholic'.

10. A. Mazon, 'Deux Lettres de la Princesse Z. Volkonsky au Prince Kozlovsky', *Revue des Études Slaves*, XXX, Paris, 1953, pp.105–6.

11. Zhukovsky, op.cit., pp.279, 283, 290, 295.

12. Gogol, *Complete Works*, Vol.XI, p.197.

13. Volkonsky Archives, Houghton Library, Harvard.

14. F. I. Jordan, *Zapiski* (Notes), Russkaya Starina, 1891, pp.247–48, quoted by Belozerskaya, op.cit.

15. Letter of 31 May 1839, Gogol, *Complete Works*.

16. V. I. Shenrok, '*Vestnik Evropi*', 1894, pp.630–31, *N. V. Gogol, Piat let za Granitsoy*, quoted by Belozerskaya, op.cit.

17. Gogol, *Complete Works*.

18. Volkonsky Archives, Houghton Library, Harvard, quoted by Gorodetsky, pp.102–3.

19. Durnovo, op.cit., p.358.

20. Shenrok, op.cit., p.630.

21. *Journal du Comte R. Apponyi*, E. Daudet, Paris, Plon, Vol.III, p.416.

22. Letter of 13 June 1841, MS at St Petersburg Public Library, quoted by Belozerskaya, op.cit.

23. Letter of 28 July 1841, ibid.

24. Letter of 8 September 1841, ibid.

25. Letter of 14 September 1841, ibid.

26. Letter of 4 December 1845, Archive of the Order of the Sisters, Adorers of the Most Precious Blood, Rome.

27. Muraviev, op.cit., pp.13–14.

28. Ibid.

29. Letter of 14 September 1841.

30. P. V. Annenkov, *Literaturniye Vospominanie i Perepiska 1835–85*.

31. A. O. Smirnova Rosset, *Vospominanie*, p.406.

32. Letter of 24 October 1845, Gogol, *Complete Works*.

33. V. G. Belinsky, *Complete Works*, Vol.X, pp.213–14.

34. Letter of 11 February 1847, Gogol, *Complete Works*.

Chapter 12 The Beata

1. Preface to Monsignor de Lobet, *Lettres et pages inédites de Mgr Gerbet*, Lyons-Paris, 1946; *Extraits des notes et des souvenirs de Soeur Marie du Sacré Coeur*, quoted by Gorodetsky, in 'Zinaida Volkonsky as a Catholic'.

2. de Bussières, *L'Enfant de Marie ou une Conversion*, Rome, 1842, pp.25 and 146, quoted by Gorodetsky, ibid.

3. The Jewish quarter in Rome remained literally a ghetto until 1870.

4. Letter to the Pope, in the Archive of the Sisters, Adorers of the Most Precious Blood, Rome.

5. *Zapiski Archimandrita Vladimira Terletskogo, 1808–58*, Russkaya Starina, LXIII, St Petersburg, July 1889, pp.1–26, September, pp.59–78, June

1891, pp.581–601, November, pp.351–92, quoted by Belozerskaya, op.cit., p.162 and Gorodetsky, 'Zinaida Volkonsky as a Catholic', p.105.

6. Ibid.

7. Letter of 10 January 1864, quoted by Don Michele Colagiovanni in *Le Quatre Evangeliste: Sorelle de Sanctis*.

8. All MS letters from Z. Volkonsky and her sister Madeleine to Mother Maria de Mattias are in the Archive of the Sisters, Adorers of the Most Precious Blood, Rome.

9. Biographical sketch of Zinaida Volkonsky, by her confessor, Don Giovanni Merlini, in the Archive of the Sisters, Adorers of the Most Precious Blood, published in *Nel Segno del Sangue*, XXVII, 5–6, 1977.

10. Ibid.

11. Ibid.

12. Moroni, *Dizionario de erudizione Storico-Ecclesiastica da San Pietro ai Nostri Giorni*, Venice Art. Scuole Pie, LXIII, p.123, quoted by Gorodetsky, 'Zinaida Volkonsky as a Catholic'.

13. Don Merlini, op.cit.

14. Letter of 20 December 1852, M. de Mattias's letters published in two vols, edited by Giovanni Merlini.

15. Merlini, op.cit.

16. Ibid.

17. Prince Sergei G. Volkonsky and B. L. Modzalevsky, *Archiv Dekabrista*, XLI.

18. Minutes of a legal act – Acta Curia generale no 44 – of 11 June 1868, signed by Giovanni Merlini and others accepts a second and last payment of 1000 scudi from Prince Alexander Volkonsky according to the wishes of 'Donna Zenaide', his mother, for the purchase of a small house, etc., in the Archive of the Sisters, Adorers of the Most Precious Blood in Rome.

19. Volkonsky Archives, Houghton Library, Harvard.

20. Ibid.

21. Ibid. Original entry: *'J'ai toujours été sensible aux beautés de la nature; ce goût ne m'a pas quitté, il a pris le caractère de la prière. Quand j'entends le chant des oiseaux je pense à Sainte Rose qui disait que le chant et même le bourdonnement des insectes lui semblaient des hymnes au Créateur. Elle disait vrai: la prière remplit l'espace de l'amour de Dieu. C'est l'échelle des anges qui vont et viennent: et Dieu est là dans les cieux et dans notre coeur. Et les arbres: comment ne pas les aimer? Ils nous ont donné la Croix! C'est la vie: cette sève ne tarit jamais.'*

22. *Giornale di Roma*, 5 February 1862.

23. 'She dedicated the memorials along this path to filial piety, to gratitude, to friendship. The same tribute is paid to her dear memory.'

Select Bibliography

PRIMARY SOURCES

Adams, John Quincy, *Memoirs of J. Q. Adams Comprising Portions of his Diary 1795–1848*, Lippincott, Philadelphia, 1874.

d'Albany, Comtesse, *Le Portfeuille de la Comtesse d'Albany*, Paris, 1902.

Alekseevea, E. G., *Zelyoni Albom*, New York, 1958.

Annenkov, P. V., *Literaturniye Vospominanie i Perepiska 1835–1885*, St Petersburg, 1892.

Belinsky, V. G. *Complete Works*, Moscow, 1956.

Berry, Mary, *Extracts of the Journals and Correspondence of Miss Berry*, ed. Theresa Lewis, London, 1865.

Boigne, Comtesse de, *Mémoires de la Comtesse de Boigne*, Paris, Plon, 1907.

Bourgeat, J. *Napoléon; Lettres à Joséphine*, Guy Le Prat, Paris, 1941.

Burghersh, Lady, *Journal and Letters of Lady Burghersh*, ed. Lady Rose Weigall, John Murray, 1897.

Castlereagh, Viscount, *Correspondence, Despatches and other Papers of Viscount Castlereagh*, William Shobel, London 1852.

Caulaincourt, A. de, *Nouvelles et on dit de St. Petersbourg 1908, & Mémoires du Général de Caulaincourt*, Paris, Plon, 1933.

Chateaubriand F. R., *Napoléon*, Egloff, Paris and *Mémoires d'Outre Tombe*, Nelson, Edinburgh.

Choiseul-Gouffier, Comtesse de, *Mémoires sur L'Empereur Alexandre I et sur l'Empereur Napoléon*, Dentu, Paris, 1862.

Clausewitz, General Carl von, *The Campaign of 1812 in Russia*, Da Capo Press, New York, 1995.

Cochelet, Mademoiselle Louise de, *Mémoires sur la Reine Hortense et la Famille Impériale*, 4 vols, Brussels, 1837.

Creevey, Thomas, *The Creevey Papers*, ed. John Gore, John Murray, 1948.

Crétineau-Joly, *Mémoires du Cardinal Consalvi*, Paris, 1866.

Czartoryski, Prince Adam, *Mémoires et Correspondence avec l'Empereur Alexandre I*, 2 vols, Paris, 1887.

Disbrowe, Charlotte, *Original Letters from Russia 1825–28*, London, 1878.

Edling, Comtesse, *Mémoires*, Moscow, 1888.

Garde Chambonas, Comte Auguste de La, *Souvenirs du Congrès de Vienne*, Vivien, Paris, 1901.

Gentz, Freidrich von, *Dépeches inédites aux Hospodars de Valachie*, Plon, Paris, 1876.

Gogol, N. V., *Complete Works*, Akademia Nauk SSSR, Moscow, 1952.

Herzen, Alexander, *Byloe i Dumi (My Past and Thoughts)*, Goslitizdat, Leningrad, 1947.

I. I. Kozlov Complete Works 1960

La Harpe F. C. de, *Correspondance de Frédéric-Cézar de La Harpe et Alexandre I*, Neuchâtel, 1978.

La Tour du Pin, Marquise de, *Mémoires d'une femme de cinquante ans*, Chapelt, Paris, 1914.

Lieven, Princess Dorothea, *Letters of Princess Lieven*, Longman, London, 1902.

Ligne, Prince de, *Mémoires, Lettres et Pensées du Prince de Ligne*, ed. F. Bourin, 1989.

Maistre, Joseph de, *Correspondance Diplomatique*, Paris, 1860, and *Les Soirées de St Petersbourg*, Paris, 1922.

Merlini, Giovanni, *Lettere à Maria de Mattias*, 2 vols, Sanguis, Rome, 1974.

Metternich, C. Prince de, *Mémoires*, 2 vols, Plon, Paris, 1880.

Mickiewicz, Adam, *Pametniki (Memoirs)*, Archivum Literackie, Paris.

Muraviev, A. N. *Znakomstvo s Russkimi Poetami*, Kiev, 1871.

Nicholas Mikhailovich, Grand Duke, *L'Empereur Alexandre I*, 2 vols, St Petersburg, 1912; *Le Comte Paul Stroganov*, 3 vols, St Petersburg and Paris, 1905; *Scenes from Russian Court Life: the Correspondence of Alexander I and his sister Catherine*, Jarrolds, Norwich.

Pushkin, A. S., *Complete Works*, Nauka, Leningrad, 1978.

La Rochefoucauld, Vicomte de, *Mémoires du Vicomte de La Rochefoucauld*, Paris, 1837.

Seaman, W. A. L., and Sewell, J. R., *The Russian Journal of Lady Londonderry 1836–7*, John Murray, 1973.

Shelley, F. Lady, *Diary of Frances Lady Shelley 1787–1817*, Edited R. Edgecumbe, London 1912

Shenrok, V. I., *N. V. Gogol, Piat let Zhizni za Granitsoy 1836–1841*, St Petersburg, 1902.

Smirnova Rosset, A. O., *Vospominanie & Pisma*, Pravda, Moscow, 1990.

Staël Madame de, *Dix Années d'Exil*, ed. Gautier, Plon, Paris, 1904; *Oeuvres Complètes*; *Corinne ou l'Italie*; *Considérations sur la Revolution Française*.

Stendhal, *Vie de Rossini*, ed. Brunel, Folio, Gallimard, Paris 1992. *Oeuvres Complètes*; *Correspondance*, Le Divan, Paris, 1834.

Talleyrand, Prince Charles-Maurice de, *Mémoires*, Paris, 1891.

Trubetskoy, Princess Lise, *Un Ambassadeur Russe à Turin, Dépêches de S. E. le Prince Alexandre Belosselsky de Bélozersk*, ed. Ernest Leroux, Paris, 1901.

Viazemsky, P. A., *Complete Works* St Petersburg, 1879.

Vigée-Lebrun, Elizabeth, *Souvenirs de Madame Vigée-Lebrun*, 3 vols, Paris, 1835–37.

Volkonsky, Princess Zinaida Alexandrovna, *Oeuvres Choisies de la Princesse Zénéide Volkonsky*, Hasper, Paris and Karlsruhe, 1865

Volkonsky, Prince Sergei G, *Mémoires*, 1902.

Volkonsky, Prince Sergei M., *Vospominanie o Dekabristakh po Semeinim Vospominaniam*, Isskustvo, Moscow, 1994.

Volkonsky, Prince Serge (trs. A. E. Chamot), *My Reminiscences*, 2 vols, Hutchinson, London.

Weil, Commandant M. H., *Les dessous du Congrès de Vienne*, Payot, 1917.

Wellington Duke of, *Despatches*, London, 1847.

Wilmot, The *Russian Journals of Catherine and Martha Wilmot, 1803–8*. Macmillan, 1934.

Wilson, Sir Robert, *Narrative of Events during the Invasion of Russia*, John Murray, 1860.

Zhukovsky, *Dnevniki*, ed. I. A. Bichkov, St Petersburg, 1901.

SECONDARY SOURCES

Alsop, Susan Mary, *The Congress Dances, Vienna 1814–1815*. Weidenfeld and Nicolson, 1984.

Angeli, Diego, *Roma Romantica*, Fratelli Treves, Milan.

Angelluci, P. *Il Grande Segretario della Santa Sede*, Roma, Scuola Typ., 1924.

Aroutunova, Bayara, *Lives in Letters: Princess Zinaida Volkonsky and her Correspondence*, Slavica Publishers Inc., 1994.

Balayé, Simone, *Madame de Staël: Lumières et Liberté*, ed. Klincksieck, Paris, 1979.

Bayley, John, *Pushkin*, Cambridge University Press, 1971.

Belosselsky-Belozersky, Prince Serge Sergeevich, *Memoirs*, ed. Marvin Lyons, Paris.

Belozerskaya N. A. *Kniginia Zinaida Alexandrovna Volkonskaya*, Istoricheski Vestnik, LXVII, 1897.

Berlin, Isaiah, *Russian Thinkers*, Hogarth Press, 1978; *The Sense of Reality: The Romantic Revolution*, Chatto and Windus, 1996; *The Crooked Timber of Humanity: Joseph de Maistre and the origins of Fascism*, John Murray, 1990.

Billington, James H. *The Icon and the Axe: An Interpretative History of Russian Culture*, Vintage Books, 1970.

Bocharov, Ivan, and Glushakova, Yulia, *Italianskaya Pushkiniana*, Sovremmenik, Moscow, 1991.

Boudou, Adrien, *Le Saint Siège et la Russie: Leur Relations diplomatiques au XIX siècle 1814–1847*, Plon, Paris, 1992.

Bruce, Evangeline, *Napoleon and Josephine: An Improbable Marriage*, Weidenfeld and Nicolson, 1995.

Bryant, Arthur, *The Age of Elegance 1812–1822*, Collins, London, 1950.

Cobban Alfred, *A History of Modern France*, 3 vols, Penguin, 1965.

Colagiovanni, Michele, *Maria de Mattias, La Ribelle obbediente*, ed. Pia Unione Prez.Sangue, Roma, 1984; *Giovanni Merlini: La Volonta di Dio mu Basta*, ed. Citta Nuova, 1996; *Le Quattro Evangeliste: Sorelle de Sanctis*, ASC Profili, 2, 1995, Centro Studi Internazionale di Spiritualita.

Cooper, Duff, *Talleyrand*, Jonathan Cape, 1947.

Custine, Marquise de, *Lettres de Russie – La Russie en 1839*, Gallimard, ed. Folio, 1975.

Dallas, Gregor, *1815*, Richard Cohen Books, 1996.

Edmonds, Robin, *Pushkin, The Man and his Age*, Macmillan, 1994.

Ellis, John T., *Cardinal Consalvi and Anglo-Papal Relations*, Catholic University of America Press, 1942.

Erickson, Carolly, *Our Tempestuous Day: A History of Regency England*, Robson Books, 1996.

Fraser, Flora, *The Unruly Queen*, Macmillan, 1996.

Fridkin, V. M., *Propavshi Dvevnik Pushkina*, Znanie, Moscow, 1991.

Gorodetsky, Nadezhda, 'Princess Zinaida Volkonsky', *Oxford Slavonic Papers*, V, 1954; 'Zinaida Volkonsky as a Catholic', *The Slavonic and East European Review*, Vol. XXXIX, No. 92, Dec. 1960; 'La Boue d'Odessa' and 'Un Episode du Romantisme Russe', *Revue de Littérature Comparé*, 1953.

Herlihy, Patricia, *Odessa: A History, 1794–1914*, Harvard University Press, 1986.

Hare, Augustus, *Walks in Rome*. V. vols. London 1871.

Hinde, Wendy, *George Canning*, Basil Blackwell, 1989; *Castlereagh*, Collins, 1981.

Hobsbawm, E. J. *The Age of Revolution 1789–1848* and *The Age of Capital 1848–1875*, Cardinal, 1988.

Horne, Alistair, *Napoleon: Master of Europe*, Morrow, New York, 1979; *How Far from Austerlitz?*, Macmillan, 1996.

Hosking, Geoffrey, *Russia, People and Empire 1552–1917*, HarperCollins, 1997.

Karlinsky, Simon, *The Sexual Labyrinth of Nikolai Gogol*, University of Chicago Press, 1976.

Kelly, Linda, *The Young Romantics, Paris 1827–37*, The Bodley Head, 1976.

Kelly, Laurence, *Lermontov: Tragedy in the Caucasus*, Robin Clark, London, 1983.

Kaïdach, Svetlana, *Liubov i Dolg: Jenskii Siloueti Russkoi Istorii*, Sovetskaya Rossia, 1989.

Kauchtschischwili, N., *L'Italia nella vita e nell'opera di P. A. Viazemsky*, Societa Ed. Vita & Pensiero, Milan, 1964.

Knapton, E., *The Lady of the Holy Alliance*, New York, 1939.

Laver, James, *Fashion and Fashion Plates 1800–1900*, Penguin, 1943.

Lemme, Ludovico Paolo, *Salotti Romani dell'Ottocento*, Umberto Allemandi and Co.

Lo Gatto, Ettore, *I Russi in Italia*, Editori Riuniti, 1971.

Longford, Elizabeth, *Wellington: The Years of the Sword*, Weidenfeld and Nicolson, 1969.

Mack Smith, Denis, *The Making of Italy 1796–1866*, Macmillan Press, 1988.

Madariaga, Isabel de, *Russia in the Time of Catherine the Great*, Yale University Press, 1981.

Magarshack, David, *Gogol: A life*, Grove Press Inc., New York, 1957.

Massie, Suzanne, *Pavlovsk: The life of a Russian Palace*, Hodder and Stoughton, 1990.

Mazon, André, *Deux Russes Ecrivains Français*, Paris, 1964 and *Zéneide Wolkonsky la Catholique*.

Mazour, Anatole, *The First Russian Revolution, 1825*, Berkeley, 1937.

Modzalevsky, B. L., *Pushkin pod Tainim Nadzorom*, St Petersburg, 1922.

Montgomery-Hyde, H., *Princess Lieven*, Harrap.

Nicolson, Harold, *The Congress of Vienna*, Viking Press, New York, 1967.

Palmer, Alan, *Napoleon in Russia*, Constable, 1997.

Poltartsky, Hermoine, *Profils Russes: Une Princesse Russe à Rome*, Librairie Académique Perrin & Cie., 1912.

Riasanovsky, Nicholas V., *A History of Russia*, Oxford University Press, 1984.

Robbins, H. C., *Beethoven, His Life, Work and World*, London, 1992.

Shilder, N. K., *Imperator Alexander I ego zhizn i tsarstvovanie*, 4 vols, Suvorin, St Petersburg, 1897.

Simmons, Ernest J., *Pushkin*, Oxford University Press, 1937.

Sutherland, Christine, *The Princess of Siberia*, Robin Clark, 1984.

Sutherland, John, *The Life of Walter Scott*, Blackwell, 1995.

Thompson, J. M., ed. and trs., *Napoleon I Letters of Napoleon*, Basil Blackwell, Oxford, 1934.

Trofimoff, André, *La Princesse Zénéide Wolkonsky*, Staderini, Rome, 1966.

Troyat, Henri, *Alexandre Ier: Le Sphinx du Nord*, Flammarion, 1980.

Webster, C. K., *The Congress of Vienna 1814–1815*, Oxford University Press, 1919.

Webster C. K., ed. British Diplomacy 1813–15. G Bell & Son 1921

Zaccagnini, Carlo, *Le Ville di Roma*, Newton Compton ed.

Ziegler, Philip, *The Duchess of Dino*, Collins, 1962.

Index